Innovation within Tradition

Innovation within Tradition

Joseph Ratzinger and Reading the Women of Scripture

Mary Frances McKenna

Fortress Press
Minneapolis

INNOVATION WITHIN TRADITION

Joseph Ratzinger and Reading the Women of Scripture

Copyright © 2015 Fortress Press. All rights reserved. Except for brief quotations in critical articles or reviews, no part of this book may be reproduced in any manner without prior written permission from the publisher. Visit http://www.augsburgfortress.org/copyrights/ or write to Permissions, Augsburg Fortress, Box 1209, Minneapolis, MN 55440.

Cover design: Alisha Lofgren

Library of Congress Cataloging-in-Publication Data

Hardcover ISBN: 978-1-5064-0020-4

Paperback ISBN: 978-1-4514-8799-2

eBook ISBN: 978-1-5064-0043-3

The paper used in this publication meets the minimum requirements of American National Standard for Information Sciences — Permanence of Paper for Printed Library Materials, ANSI Z329.48-1984.

Manufactured in the U.S.A.

This book was produced using PressBooks.com, and PDF rendering was done by PrinceXML.

To my husband Theo, with love.

If I have prophetic powers, and understand all mysteries and all knowledge, and if I have all faith, so as to remove mountains, but have not love, I am nothing.

1 Corinthians 13:2

Contents

	Foreword	ix
	Introduction	1
1.	Joseph Ratzinger's Theological Perspective	11
2.	The Female Line Foundations and Methodology	99
3.	The Female Line in the Old Testament	135
4.	The Female Line in the New Testament	163
5.	The Female Line in the Bible Innovation within the Tradition of the Church	215
	Bibliography	227
	Index of Names and Subjects	245
	Index of Scripture References	259

Foreword

After Joseph Ratzinger was elected pope in 2005, taking the name Benedict XVI, I began reading his writings to understand who this man was and what he was about. I found a writer who offers coherent, comprehensive answers that get to the heart of the challenging questions facing not just theology, but also contemporary society. I hope that this book offers the opportunity for others to explore Ratzinger's theological thinking so that his ideas and approach may contribute to new and fresh ways of responding to the problems facing modern theology and society.

I am delighted to be afforded the opportunity to publish this book and share my research both with the academic community as well as those in the wider community who have an interest in theological debate since Vatican II. The book is based on my PhD dissertation, which I defended in 2012. Material has been added to expand on a number of important themes covered in the original document and other material, more in keeping with a dissertation, has been removed. However, the substantive arguments are anchored in and remain in continuity with those of my dissertation.

The research for this book began when Siobhan Clarke, of the Patricians group in Beechwood parish church, Ranelagh, Dublin, suggested that I give the next monthly talk to that group in March

2007 on a topic of my choosing. I chose to present on some interesting ideas that I had come across in the newly elected pope's earlier writings. The title of the paper, "The Women of the Bible," served as the beginning of this research and book. I thank Siobhan and the Patricians group for affording me the opportunity to present the paper, and, as a result, commence a very fulfilling period of my life.

I want to acknowledge a number of people who provided important support and guidance to me, without whom this research would not have been completed, let alone started. First, I thank Dr. Tom Dalzell, my thesis supervisor, for providing critical input to this research project and for guiding me through the difficult doctoral journey. I also thank Dr. Bernadette Flanagan, former director of research at All Hallows College, Dublin City University, for her support, particularly as I began this research project.

As I began the research for this book, Dr. James Corkery, who also has a research interest in Joseph Ratzinger's writings, generously spent time discussing "all things Ratzinger" with me, which I found very helpful. I also acknowledge the contributions Dr. Brendan Leahy, former professor of systematic theology at the Pontifical University Maynooth and now bishop of Limerick, and Dr. Tony Draper of All Hallows College made to the finalization of my thesis.

I also acknowledge, and thank most sincerely, the very significant help and support provided to me by Dr. Teresa Whitington, head librarian of the Central Catholic Library in Dublin. Dr. Whitington on numerous occasions responded very thoroughly to my inquiries about the availability of texts from the library, and at times suggested additional texts that were highly valuable to the development of my research. I thank as well Trinity College Dublin's School of Religions and Theology and the Loyola Institute for providing me with valuable access to the library as I completed this book.

Finally, I would like to thank and acknowledge Michael Gibson and Lisa Gruenisen of Fortress Press for their generous support, guidance, and wisdom as I translated, and further developed, my doctoral thesis into this book.

Introduction

Joseph Ratzinger's notion of "the female line in the Bible" retrieves the voice of the women of Scripture for Christian faith and theology, placing the women of the Bible at the heart of salvation history. Ratzinger describes his idea as follows:

> [I]n the Old Testament, alongside the line from Adam through the Patriarchs down to the Servant of God, there appears another line from Eve through the Matriarchs to figures like Deborah, Esther, Ruth and finally to the personified Divine Wisdom. . . . The line from Adam receives its full meaning in Christ. Similarly, the significance of the female line in its inseparable interaction with the Christological mystery is revealed in Mary and in the symbolism applied to the Church.[1]

What Ratzinger argues is that the male line of salvation, Adam to the second Adam, is accompanied by a female line, Eve to Mary. Salvation history does not consist of a male line alone, but a line of women, the female line, of equal and conjunctive significance.

---

1. Joseph Ratzinger, "The Sign of the Woman," introduction to *Mary: God's Yes to Man: John Paul's Encyclical Letter* Redemptoris Mater, trans. Lothar Krauth (San Francisco: Ignatius, 1988), 17–18; also published in Joseph Ratzinger and Hans Urs von Balthasar, *Mary: The Church at the Source*, trans. Adrian Walker (San Francisco: Ignatius, 2005). Two different translators were used to translate the article for the two publications, so, in the latter, the word *female* is translated as *feminine* so it reads "the feminine line in the Bible" (43–44). As will be discussed in chapters 3 and 4, Ratzinger, with his concept, is referring to the line of women in the Bible and the meaning they point to and represent within salvation history. In this regard, the English word *female* is the appropriate word to describe the concept Ratzinger is articulating.

Ratzinger's advocacy of a female line, understood within the context of the relational nature of his theology, offers an intriguing response to the question of women in Christianity and the role of the female in salvation. Underscoring the women of the biblical stories, Ratzinger points toward a new path that charts its course from Scripture while, at the same time, it develops and refines the Church's tradition.

Ratzinger's renewed articulation of the fullness of salvation history has significant implications for clarifying and illuminating the place of women, including Mary, in Scripture, tradition, and Christianity. *Lumen Gentium*, the Vatican II document promulgated by Pope Paul VI in 1964, explicitly acknowledges that there are unanswered questions in relation to Mariology,[2] which means that the Catholic Church's Mariology is a work in progress. Ratzinger's female line offers an interpretative tool in which the open, unresolved issues of Mariology can be explored afresh. But it goes further than just Mariology: by integrating the female line with the male line, Christianity itself is placed in a renewed context. An investigation of the meaning and implications of a female line parallel to and integral with the male line in salvation history opens new perspectives on salvation history and Christianity as a whole. A richer, fuller evaluation and assessment is available through this articulation of God's activity within history.

This book responds to a hope expressed in the Congregation for the Doctrine of Faith's 2004 "Letter to the Bishops of the Catholic Church on the Collaboration between Men and Women in the Church and the World": "These reflections are meant as a starting point for further examination in the Church, as well as an impetus for dialogue with all men and women of good will, in a sincere search for the truth and in a common commitment to the development

---

2. *Lumen Gentium*, no. 54, in Austin Flannery, ed., *Vatican Council II: The Basic Sixteen Documents: Constitutions, Decrees, Declarations* (Dublin: Dominican Publications, 1996), 81.

of ever more authentic relationships [between men and women]."³ While the Letter itself does not address the unanswered questions of Mariology, this book responds to the Letter's call for further examination by seeking to contribute to a deeper understanding of the women of the Bible. Exploring Ratzinger's notion of the female line in the Bible, the book contributes to the development of the Church's understanding of salvation history through the women of the Bible; and through this renewed understanding of salvation history a renewed understanding of humanity, of `adam, the human being, may be generated. Ratzinger interprets the Hebrew word `adam as meaning the human being who represents every human being.⁴ By returning to the Hebrew roots of the creation accounts, Ratzinger's understanding of `adam, the human being, is a starting point, anchored in Scripture and tradition, that offers the opportunity for a more authentic view of humanity and the relationship between "man" and "woman" that the Letter seeks to achieve.

The objective of this book is to synthesize into a coherent whole Ratzinger's writings on the biblical women through the lens of his concept of the female line in the Bible. With this synthesis I will propose an explanation of what these women say to us about humanity's relationship with God. Do these women tell us something that is unique to women or do they speak about both men and women? Do these women represent women or humanity? Ultimately, the core question is: How do the women who make

---

3. "Letter to the Bishops of the Catholic Church on the Collaboration between Men and Women in the Church and the World" (2004), http://www.vatican.va /roman_curia /congregations /cfaith /documents /rc_con_cfaith_doc_20040731_collaboration_en.html. This Letter was issued by the Congregation for the Doctrine of the Faith when Ratzinger was its prefect in the year before he was elected pope.
4. Joseph Ratzinger, "Man between Reproduction and Procreation," trans. T. A. Caldwell, *Communio* 16, no. 2 (1989): 206–7. This interpretation is congruent with current biblical interpretation. Pauline A. Viviano states that the Hebrew word `adam "is not to be understood as an individual named Adam; rather, 'the Human' is the whole of humanity." Viviano, *Genesis*, Collegeville Bible Commentary, vol. 2 (Collegeville, MN: Liturgical, 1985), 15.

3

up the female line in the Bible contribute to our understanding of salvation history, to Christianity? Do they tell us something new or retell what is already known? The emphasis throughout the book will be on organizing the discussion into a new synthesis. Building upon Ratzinger's notion of the female line in the Bible and older traditions of theological exegesis and reflection, I hope to enable a new pathway to emerge—one that provides a glimmer of how we can move toward a deeper understanding and appreciation, not only of the women of the Bible, but, through them, of salvation history and inclusive, relational anthropology.

The book consists of five chapters. In chapter 1, I explore the nature, framework, and structure of Ratzinger's theological development and his theology in general. The aim is to situate his concept of the female line in the Bible within the overall context of his writings and theological evolution. Chapter 2 examines the development and basis of the female line. As part of that discussion I explore the hermeneutical principles that underpin Ratzinger's work with a particular emphasis on the issue of faith in history and biblical interpretation. Chapters 3 through 5 look specifically at Ratzinger's writings on the women of the Bible as interpreted through the lens of the "female line" concept. Throughout the exploration of Ratzinger's theological thought I will discuss each theme in relation to other theologians seeking to address the same issue, with the aim to identify fruitful areas for further development.

The topic of "the feminine" is closely associated with the central concern of this book. It is, however, a topic that is outside this book's scope because Ratzinger's writings focus on the women of the Bible rather than on the concept of the feminine in general. Interestingly, the aforementioned "Letter on the Collaboration between Man and Woman" notes in this regard that:

> It is appropriate however to recall that the feminine values mentioned here are above all human values: the human condition of man and woman created in the image of God is one and indivisible. It is only because women are more immediately attuned to these values that they are the reminder and the privileged sign of such values. But, in the final analysis, every human being, man and woman, is destined to be "for the other." In this perspective, that which is called "femininity" is more than simply an attribute of the female sex. The word designates indeed the fundamental human capacity to live for the other and because of the other.[5]

The Letter acknowledges that "the feminine" does not directly translate into "female" or "woman" but, rather, that femininity refers to the human disposition of being and living "for the other," which points to the fundamental essence of humanity. This book seeks to understand—through the lens of Ratzinger's "female line"—what the women of the Bible tell us about salvation history and anthropology, so the topic of the feminine will only be touched upon where it is relevant to the discussion in connection to Ratzinger's work.

A Short Overview of Joseph Ratzinger's Life

Before commencing on our task, a brief biographical note on our main subject is in order. Joseph Ratzinger, Pope Benedict XVI, has played many roles in his life: son of a local Bavarian policeman, teenage soldier, priest, lecturer and professor, bishop, prefect of the Congregation for the Doctrine of Faith, pope, and now pope emeritus. Yet, for a man who has had such a dominating influence on the Catholic Church for the last number of decades, relatively little is known about him personally. How can we reconcile the variegated images of the man hailed as a progressive theologian at the beginning of his ministry, but later accused of being an archconservative, a *Panzerkardinal*?

---

5. "Letter on the Collaboration between Man and Woman," no. 14.

Ratzinger was born in Bavaria, in 1927, at a time of unprecedented tumult for the German people. Military defeat, the Versailles Treaty, and financial turmoil dominated his native nation just prior to his birth. Six years after Ratzinger's birth Adolf Hitler was appointed chancellor, and he was twelve when World War II broke out. He subsequently served in the German army as a teenage soldier and the American army held him, for a short period, as a prisoner of war. His brother, George, who also served in the German army, survived the war as did his sister and parents. The impact of the turmoil, war, and the Holocaust on Ratzinger as a person, theologian, and Church leader is difficult to judge. He and his brother entered seminary after the war and both became priests in 1951. This path does not appear to have been primarily influenced by their war experience; rather, the piety of their parents and family life appears to be the determining factor that gave rise to their vocation. Any statement on the impact of the dire political environment of his youth is complicated, not just because it is what happened during his youth, but also because of how he responded. It also risks descending into conjectural psychology without Ratzinger himself making a definitive statement on the matter. All that can really be said is that, like Plato, he experienced traumatic political events in his youth that drove his search for answers to the questions regarding ultimate reality and authentic humanity.

Although he served for a year in a parish after his ordination, Ratzinger has spent most of his priesthood working as a theologian in universities and as prefect of the Congregation for the Doctrine of Faith. He was appointed a professor of fundamental theology at the University of Bonn in 1959 and subsequently worked at Münster, Tübingen, and Regensburg Universities. He was viewed as a progressive theologian at the start of his career but a conservative after Vatican II. The world of the 1950s was radically different from that of post–Vatican II. The impact of the revolutionary movements of 1968 and other social changes had profound consequences not only for society, but for the relationship between society and the Church as well, which sharply affected Ratzinger's worldview. Nonetheless, as will be seen, Ratzinger did remain an innovative and nuanced theologian throughout his career.

Ratzinger has held a high profile in the Catholic Church since Vatican II when he acted as *peritus*, chief theological adviser, to Cardinal Josef Frings of Cologne. He contributed to the development of major Vatican II documents and wrote commentaries on the four sessions of the Council. Subsequently, he served on the International Theological Commission from its establishment in 1969 and became president when appointed prefect of the Congregation for the Doctrine of Faith in 1981. In response to what he perceived as misguided theological trends post–Vatican II, he, along with Hans Urs von Balthasar, Henri de Lubac, and others, set up the journal *Communio* in 1972. Although he has published significantly and written major theological treatises, such as *Eschatology*, before his appointment as archbishop of Munich in 1977, much of what was published were collections of lectures, essays or talks on particular topics. These reflect his theological concerns and prefigure his work as prefect and pope. In 1981 Saint John Paul II appointed Ratzinger as prefect of the Congregation for the Doctrine of Faith. He held this position until his own election as pope in April 2005. On February 28, 2013, Benedict resigned as pope, the first to do so since Celestine V in 1294, opening a new chapter for the Church.

Two final points of clarification are required before commencing our discussion on the female line in the Bible. First, in the book I have not sought to distinguish between Ratzinger's theological thinking and his approach as pope. Instead, I draw on his writings as pope when I think they reflect the thinking of Ratzinger the theologian.

One text I do make use of, *Jesus of Nazareth* (2007),⁶ he himself makes clear in the foreword that it is to be considered his own personal work as a theologian rather than a papal document. Second, a point of clarification is required on Ratzinger's use of the term *man*. When using the term *man*, Ratzinger is not just referring to the human male; instead, he uses it to refer to humanity as such. This use reflects his use of the Hebrew word `adam` to refer to the whole of humanity. But it also reflects a Germanic approach. Erich Fromm also uses the term *man* to describe humanity. In *To Have or To Be?* Fromm addresses this "point of style" that is specific to the English language and not the German. Fromm states, in relation to the generic use of "man" and "he" as the term of reference for the species *homo sapiens*, that:

> The use of "man" in this context, without differentiation of sex, has a long tradition in humanist thinking, and I do not believe we can do without a word that denotes clearly the human species' character. No such differentiation exists in the German language: one uses the word Mensch to refer to the non-sex-differentiated being. But even in English the word "man" is used in the same sex-undifferentiated way as the German Mensch, as meaning human being or the human race. I think it is advisable to restore its non-sexual meaning to the word "man" rather than substituting awkward-sounding words. In this book I have capitalised "Man" in order to clarify my non-sex-differentiated use of the term.⁷

Although I would welcome the development of a unique word in the English language that would directly translate the meaning of the German word Mensch, here in this book, to avoid confusion and a lack of consistency, I will follow Ratzinger's own use of the term *man* to refer to humanity when referring to his work. Now we will

---

6. Joseph Ratzinger, *Jesus of Nazareth*, trans. Adrian J. Walker (London: Bloomsbury, 2007), xxiii–xiv.
7. Erich Fromm, *To Have or To Be?* (London: Abacus, 1979), 9–10.

commence exploring his notion of a female line in the Bible, starting with Ratzinger's theological ideas and positions.

1

Joseph Ratzinger's Theological Perspective

To place Ratzinger's notion of a female line in the Bible within the context of his overall theological project, this chapter will explore the main contours of his thought as well as the framework and structure of his theological approach, beginning with his thinking on the God of Jesus Christ. Jesus Christ, fully human and fully divine, one person in two natures, mediates Ratzinger's thought on God and humanity, and the relationality he identifies as essential to Christ is at the core of that thought. I will first explore Ratzinger's Christology and then his thought on the meaning of God's self-revelation in the persons of Father, Son, and Spirit. From there I will turn to the role that Mary plays in his thought and how she personifies a number of its important developments and characteristics. Together these will show how all aspects of his thinking interconnect. The framework and structure of Ratzinger's theology are crucial here, too, particularly the interplay of faith, theology, and tradition, in which the Church continually deepens and develops its understanding of tradition through the Spirit's guidance, which creates a generative structure for Ratzinger's own constructive vision.

The God of Jesus Christ

A Pauline Augustinian Christology

Ratzinger's theological thinking is christocentric in nature: Scripture is interpreted through the light of Christ, which illustrates his view that Christ is the determining factor for the meaning of the whole of Christianity.[1] For as he says, "... if it is indeed true that Jesus *is* the Son of God. Precisely this *Being* is the tremendous *event* on which everything else depends."[2] It is through the lens of Jesus' *Being* and the event of the incarnation, by which he is the Son of God, that Ratzinger views and understands the whole of Scripture, revelation, and tradition. This Jesus Christ is a radical challenge, as well as the answer for all humanity: "The Jesus who makes everything OK for everyone is a phantom, a dream, not a real figure. The Jesus of the Gospels is certainly not convenient for us. But it is precisely in this way that he answers the deepest questions of our existence."[3] Ratzinger anchors his Christology in the Pauline interpretation of Jesus as the second Adam in such a way that it can be described as an interplay of the Gospels and the Pauline material.[4] This has implications for his overall theology and his understanding of salvation through Jesus Christ. Jesus is the apex and fulfillment of salvation history, such that the movement from creation and the fall

---

1. Joseph Ratzinger, *Eschatology: Death and Eternal Life*, 2d ed., trans. Michael Waldstein and Aidan Nichols (Washington, DC: Catholic University of America Press, 1988), 12.
2. Joseph Ratzinger, *The God of Jesus Christ: Meditations on the Triune God*, trans. Brian McNeil (San Francisco: Ignatius, 2008), 88.
3. Joseph Ratzinger, *On the Way to Jesus Christ*, trans. Michael J. Miller (San Francisco: Ignatius, 1987), 8.
4. Joseph Ratzinger, *Introduction to Christianity*, 2d ed., trans. J. R. Foster (San Francisco: Ignatius, 2003), 234–43.

to incarnation and resurrection are essential to his understanding of the full meaning of Scripture and the theological enterprise to understand and interpret them. This movement from Adam to Adam gives direction to Ratzinger's theological work and is the principle and starting point of his Christology and soteriology. It is not Jesus Christ as a stand-alone individual, but Jesus Christ as the fullness of time in relation to the whole of Scripture and faith and also the fullness of the meaning and interpretation of humanity itself.

The Pauline aspect of soteriology plays an important role in this interpretation in that humanity requires conversion from the alienation of the fall and each human being's salvation arises not from his own activity but God's self-gift in Jesus Christ, even if the human response to God's initiative is essential. Ratzinger's thinking here is influenced by what can be called Pauline-Augustinianism, counter to the criticism that identifies his soteriology as influenced by (neo-)Platonic-Augustinianism.[5] His view is that salvation cannot be achieved or brought about within history, and when such is attempted, it becomes totalitarian. This has had important consequences for his engagement with political theologies during his time as prefect of the Congregation for the Doctrine of Faith. It could be argued that Ratzinger's style led to a narrow theological approach, while political theologies' focus is greater than just theology, and includes an active response to the suffering of the world, such as in liberation theology's desire to respond to the appalling poverty and suffering of the people of South and Latin America.

Critical for Ratzinger's Christology is his affirmation of the incarnation, that God became flesh and dwelt among us; this is the central proposition of the Christian creed and Christianity.[6] It also

---

5. James Corkery, *Joseph Ratzinger's Theological Ideas: Wise Cautions and Legitimate Hopes* (Dublin: Dominican Press, 2009); Thomas P. Rausch, *Pope Benedict XVI: An Introduction to His Theological Vision* (New York: Paulist, 2009).
6. Ratzinger, *God of Jesus Christ*, 69.

points to the historical nature of Christianity and to the notion of person, and hence relation: "The person of Jesus *is* his teaching and his teaching is he himself. Christian faith, that is, faith in Jesus as the Christ is . . . the acceptance of this person who is his word; of the word as person and of the person as Word."[7] The ontological portraiture of Jesus' being is most clearly manifest in his dialogue with God the Father: The communion with the Father through prayer determines who Jesus is, so that Ratzinger maintains, "the centre of the life and person of Jesus is his constant communication with the Father," and "the centre of the person of Jesus is prayer."[8] It is not Christ's being or person as an abstract quality; rather, it is the relationship of Christ's being and person with the Father that determines his being and person. The central emphasis on the relational nature of Jesus with the Father is highly significant to Ratzinger's thinking. It also provides crucial, dynamic dimensions to his Christology and anthropology, and, as will be seen, his concept of "the female line of the Bible."

God's Self-Revelation as a Relational, Personal Being

The Triune God—Father, Son, and Holy Spirit—is, for Ratzinger, fundamentally relational and personal. God as a relational being is foremost a scriptural notion, reflected in the self-revelation of God in the Old Testament as the God of Abraham, Isaac, and Jacob, and God's covenantal relationship with Israel. God's response to Moses—"I am who I am"—means that God *is*: God is at work, God acts, God can act, God is an "I," God is a person. This implies that God is neither abstract nor impersonal, like a mathematical formula, nor is God "nothingness."[9] Likewise, the relational reality of God is

---

7. Ratzinger, *Introduction to Christianity*, 205; see also 204.
8. Joseph Ratzinger, *Behold the Pierced One*, trans. Graham Harrison (San Francisco: Ignatius, 1986), 15, 25.

in total opposition to the beast of the book of Revelation who, as he says, is a number and makes men nothing but numbers.[10] God as a personal relational being is most fully actualized and revealed in Jesus Christ, God's Word.

Ratzinger outlines a relational anthropology in an important 1973 article,[11] in which he addresses similar issues to those raised by the Russian Orthodox theologian Vladimir Lossky.[12] Ratzinger and Lossky each offer a constructive examination of the topic and both provides important direction to the development of insights in the theological notion of person and its application to the human being. Lossky's work takes up "a group of extremely important questions" that Hans Urs von Balthasar touches upon in discussing post-Chalcedonian theology in his considerations on Maximus the Confessor, but which Balthasar does not pursue in detail. The questions, according to Lossky, relate to the distinction between essence and existence and how they relate to the created human being,[13] which is Lossky's point of departure. Ratzinger, too, is influenced by Maximus and Balthasar; indeed, Ratzinger contends that Maximus provides the most significant positive clarification of the christological concept of person.[14] Where Balthasar remains on the surface, as Lossky contends, on the level of Greek (Aristotelian) philosophy, Lossky's and Ratzinger's considerations seek to move beyond that and to appreciate how person as revealed in God's self-

---

9. Ratzinger, *God of Jesus Christ*, 21–22, 28.
10. Ibid., 24.
11. Joseph Ratzinger, "Retrieving the Tradition concerning the Notion of Person in Theology," trans. Michael Waldstein, *Communio* 17, no. 3 (Fall 1990): 439–54. The article in its original form was a lecture given at a congress on the understanding of the person in educational theory and related disciplines; it was subsequently published in 1973 in his book *Dogma und Verkundigung*.
12. Vladimir Lossky, "The Theological Notion of the Human Person," in *In the Image and Likeness of God* (Crestwood, NY: St. Vladimir's Seminary Press, 1974).
13. Lossky's reference to Balthasar is: Hans Urs von Balthasar, *Liturgie comsmique* (Paris, 1947), 21.
14. Ratzinger, "Retrieving the Tradition," 450–51 n. 8.

revelation in Jesus Christ fully transitions to the human being. How, based on theological consideration on the triune God, is "person" appropriately applied to the human being? As we will see, both determine this based on Christology, but each takes a different, if complementary, approach. Lossky's and Ratzinger's considerations cannot be explored here in the detail required to draw out the full depths and potential of their thought. I can only attempt to identify some lines of thought on divine person and how those are applicable to the human being, which will later help illuminate our main theme, the female line in the Bible. I will first consider Lossky's and then Ratzinger's thought.

Lossky on Person

Vladimir Lossky, in his classic essay on the theological notion of person in the divine and human, notes that in the Greek father's comprehensive doctrine on divine person to express "the absolute and primordial condition of a Trinitarian God in His transcendence," they used a pair of synonyms, *ousia* and *hypostasis*, which denote absolute identity and absolute difference. This "terminological discovery," as Lossky refers to it, expresses "the irreducibility of the hypostasis to ousia" without "opposing them as two different realities."[15] Lossky argues that, where scholars create distinction between them, they "fall back into the domain of conceptual knowledge: one opposes the general to the particular."[16] Against this Lossky argues that the distinction between these two terms cannot be found in concepts; rather, their theological truth exists beyond concepts that "become signs of the personal reality of God."[17]

---

15. Lossky, "Theological Notion," 113.
16. Ibid.
17. Ibid., 115.

The issue of the appropriate application of person to the human being arises when, in the theological language of East and West, the human person coincides with the human individual, "an individual numerically different from all other men."[18] This situation, Lossky rightly notes, fundamentally distorts the notion of divine person. Lossky asks how "person" sits within Jesus Christ, who is both fully human and fully divine, but whose humanity began at the "moment of Incarnation," while his person is that of the Son of God which preexisted his humanity in eternal communion with the Father and Spirit. When considering this, Lossky accepts that Jesus' humanity does have "the character of an individual substance."

To avoid the errors of Nestorius and Apollinarius of Laodicea, Lossky argues that there is an irreducibility of Christ's person to his human nature.[19] This means that in the human being, the person must also be distinguished from its nature or, in other words, its individual substance. A human person, then, is "someone who goes beyond his nature while still containing it." Such a person exists in his or her nature while constantly exceeding it.[20] Lossky concludes that "'person' signifies the irreducibility of the person to his nature." This is *irreducibility* rather than an individual person being irreducible to their nature because that would indicate another nature,[21] there would be two rather than one nature. Lossky's concern is always to *distinguish* the person from its nature while never allowing a distinction between the two. The tree persons of God do not make God into three but reveal God as Tri-Unity. As a result, Lossky rightly insists we should abandon designating the human person with individual substance of reasonable nature. This is the opposite of the construal of Karl Rahner's approach to the disconnect between the

---

18. Ibid., 116.
19. Ibid., 118.
20. Ibid., 120.
21. Ibid.

notion of divine person and how to date person has been applied to the human being. Rahner, wrongly in my view, argues that the addition of the term, "distinct manner of being" is required to clarify the notion of person in relation to God.[22] Lossky's, and Ratzinger's, approach, which works to identify how person *is appropriately applied to the human being*, protects the fullness of person for the human being, discovered in the divine.

The implication of all this is that, in the union of person and nature, human beings are not enclosed in themselves but can transcend, in grace, the limits of their individuality. As Lossky puts it:

> The creature, who is both "physical" and "hypostatic" at the same time, is called to realise his unity of nature as well as his true personal diversity by going in grace beyond the individual limits which divide nature and tend to reduce person to the level of the closed being of particular substances. Thus the level on which the problem of the human person is posed goes beyond that of ontology as we normally understand it; and if it is a question of metaontology, only God can know—that God whom the story of Genesis shows stopping his work to say in the Council of the Three Hypostases: "Let us create man in our image and likeness".[23]

Lossky provides important technical clarification on the theological notion of divine person, how it can to be applied to the human being, and what it means for the human being. But he does so in an apophatic way, which leaves the question of the true nature of the human person beyond our reach and access. What is strikingly absent from Lossky's considerations here is the notion of relationality that Christian theology discovered in the triune God. He focuses

---

22. Karl Rahner stated in relation to this that: "When *today we* speak of person in the plural, we think almost necessarily, because of the modern meaning of the word, of several spiritual centres of activity, of several subjectivities and liberties. But there are not three of these in God—not only because in God there is only one essence, hence *one* absolute self-presence, but also because there is only *one* self-utterance of Father, the Logos." Rahner, *The Trinity*, trans. Joseph Donceel (New York: Herder & Herder, 1997 [1967]), 106; also see 56–57 and 103–15 for discussion on the issues related to the term *person*.
23. Lossky, "Theological Notion," 122–23.

instead on how the Greek fathers acknowledged the three persons, or hypostases, in the one nature of God and how that is applied to the human being. His primary concern is to ensure person can be acknowledged and expressed while ensuring that person is not distinct from its nature, as if it were another nature. Lossky does not call upon the relationships of the Father and Son in the Holy Spirit to extrapolate how to distinguish the persons of God from the one divine nature. The relations of the person of the triune God are peripheral to Lossky's considerations.

Ratzinger on Person

Ratzinger, in contrast to Lossky, insists that the true nature and meaning of God as person is accessible to humanity precisely through the person of Jesus Christ. He constructs an anthropology that is fully determined by a relational Christology, in which personal being—the human as image of God—is constituted and defined by Jesus Christ as the second Adam. Person, Ratzinger argues, is a notion that arose out of Christian faith through two questions that presented themselves to the Fathers: What is the God of Scripture? And, Who is Christ? The notion of person develops from the answers to these questions.[24] Of significance is the scriptural portrayal of the God who speaks. Utilizing prosopographic exegesis,[25] which underscores the dialogical dimensions and effects of story, ancient and medieval interpreters imported from Greek culture *prosopon*, or *persona*, which originally meant "the role or mask of the actor who describes dialogical scenes," and imbued it with theological meaning.[26] Christian scholars appropriated, and radically transformed, this word as a mechanism

---

24. Ratzinger, "Retrieving the Tradition," 439.
25. Ratzinger argues, in reference to Sjoberg, that the rabbinic antecedents to prosopographic exegesis should be investigated as this may be an additional basis of the concept of person.
26. Ibid., 441.

to interpret the God Scripture describes. As Ratzinger puts it, "The phenomenon of *intra*-divine dialogue gives birth here to the idea of person who is person in an authentic sense."[27] We immediately see the relationality that is central to Ratzinger's notion of person associated with Tertullian's term *prosopon*, which is not as readily available through the terms *hypostasis* and *ousia*.

Two hundred years after Tertullian, Ratzinger argues that Augustine further developed this specifically Christian idea. Augustine identified that person in God means relation, being related, and, even more, that the person *is* relation. Ratzinger posits that the person exists as relation such that the person is the deed of generating, the act of self-donation. He refers to this as the pure reality of act or pure act-being. God is "the act of relativity toward the other. In God, person is the pure relativity of being turned toward the other."[28] The importance of this, for Ratzinger, is that the person is relation, not substance. God remains one substance, while as person-in-relation is "Tri-Unity," not three (as Lossky insists). This is where through person Christian thought moves beyond the boundaries of Greek philosophy to something uniquely Christian that is based on God's self-revelation through Jesus Christ.

The phenomenon of pure relationality, which is "absolute openness of existence without any reservation,"[29] appears for Ratzinger most particularly in John's Gospel. Jesus' words, "The Son can do nothing of himself" (5:19) and "I and the Father are one" (10:30), demonstrate that the Father and Son are one because Jesus exists in total relativity toward the Father without any delimiting of substance. Furthermore, this is transferred to the disciples through Jesus' words, "Without me you can do nothing" (15:5) and "that they

---

27. Ibid., 442.
28. Ibid., 444.
29. Ibid., 446.

may be one as we are one" (17:11). The disciple does not create a self-enclosed existence but, rather, seeks to be in pure relation with the other and with God. In Ratzinger's view, this phenomenon of God as person, as pure relationality, transforms anthropology through Christology and "indicates the direction of all personal being."[30]

Christology, in fact, undergirds for Ratzinger an additional, yet fundamental, evolution of the notion of person in the tradition's development of two-nature Christology—that is, Jesus has two natures, one human and one divine, in a single subject. Explicating the landmark definitions of the fourth and fifth centuries, Ratzinger turns to critique Boethius's concept of person as the individual substance of a rational mind, contrasting this with Richard St. Victor's definition of person as "the incommunicably proper existence of spiritual nature," a critique Lossky also makes. For Ratzinger, Richard correctly sees person on the level of existence, not essence, or, in other words, relation rather than substance, which then breaks out of the limits of Greek philosophy. The person does not fit within the category of substance, person identifies an entirely new category which Scholastic theology developed; antiquity only knew of the category of essence. Where he criticizes Scholasticism most on this matter is its limitation of existence as an ontological category of explanation for Christology and the doctrine of the Trinity. Ratzinger, in contrast, argues that Christology should not be seen as a unique ontological exception but, rather, as the model and fulfillment of anthropology: Christology is normative for the understanding of the human person.[31] This implies, first, that there are primary christological grounds of anthropology by which person and being human are given definition and actualization as opposed to the derivation from a priori analytic or generic/abstract categories of

---

30. Ibid., 445.
31. Ibid., 449–50.

being. Second, by fully applying the category of relation to humanity, Ratzinger introduces relation to intellectual thought in general, which, if fully realized, will transform it. By giving the category of relation grammar and language, using terms, phrases, and thought patterns to express and describe what it is, something that has hitherto not been integrated into the lexicon of accepted intellectual language, new horizons of reality will open. Faith in the personal, dialogical, and relational God, from the perspective of modern intellectual discourse, will then have solid ground, and cannot nor could not be viewed as "irrational."[32]

This reconstruction of anthropology through Christology is given further definition and clarity in connection with two-nature Christology. Ratzinger offers three insights to clarify in a positive way what it means for Jesus to be constituted by two natures in a single subject. First, the essence of the Spirit is going beyond itself, such that by being with the other it comes to itself: the human person actualizes his or her nature in total relationality with God and others without reserve. Thus, Ratzinger can say: "The more the person's relativity aims totally and directly at its final goal, at transcendence, the more the person is itself."[33] Second, in Christ being with the other is radically realized and that being-with-the-other brings being-with-himself to its fullness. Jesus' humanity is brought fully to itself and demonstrates the human being's greatest possibility, that of "transcending itself into the absolute and in the integration of its own relativity into the absoluteness of divine love."[34] As with Christ, in doing so the human being is not subsumed into

---

32. See the description of faith in *Lumen Fidei*, whose initial drafts were developed by Pope Benedict XVI. Francis I, *Lumen Fidei* (Dublin: Veritas, 2013), http://www.vatican.va/holy_father/francesco/encyclicals/documents/papa-francesco_20130629_enciclica-lumen-fidei_en.html.
33. Lossky, "Theological Notion," 451–52.
34. Ibid., 452.

God; rather, the "I" of a human being remains fully an "I" while being in total relation with God. Relationalilty with the Other and others, by connecting with the Other and others, allows the human being to transcend its individual limits: person denotes this reality.

Jesus as the final Adam, then, provides the space for humanity to gather on its way to relational communion with the triune God. In this way, God, as eternal communion of being, provides the space for the human, such that the divine "we" is opened to and united with the human "we." The "we" of God is God *for* (Father), *from* (Son), and *with* (Holy Spirit). God is a God turned toward the other, not turned in and consumed by the self. The internally communal being of God, opened outward toward humanity, grounds the definition of humanity as the image of God.[35] At the same time, relationality does not abrogate individuality, nor does it subsume humanity *into* divinity—divine and human being are noncompetitive and asymmetrical in character and relation.

The additional aspect of freedom or, more precisely, free relation needs to be included here. Freedom is an essential aspect of Ratzinger's notion of person. A person is free only where relationship is self-giving rather than a means to an end. In self-giving, humanity is free as God is: freedom means, for Ratzinger, that in self-possession we have the possibility for self-realization of our being and true nature.[36] In being so, we are at one with truth and thus "essence, willing, and acting have at last coincided."[37] True freedom, like person, is revealed through God—through God's free relation to humanity in Jesus Christ—and is available to the human being as the image of God. Person is relation and that relation demonstrates true

---

35. Joseph Ratzinger, "Truth and Freedom," trans. Adrian Walker, *Communio* 23, no. 1 (1996): 16–35.
36. Joseph Ratzinger, "Freedom and Liberation," in *Church, Ecumenism, and Politics: New Endeavors in Ecclesiology*, trans. Michael J. Miller, et al. (San Francisco: Ignatius, 2008), 182–83.
37. Ibid., 245, 247, 255.

freedom, which, for Ratzinger, is related not to the capacity to do but to being and existing in truth.

Ratzinger's christological recalibration of anthropology here contains four specific contributions. First is the notion that person is constituted by pure relationality and is not simply an attribute of substance. Second, that relationality does not consume the human being but, rather, brings the human being fully to itself. Third, Jesus Christ fully realizes relationality *as the* human being for all humanity and does so in such a way that mediates the relationality constitutive of God *in se* as triune and in direct expression of what it means to be a person in relation to others, applicable to every person. Fourth, the full introduction and application of the category of relation is a theological matrix for intellectual thought, both Christian and secular. In particular, Ratzinger achieves the latter by broadening relation from its unique and limited use in Christology and the doctrine of God, and applying it to anthropology. Ratzinger's own theological work applies it even more widely, infusing every aspect of his thinking.

Complementary Visions of Person

Ratzinger and Lossky offer two different, but complementary, presentations of the theological notion of person. One emanates from the Greek tradition and the other from the Latin, or Tertullian-Augustinian, tradition. Based on the doctrine of divine person developed by the fathers, each theologian seeks to clarify and develop how divine person is appropriately applied to the human being. Lossky's is a more technical discussion, concerned with ensuring that the notion of person applied to the human being in Christian thought aligns fully to the notion of person discovered in trinitarian theology. Specifically, that person can be distinguished without creating a distinction of natures. Lossky shows that person in the human being, as in God, means the irreducibility of the person to one's nature. The person is not distinct from their nature rather they remain one with their nature while nonetheless can be distinguished from their nature. The irreducibility of the person enables the human being to transcend their nature. The human being is not trapped in their nature but can go beyond their nature while remaining itself. Ratzinger, on the other hand, is concerned with demonstrating how the christological relationality provides for the notion of person and how that applies through Christ without reserve to the human person. In this way, Ratzinger draws out the meaning of person as relation, communion, and dialogue. Ratzinger's considerations, while drawing on Augustine's thought on person, is also critical of it, in this case Augustine's projection of the divine persons into the interior life of the human person.[38] By contrast, Ratzinger applies those relations fully to the human being through Christ.

Together we can say of Ratzinger's and Lossky's reflections on the theological notion of person, that there are not two types of person but one, even if the full theological realization of person in the human being is occurring long after the articulation of the notion of person in relation to the divine. Person as the act of pure relationality toward the other is that irreducibility of the person to its nature. The person is relatedness, and it is that potential for relationship with the Other and others that distinguishes the person from their nature. The human being's person and nature are not distinct as it two natures—two different things—rather the relationality is not contained within or by the nature. This means the individual human being is not imprisoned in itself, but in grace can break out of its limits through and in relationality, by encountering or connecting with the Other and others. Their considerations together inform each

---

38. Ratzinger, "Retrieving the Tradition," 454.

other and provide a more complete view of the theological notion of person and its appropriate application to the human being than either does alone. Importantly, though, Ratzinger provides a critical addition, namely, that the true meaning of person is not limited simply to God, as per Lossky, but is available to us through God's self-revelation to humanity. Each human being has the free choice to be an individual or a person. By choosing to be person, the human being in relationality remains oneself while going beyond oneself. Both Ratzinger and Lossky's work on the notion of person in the divine and the human are important contributions to and impetus for the Church's continuing development and deepening of its comprehension of God's self-revelation and the true meaning and potential of Christian anthropology. Needless to say, much is left to consider, including whether the way in which person applies to the human being has any implications for our understanding of the body of Christ.

Person and Individualism in Community

Before concluding this discussion of the meaning of person in relation to God and humanity in Ratzinger's thought, let us compare two other perspectives on the notion of the human person in concrete reality that offer the possibility of extending both Ratzinger's and Lossky's considerations. First, Rowan Williams, former Archbishop of Canterbury, explicitly responds to Lossky's argument that Christianity has yet to develop the vocabulary to distinguish between "two things that its absolutely vital to hold apart": between the subject (or the unique instance) of God and the quality of God, or between *hypostasis* and *ousia*.[39] Williams concern

---

39. Lossky, "Theological Notion," 113. Rowan Williams, "The Person and the Individual," presented at the Theos annual lecture, October 1, 2012, http://www.theosthinktank.co.uk/comment/2012/10/09/theos-lecture-transcript.

is how the nature of a thing is distinguished form the unique consciousness of the person: "when we talk about being 'a person,' we're talking of something about us as a whole that isn't specified, that isn't defined just by listing facts that happen to be true about us."[40] Williams maintains that the critical distinction in relation to the individual is primarily that between individual and person, not between the individual and the community. This is an important contribution to the idea of person and the place of the human being in the community. Williams places the distinction on the human being's way of living and existing, between being in relation and being closed in on oneself. Williams describes person as the mysterious, relational, conversational, environment-building activity, which is set up against the individual who sets one's own agenda disconnected from others. Person involves an act of faith, wherein we step out of our individual existence into the midst of a network of relations. For Williams, theology is probably the only true way of speaking of the human being in relationship because God, and our relationship with God, is at the root of everything. We are persons rather than individuals because of God. As he puts it:

> It is in turning away from an atomised artificial notion of the self as simply setting its own agenda from inside towards that more fluid, more risky, but also more human discourse of the exchanges in relations in which we're involved, and grounding that on the basic theological insight that we are always already in advance spoken to, addressed, and engaged with by that which is not the world and not ourselves.[41]

In Williams's reading, not only does person mean relation, but those relations create connections with others that bring into existence a network of persons operating together. This resonates with what we

---

40. Rowan Williams, "The Person and the Individual," presented at the Theos annual lecture, October 1, 2012, http://www.theosthinktank.co.uk/comment/2012/10/09/theos-lecture-transcript.
41. Ibid.

noted in relation to Ratzinger and Lossky, that relationality allows the individual to remain oneself while bursting through one's individual limits.

Mauro Giuseppe Lepori, a Cistercian monk, offers an additional perspective. He explores the individual in community, specifically religious community, but in a way that is also relevant to community in general.[42] He views individualism as "a flight one takes before the misery of one's own heart," when a human being makes the choice for "sterile autonomy." But for him, it is not just the individual human being that can make this choice. Communities, which are closed in on their own project and image, rather than God's work, also choose individualism. It is in communion with the Trinity, through Christ and the grace of the Holy Spirit, "in the Love that God is, the Love that unites the Father and the Son," rather than in the community itself that the true meaning of the individual and the community is to be found. Lepori distinguishes communion in relation with others and with God from simply being and existing in a community: unless a community offers and asks of an individual only that which is of the origin and ultimate end, a distortion of true community results. Lepori sees that the mission of the religious (consecrated person, monks, nuns, priests), and I would add all Christians, is to live in such a way that individuals experience the communion of love that is the Trinity. The mission is not to solve the problems of the world; rather, it is to offer the world access to salvation through Jesus Christ.[43]

Williams sets the individual against the person rather than community, and for good reason. Individualism, as per Lepori's contribution, is not confined to the individual but can be pursued by

---

42. Mauro Giuseppe Lepori, "The Individual and Community," trans. Carol Dvorak, *Cistercian Studies Quarterly* 48, no. 3 (2013): 369–79.
43. Ibid., 374–79.

a community. Person, whether as an individual or community, is a way of living and existing. It is relation with others, which means being in communion, not a community, with others. The human being as person is openness rather than closure, and this openness connects with the openness of others to form a web of relatedness. This relatedness, however, is ultimately a relatedness through and with the communion of the Father, Son, and Holy Spirit. The person who is in true relation toward the other, who transcends itself by going beyond itself in relatedness, as we learn from Ratzinger and Lossky, is a we, not simply with God and the Church, but a "we" open to communion with the wider community. Ratzinger and Lossky clarify the meaning of the person, and Williams and Lepori offer clarity on the person vis-à-vis individualism, which allows us to posit that, for the human being, person is communion in relation with other persons through God the Father, Son, and Holy Spirit. We see here the "we" of God to which Ratzinger points, around which humanity gathers.

Finally, Ratzinger not only provides an historical outline of the development of theological anthropology but also reveals crucial elements of his own theological approach. First, as noted earlier, the Augustinian influence on Ratzinger is quite apparent, which is inflected by Pauline, rather than Platonic or neo-Platonic, notes, as per much criticism of his thought.[44] Second, Ratzinger starts his consideration not from modern thought but, in a signature methodological approach, he commences by exploring the origins, in this case with the fathers, to identify the meaning of specific aspects of Christian thought. His point of departure for his engagement with modern theological thought is through understanding why and how something in theology developed and exists. In this way, his

---

44. Corkery, *Joseph Ratzinger's Theological Ideas*; Rausch, *Pope Benedict XVI*.

thought remains anchored within the river of tradition that provides for a deep comprehension of theological issues, which is then used to respond to how those issues present themselves in the modern period.

Mary, an Essential Element of Authentic Christianity

The God of Jesus Christ, for Ratzinger, as we have seen, is mediated through God's self-revelation in the Son. The incarnation is the point of entry of the Son into history. This was not simply God's act, but critically an act that sought a response from created humanity. Mary, in her yes, provided that positive response and is an essential aspect of the God of Jesus Christ. What is noteworthy here is that there has been a movement with regard to the importance of Mary in Ratzinger's thinking. So, while the christocentric nature of his thinking has remained a constant, the place of Mary has evolved from being an aspect, though not central, to becoming a central aspect of his thinking, and this has profoundly shaped his post–Vatican II theology. What changed was the context within which Christ is to be placed. According to his own assessment, early in his career he was influenced by the primacy of the christological in Christianity associated with the liturgical movement and the dialogue with Protestantism,[45] but this evolved when he appreciated the critical nature of the link between Mary and the Church. In *The Ratzinger Report*, this intellectual journey is described as somewhat like a conversion.[46] As a young theologian, before and during Vatican II, he had reservations about certain ancient Marian doctrines, and was critical of pre–Vatican II Catholic Mariology, namely, a Mary

---

45. Joseph Ratzinger, *God and the World: Believing and Living in Our Time: A Conversation with Peter Seewald*, trans. Henry Taylor (San Francisco: Ignatius, 2000), 296; also see idem, *Daughter Zion: Meditations on the Church's Marian Belief*, trans. John M. McDermott, S. J. (San Francisco: Ignatius, 1983), 26.
46. Joseph Ratzinger with Vittorio Messori, *The Ratzinger Report*, trans. Salvator Attanasio and Graham Harrison (San Francisco: Ignatius, 1985), 105.

or Marian piety disconnected from Christ. Mary as Mary in and for herself means absolutely nothing for Christianity; only Mary in relation to Christ is meaningful for theology. His earlier concern was what he saw as Catholic Mariology's negative impact on ecumenical dialogue; this concern is evident in his commentaries on sessions two and three of Vatican II (1963/64).[47]

Ratzinger's thinking at the close of Vatican II is seen in his 1965 article "Das Problem der Mariologie,"[48] where he draws on René Laurentin's criticism of the exaggeration and misunderstanding of Mariology for his own critique of pre–Vatican II Mariology. Ratzinger highlights Laurentin's observation that such intense zeal for the Virgin in herself, evident in the Catholic Church, does not appear in the Eastern Orthodox Churches. Laurentin is highly critical of the term *Ordo hypostaticus*, or "hypostatic order," in reference to Mary, which Mariologists at the time, such as José Antonio de Aldama, had promoted. The use of such language, Laurentin argues, blurs the boundaries between Christology and Mariology and waters down the mystery of Jesus, a situation that is illustrated in Aldama, where titles given to Christ are also used for Mary. In rejecting this term, Laurentin notes that the early church's struggle to articulate the reality of Jesus was a struggle to identify exact and precise wording which could not be misunderstood—for example, *homoousios*.[49] For Laurentin and Ratzinger, teachings on Mary must emanate from the Bible. Ratzinger points to John XXIII's call for Marian piety and devotion to be based on Scripture, wherein Mary's virginity and motherhood are found at her place at the foot of the cross. Ratzinger's view, as per John XXIII, is that Catholic Mariology needs to be

---

47. Joseph Ratzinger, *Theological Highlights of Vatican II*, trans. Gerard C. Thormann (New York: Paulist, 1966). The commentaries on the sessions were published in German after each session of the council and published in English by Paulist as one book in 1966.
48. Joseph Ratzinger, "Das Problem der Mariologie," *Theologische Revue* 2, no. 61 (1965): 74–82.
49. Ibid., 78–80.

cleansed and deepened, not expanded. John XXIII's Mariology, to Ratzinger, marks a decisive point in the development of Catholic Mariology. Indeed, although a scriptural Mariology was not in the first draft of chapter 8 on Mary in *Lumen Gentium*, it was in the subsequent and final drafts.[50] And it is this Mariology upon which Ratzinger's "Marian conversion" is based, along with his concept of a female line.

The debate at Vatican II on whether Mariology should be part of the constitution on the Church or form a separate document reflected, in Ratzinger's view, the profound crisis of the Church's understanding of Mary. In an article Ratzinger published in 1979, on the correct place and role for Mary in Christian faith and theology, he argues that the crisis in relation to Mary arose from a conflict between the Marian movement and the liturgical movement. The dynamic played out not just in relation to the Marian question, but also other major theological issues, so much so that Ratzinger asserts that "one cannot properly understand the wrestling of the first half of the Council—the dispute about the Constitution on the Liturgy, the doctrine of the Church and the correct place of Mariology, about revelation, Scripture and tradition, and the ecumenical dimensions—except against this background of tension between these two forces."[51]

The chapter on Mary in *Lumen Gentium*, according to Ratzinger, was deliberately written as an inner parallel to the chapters on the structure of the Church. The decision to integrate the texts cannot, for him, be overestimated, as it meant that the Marian and liturgical movements were seen as complementary, neither being absorbed by

---

50. Ratzinger, *Theological Highlights of Vatican II*, 141.
51. Joseph Ratzinger, "On the Position of Mariology and Marian Spirituality within the Totality of Faith and Theology," trans. Graham Harrison, in Helmut Moll, ed., *The Church and Women: A Compendium* (San Francisco: Ignatius, 1988), 69.

the other. To his mind, however, in practice, this resolution led to the opposite of what was intended: Mariology was absorbed into ecclesiology. Paul VI's attempt to address the fall-out from Vatican II's decision, by declaring Mary the Mother of the Church, was incapable, according to Ratzinger, of addressing the subsequent crisis. This crisis arose in part because Church-centered Mariology was alien to those who had advocated the Marian position, in the sense that they were promoting a Mary in herself—a stand-alone Mary, if you will—and hence wanted a document dedicated to her, rather than a Mary indelibly linked with Christ and the Church. In addition, there was a misunderstanding of tradition, which had a negative impact on Mariology. This misunderstanding of tradition viewed the Church's later theological insight as inferior to the earlier. Ratzinger rejected this process because, in his view, it meant that the Church was not capable of development in all ages. This would have an important bearing on his approach to biblical interpretation, as will be seen in chapter 2.

This crisis, and Ratzinger's assessment of it, form the matrix for the development of his own Mariology[52] and illuminate, as well, his theological evolution. Ratzinger came to embrace Church-centered Mariology, in which Mary and the Church are viewed as one figure by Scripture and the Fathers. Twenty years after the Mariology debates at Vatican II, Ratzinger reported:

> It seemed exaggerated to me. So it was difficult for me later to understand the true meaning of another famous expression (current in the Church since the first centuries when—after a memorable dispute—the Council of Ephesus, in 431, had proclaimed Mary Theotokos, Mother of God). The declaration, namely, that designated the Virgin as "the conqueror of all heresies." Now in this confused period where truly every type of heretical aberration seems to be pressing upon the doors of the authentic faith—now I understand that

---

52. Ibid., 67–71.

it was not a matter of pious exaggerations, but of truths that today are more valid than ever.

Yes . . . it is necessary to go back to Mary if we want to return to that "truth about Jesus Christ," "truth about the Church" and "truth about man."[53]

Mary is not just about Mary for Ratzinger; rather, Mary is an integral aspect of Christianity. Mary has an impact on every aspect of Christian faith and theology because it is part of Christianity's DNA, so to speak. Mary is important solely in reference to Christ, but Mary is essential to Christology. The realization of the widespread implication of this for Christianity became the fulcrum of Ratzinger's approach to Mariology and changed his attitude to her, Christology, and ecclesiology.

An important catalyst for Ratzinger's Marian conversion was Hugo Rahner's book *Our Lady and the Church*, originally published in 1951.[54] In this work Rahner explores the patristic writings on the Church and the interconnection early Christian interpreters drew between the ecclesial body and Mary. Ratzinger reports that in Rahner, and in other's[55] work on this issue, "[The] rediscovery of the inter-changeability between Mary and the Church, the personification of the Church in Mary and the universal dimension acquired by Mary in the Church, is one of the most important theological rediscoveries of the twentieth century."[56]

Ratzinger's theology developed in response to this rediscovery of the patristic relationship between Mary and the Church, and this Church-centered Mariology became a dominant theme. The development this rediscovery generated can be seen in Ratzinger's

---

53. Ratzinger and Messori, *Ratzinger Report*, 105–6.
54. Hugo Rahner, *Our Lady and the Church*, trans. Sebastian Bullough (Bethesda, MD: Zaccheus Press, 2004).
55. Alois Muller, Karl Delahaye, René Laurentin, and Otto Semmelroth. Ratzinger, "On the Position of Mariology," 69–70.
56. Ratzinger, *God and the World*, 353.

Introduction to Christianity (1968). There Mary is discussed in relation to the incarnation, while the Church is considered in connection to the Spirit.[57] Following the evolution of his thought Mary does not replace the Spirit; rather, Mary and the Church are to be understood in relation to the activity of the Spirit. Church-centered Mariology clarified tradition in relation to Mary, opening up a new vista on Mary through ecclesiology, a vista that the rediscovery of Mary as type of the Church facilitated. This, more than anything, answered Ratzinger's concerns with Mary and the implicit question of Marian thought as reflected and anchored in Scripture. In doing so it demonstrated how the nineteenth- and twentieth-century Marian dogmatic developments (immaculate conception and bodily assumption) were not in fact the departure from the wider historical tradition of the Church that some theologians had thought them to be. Mary was seen from Gospel times to be one figure with the Church, so what is said of Mary is said of the Church and vice versa, which provides the basis for the declaration of these later dogmas. Mary, for Ratzinger, was no longer a spontaneously self-generating aspect of tradition inappropriately and bizarrely maintaining a stubborn presence within the tradition of the Church, but very much part of the apostolic tradition received and nurtured by the Church.

Henri de Lubac's *The Motherhood of the Church* discusses the meaning of its title subject.[58] Originally published in 1973, de Lubac's discussion of the motherhood of the Church in large measure is undertaken in Mary's absence. He argues that the motherhood of the Church derives from the New Testament, and that the Church is personified by the title of "mother." De Lubac refers to the *parallel* between the Church and the Virgin Mary, rather than Mary as

---

57. Ratzinger, *Introduction to Christianity*, 272–80.
58. Henri de Lubac, *The Motherhood of the Church*, trans. Sergia Englund (San Francisco: Ignatius, 1982 [1973]), 40, 53.

type of the Church, as Hugo Rahner identified in patristic literature and taken up by *Lumen Gentium*. The minimal reference to Mary, specifically as type of the Church, is underscored by de Lubac's assertion that the Church's motherhood is "not connected with any sensible experience," even if it does generate an experience. Mary's role comes to the fore in de Lubac's narrative as a mechanism to fight the phenomenon of abstraction and the impersonalization of the Church. It is here that de Lubac refers to Karl Rahner's comments, that what is said of the Church is said of Mary.[59] Why de Lubac focuses on the motherhood of the Church with minimal reference to Mary is not entirely clear, but it may be that, following Hugo Rahner and other's work on Mary as type of the Church, he felt a gap remained in the elucidation of the meaning of the Church as mother. However, the lack of "earthing" of the Church in the person of Mary, in the manner that Ratzinger and Hugo Rahner do, has important consequences, in that de Lubac links both the Church and Mary to the eternal feminine, as we will discuss later. Perhaps it was this link with the eternal feminine that led de Lubac to focus on the motherhood of the Church rather than necessarily on Mary in relation to the motherhood of the Church and Mary as type of the Church. The Church, for de Lubac, encompasses the eternal feminine archetype.

Karl Rahner, in *Mary, Mother of the Lord*, seeks to outline, as does Ratzinger, Mary's proper place and role in faith and theology. Rahner's thinking on Mary could be described as a trinitarian discourse on Mary, as he focuses on Mary in relation to the Father, Son, and Spirit. As Rahner says: "A doctrine of God involves a doctrine of man, and as part of it, a doctrine of Mary."[60] Such an

---

59. Ibid., 92, 113, 153, 158, 164.
60. Karl Rahner, *Mary, Mother of the Lord*, trans. W. J. O'Hara (Edinburgh & London: Nelson, 1963), 29.

approach reflects that found in his *Theological Investigations*, volume 1: *God, Christ, Mary and Grace*.[61] Rahner sees Mary as the perfect Christian and this, for him, is the fundamental idea of Mariology from which all else follows. According to Rahner, "all that faith says about the realisation of redemption, about salvation and grace and the fullness of grace, is realised in Mary."[62] Mary received the eternal Word of the Father through the faith of her spirit. In her the perfect correspondence between personal life and role in salvation history is realized.[63] Karl Rahner's reflections in *Mary, Mother of the Lord* originally were eight devotions delivered during conferences in Innsbruck, and his purpose was "doctrinal instruction." It is unfortunate that the ecclesial aspect of Mary as type was not considered in these reflections. Certainly, Mary presented as the perfect Christian in itself points to the Church; indeed, in his scheme for a treatise of dogmatic theology, outlined in *Theological Investigations*, he refers to her as the perfection of the Church, but the full reality of Mary as type of the Church remains implicit, awaiting a fuller explicit expression. The basis of that expression is in the trinitarian emphasis on Mary's relationship with God the Father, Son, and Spirit as the basis for her role in Christianity. However, this expression requires the relationship of Mary and the Church, that Mary is type of the Church, to enable it to be realized in its full potential and implications. This is something that Ratzinger's female line facilitates. Similar to de Lubac, Rahner does not integrate Mary as *type* of the Church into his Marian theology, although he mentions Mary as type of the Church in relation to Mary's assumption. Here he is considering the Church's eschatological nature and how Mary

---

61. Karl Rahner, *Theological Investigations*, vol. 1: *God, Christ, Mary and Grace*, trans. Cornelius Ernst (London: Darton, Longman, and Todd, 1961 [1954]).
62. Rahner, *Mary*, 38.
63. Ibid., 37.

as the Church type illuminates "her own future in the resurrection of the body."[64]

This notion of the assumption as eschatological is an aspect of Karl Rahner's thought that, due to the embarrassment with which Mariology is generally viewed in modern theology, unfortunately has not been taken up and developed by subsequent theologians. Rahner, in volume 1 of *Theological Investigations*, maintains that Protestantism rejects the assumption because it knows of the theology of the cross but not the theology of glory, to which the dogma refers. It knows salvation as a promise rather than something that exists "even now," even if it has not embraced everything and has not become apparent to us below. Rahner, in contrast, maintains that this state of salvation should apply to Mary in its entirety and fullness. For Rahner, Mary's assumption has significance for ecclesiology and eschatology, which means it has significance for Christianity as a whole.[65] This ecclesial eschatological reality that Mary personifies, which is underpinned by Mary as type of the Church, means the assumption needs to be revisited and further developed through the very trinitarian framework by which Rahner's Mariology is constructed.

The absence of Mary from de Lubac's *Motherhood of the Church* and the church in Karl Rahner's *Mary, Mother of the Lord* is interesting given that Max Thurian considers the two, Mary as Mother and Mary as type of the Church, together in his *Mary, Mother of the Lord, Figure of the Church*. This is particularly striking given that Thurian was a brother of Taizé in the Presbyterian tradition. Thurian's discourse on Mary is thoroughly and completely intertwined throughout with the Church, such that the Church is understood through Mary and Mary understood through the Church. For him, in speaking of Mary we speak of the Church. We see an example of this when, in relation to

---

64. Ibid., 92.
65. Rahner, *Theological Investigations*, 1:226–27.

the fusion of the images of the Daughter of Zion and the Dwelling of God (Jer. 31:3-6; Isa. 62:5, 11-12) in the Old Testament when speaking of Israel, and the application of these titles to Mary, in whom God's final visitation of his people takes place, Thurian maintains that this completes the "symbolism relating to the Church in the last time, when the people of God (of who Mary is the type) shall be renewed.[66] Ratzinger's female line sits within the framework that Thurian articulates, even if Thurian does not inform Ratzinger's thought, and does so because Mary as type of the Church links all these aspects together and thereby illuminates such a perspective. In fact, both Ratzinger and Thurian are drawing on similar sources, particularly Hugo Rahner and René Laurentin but also Karl Rahner. This demonstrates that development of thought on Mary in the pre–Vatican II era was shaped by both Catholic and Protestant thinking and shows how Ratzinger's thought drew and built on those developments.

Ratzinger's Conversion to Truth and Tradition

Ratzinger's thinking on Mary is not the only evolution that occurred in his thought. Development can also be seen in his thinking on tradition and truth, which run parallel to that on Mary. Ratzinger came to fully accept that Christianity speaks of the truth and that the tradition of the Church carries within itself this truth. Ratzinger's research activities, particularly in relation to eschatology, over a twenty-year period to the mid-1970s, led him to accept the Church's tradition. We will see later that critical engagement with tradition through reason, such that tradition is protected from traditions, is an important aspect of this acceptance. He explained this process in *Eschatology*, in relation to his attempt to construct a "de-Platonized"

---

66. Max Thurian, *Mary, Mother of the Lord, Figure of the Church*, trans. Neville B. Cryer (London: Faith Press, 1963), 9, 51.

eschatology: "The more I dealt with the questions and immersed myself in the sources, the more the antitheses I had set up fell to pieces in my hands, and in their place I saw the inner logic of the Church's tradition stand forth."[67] This move to embrace the Church's tradition came through an intellectual process that led him to view the Catholic faith as the truth. This was not an easy journey for him, but it has had a profound impact on his theological framework and starting point.

In his earlier years as a professor, Ratzinger admits that he was uncomfortable embracing Christianity's claim to truth: "I felt very strongly within myself the crisis of the claim of truth during the decades of my teaching work as a professor."[68] He feared that the way Catholicism talked about truth was "sheer arrogance" and showed a "lack of respect for others." These reservations led him to investigate the issue of truth thoroughly. The question he asked himself was, "How far may we still use it?" The answer at which he arrived was that truth is the very foundation of Christianity. It is so because Christianity's claim is to tell us "something about God, the world and ourselves—something that is true and enlightens us."[69] Truth, for Ratzinger, is ultimately about the God of Jesus Christ, who is Truth. This conversion to the truth is reflected in Ratzinger's episcopal coat-of-arms, whose motto, "co-worker of the truth," is taken from John's third letter. This text, he says, "fascinated me right from the beginning."[70] In explaining why he chose this motto, he writes:

> For one, it seemed to be the connection between my previous task as teacher and my new mission. Despite all the differences in modality, what is involved was and remains the same: to follow truth, to be at its service. And because in today's world the theme of truth has all

---

67. Ratzinger, *Eschatology*, xxv.
68. Ratzinger, *God and the World*, 262.
69. Ibid., 263.
70. Ibid., 262.

but disappeared, because truth appears to be too great for man and yet everything falls apart if there is no truth, for these reasons this motto also seemed timely.[71]

There are two important phrases in this statement which reveal the role that the issue of truth played for Ratzinger as a theologian and bishop. The first phrase, "the theme of truth has all but disappeared," reveals the context in which he understands himself to be operating. The second phrase, "yet everything falls apart if there is no truth," indicates the structural impact of truth on theology, and on reality in general, for Ratzinger. Truth holds everything together; it provides the linchpin of Christianity's inner logic, and hence the whole of reality.

So, for Ratzinger, in the modern world there is nothing holding our existence together, the result of which is a falling apart of that existence due to the lack of an integrating framework through which reality makes sense and is rational—reasonable, if you will. His emphasis on truth, then, can be understood as an attempt to demonstrate what it is that gives form to existence and makes it reasonable, makes it meaningful. He strives to articulate to the Church and the world the one thing that transforms the seeming arbitrariness of our existence into the reality of God's creation and, hence, freedom and love. He wants to share this ingredient of the Christian tradition which transfigures everything it touches so as to counter the prevalent claim that we must make our own meaning and order, which to his mind is nonsense. In Ratzinger's work, this theme of truth faces in two directions, to two audiences, two themes but one message. One audience is the Church, and the other is the world. The theme is truth, but the message is tailored to the audience. As a result, his concern with ecumenical issues, evident in

---

71. Joseph Ratzinger, *Milestones: Memoir 1927–1977*, trans. Erasmo Leiva-Merikakis (San Francisco: Ignatius, 1988), 153.

his commentaries on the sessions of Vatican II, was replaced by this search for a correct understanding of Christian faith and theology. This is a monumental shift in Ratzinger's thinking: no longer being primarily concerned with Protestant criticisms of Catholic excesses, even if this nonetheless remains a concern for him. Rather, the starting point of his ecumenical dialogue is the truth of Christian faith, and the search for the truth is the mechanism to address and resolve ecumenical disputes. The inner logic and unity that became evident for him, resulting in his realization that the theology of the Church's tradition is interconnected and interdependent, arose in part from the failure of his own attempt to develop a theology somewhat in reaction to the Church's tradition. This, in turn, led him to embrace that tradition. In this way, to a certain extent, he could be said to be a "poacher turned gamekeeper," which, perhaps, explains the zeal that he brought to the post–Vatican II debates.

In opening to the Church's tradition Ratzinger found a critical aspect of tradition, Mary's relationship with the Church, which linked together essential aspects of Christian thinking in a far-reaching manner. It is in this way that Ratzinger's theological thinking, while remaining christocentric, embraced both Christianity as the truth and the Church's tradition, while moving away from his primary concern for dialogue with Protestantism and with the Catholic and Protestant emphasis on *Solus Christus*, to embrace a wider vision of Christology. That wider vision illuminates the incarnation, which points to Mary and the Church, Mary as type of the Church, and provides for a Church-centered Mariology that provides the backdrop to Christology.

The Framework and Structure of Ratzinger's Theological Thinking

Faith, theology, and tradition in Ratzinger's thinking are each interlinked and provide the framework and structure of his theological engagement. Integration, synthesis, connection, and continuity, combined with ongoing refinement through critical reason, are the dynamics operative within this framework. The relational nature of the God of Jesus Christ is the core material principle of this framework. I will now explore each element of this framework in turn.

Faith in Ratzinger's Theology

Faith is about knowing God and, hence, believing in God; it is not something abstract. Faith has two components. The first is that God reaches out to the human being; we are touched by God. The second is the human being's response in thought and deed.[72] The human being is both passive and active in the process of faith: God's self-gift is first given and, second, the human being responds in the manner of one's choosing. Knowing God and believing in God, Ratzinger argues, arise when the human being responds to God's self-gift. Specifically, Christian faith consists in the "confession of the triune God in the communion of the Church."[73] To confess God is triune is to confess that God is self-transcendent and self-giving, and in knowing this God, human beings reflect this nature.[74]

This confession of faith in the triune God is ecclesial. It is something we receive from the Church, which the Church in turn has received from the Lord. This faith is a gift that can only be

---

72. Joseph Ratzinger, *Principles of Catholic Theology: Building Stones for a Fundamental Theology*, trans. Sister Mary Frances McCarthy, S.N.D. (San Francisco: Ignatius, 1987), 67–69.
73. Ibid., 26.
74. Ibid., 350.

received from others. This aspect of faith is demonstrated clearly for Ratzinger in the sacrament of baptism, which we receive from another person. The confession of faith brings about a communion in faith with others because it is through the Son that we becomes sons. Becoming a son means that through the confession of faith the "I" is incorporated into the communion of the body of Christ[75] without, as we saw earlier, being consumed by the new subject. As Ratzinger puts it: "Faith flows from the Church and leads back to the Church. The gift of God, which is faith lays claim both to mans' own will and to the activity and existence of the Church. . . . Faith is a process of death and birth—an active passivity and a passive activity that need other persons."[76]

Interestingly, Yves Congar, drawing on parallels to natural biospheres, describes this interdependence of faith and Church by saying that faith exists in an "ecclesiosphere."[77] Faith is received from others, but Ratzinger insists faith also requires conversion: death to the isolated I allows for an acceptance of a new I "within the unity of a new subject," the Church. Ratzinger sees this process as Paul describes in Galatians 2:20: "it is no longer I who live, but Christ who lives in me."[78] This conversion is the acceptance of a new beginning, not one we commence on our own initiative but through God's. The Pauline formula of transformation is the template for Ratzinger's notion of faith: an individual is transformed into the subject of Christ when one responds with acceptance to God's self-revelation. Faith creates something new through the acceptance of something that

---

75. Ibid., 27–41.
76. Ibid., 41.
77. Yves Congar, *Tradition and Traditions*, trans. Michael Naseby and Thomas Rainborough (London: Burns & Oates, 1966 [1960/1963]), 256.
78. Joseph Ratzinger, *The Nature and Mission of Theology: Essays to Orient Theology in Today's Debate*, trans. Adrian Walker (San Francisco: Ignatius, 1995), 51.

is before me and beyond me. Ratzinger shares with Hans Urs von Balthasar this centrality of the Pauline process of faith for faith.[79]

For Ratzinger, faith is a going beyond the self, a transcending of the self to something that is not of the self, and it is in Christ through the Holy Spirit that this transformation occurs. This is the disposition of faith that makes Christians the salt of the earth. What this means is that faith is the acceptance of and obedience to a reality that does not come from me, but which transforms me.[80] Faith is receiving God's self-gift and is known through that self-revelation.[81] In other words, it is God's initiative, God's action, through which humanity comes to know the triune God. This creates a particular theological dynamic in Ratzinger's thinking, where the human being as receiver is the primary starting point of Christian faith. Even if once received, faith is responded to and interpreted; he shares this view with Congar.[82] The process of faith always commences with God, and is followed by personal response. The consequences are that subject and object are acknowledged and delineated: there is objective truth to which the subject is orientated but is never subsumed by nor subsumes.

Given that Pope Francis acknowledges that the encyclical *Lumen Fidei* ("The Light of Faith," 2013) is essentially the work of Benedict, and I would argue that it very much reflects his work as a theologian, I will explore it for our discussion on Ratzinger's notion of faith. Although *Lumen Fidei* is a papal document, it should not be divorced from Ratzinger's overall corpus of writings. *Lumen Fidei* first outlines the basis of faith that commenced with Abraham's journey into an unknown land. Second, it speaks of knowledge from faith. The encyclical acknowledges that faith in the modern world is seen as

---

79. Hans Urs Von Balthasar, *The Glory of the Lord: A Theological Aesthetics*, vol. 1: *Seeing the Form*, trans. Erasmo Leiva-Merikikis (Edinburgh: T&T Clark, 1982 [1961]), 220–22.
80. Ratzinger, *Nature and Mission*, 50–61.
81. Ratzinger, *Principles of Catholic Theology*, 316.
82. Congar, *Tradition and Traditions*, 240–56.

an illusionary light, a barrier to knowledge which is now associated with darkness. As a result of this link between faith and darkness, the search for truth is abandoned. In stark contrast, *Lumen Fidei* maintains that faith is a light from the past and, because of Jesus Christ, of the future. The relational nature of faith that is contained within what was referred to above as the process of faith is evident in the encyclical and operates as the dynamic energy of faith in the history of salvation. Faith comes from God and illuminates the entirety of human existence. That faith in God is best understood through the journey of believers, and in this, Abraham holds a unique place.

> Something disturbing takes place in his life: God speaks to him; he reveals himself as a God who speaks and calls his name. Faith is linked to hearing. Abraham does not see God, but hears his voice. Faith thus takes on a personal aspect. God is not the god of a particular place, or a deity linked to specific sacred time, but the God of a person, the God of Abraham, Isaac and Jacob, capable of interacting with man and establishing a covenant with him. Faith is our response to a word which engages us personally, to a "Thou" who calls us by name.[83]

Abraham's faith is a response to hearing God's call to him, something that is contrasted to the seeing or sight of Greek thought. It is also a remembrance of the future because of God's promise, "Your descendants will be great in number" (Gen. 13:16; 15:5; 22:17). The voice of the word spoken to Abraham is one that is present at the core of his being. So, although it is something that is "new," it is not alien, and discloses both the origin of everything and what sustains it. The faith that *Lumen Fidei* speaks of, however, is alien to the modern world: we seek to see the face of God as a response to hearing God, but such hearing and seeking do not fall within the boundaries of modern thought. The faith and the acceptance of the specific Judeo-Christian nature of God's relationship with humanity

---

83. *Lumen Fidei*, no. 8.

that underpins Benedict's thinking makes him appear alien to the modern world, which views such faith and the relationship it creates with incredulity.

The gap between the modern world and Israel's faith is evident again from how the encyclical describes the blossoming forth of that faith, in which relation is the connecting thread. The encyclical outlines that Israel's faith is one of God's deeds in the lives of its people, which are passed down through generations, setting them free and acting as their guide. Israel's faith is a remembrance of God's acts and the continuing fulfillment of God's promises, but it is also a faith mediated by figures such as Moses. This mediation makes faith a communal endeavor in which the knowledge of faith is shared. Belief is not possible on our own; rather, because faith needs to be witnessed, it is communal. Only through the witness of an "unbroken chain" down through every generation is the faith passed on. It means that faith is relational and its setting is the "we" of the Church.[84] The sacraments celebrated in the Church's liturgy point to this "we," and it is through these that the transmission and communication of the faith is carried out: we do not perform sacraments upon ourselves, but others administer sacraments to us.[85] Jesus brings a new dimension to the faith of Israel as the eternal Word of God. Christian faith is a faith in "perfect love" which can transform the world and can act in the history of the world, such that Jesus is the foundation of all reality as well as its final destination. Faith in Jesus is a participation in seeing as Jesus sees, and it is this that enables us to see God's love and how God guides us to Godself. Faith leads to new creation, but it is a gift that must be accepted, and through this acceptance we are "transformed, experience salvation and bear good fruit."[86]

---

84. *Lumen Fidei*, nos. 37–39.
85. *Lumen Fidei*, nos. 40–41.
86. *Lumen Fidei*, no. 19.

Lumen Fidei maintains that faith knowledge arises from truth and love, meaning that reason is not the only basis of knowledge even if faith knowledge must be purified by reason: love and truth are also sources of knowledge. The consequences of this are profound, for love "is a relational way of viewing the world, which then becomes a form of shared knowledge, vision through the eyes of another and a shared vision of all that exists."[87] Faith knowledge is born of God's covenantal love, which lights up the path of history. The unity of faith, truth, and love is contrasted with both the fleeting notion of love today and the subjective nature of truth. "Since it is born of love, it can penetrate to the heart, to the personal core of each man and woman. Clearly, then, faith is not intransigent, but grows in respectful coexistence with others."[88] The significance for the place of faith in theology is that faith allows reason to be guided by truth and love, which transforms its potential and opens up a new horizon. Furthermore, theology is not solely based on "human effort"; rather, God's word is accepted, it is first, and human effort subsequently seeks an understanding of God's self-revelation. Importantly, God can be known in "interpersonal relationship." Drawing on Bonaventure, *Lumen Fidei* states that God is an eternal dialogue of communion and we are allowed to enter this communion. So, while there are limits to theology, it is only through reason that we can investigate "the inexhaustible riches" of the mystery of God's self-gift and self-revelation.[89] Thus, reason enables faith to explore the true nature of the God of Jesus Christ.

Hans Urs von Balthasar, in *The Glory of the Lord*, addresses the issue of what faith allows Christians to perceive. Strikingly, Balthasar entitles the section on faith *Lumen Fidei*. Although the fathers and

---

87. *Lumen Fidei*, no. 27.
88. *Lumen Fidei*, no. 34.
89. *Lumen Fidei*, no. 36.

Scholastics also used the term *Lumen Fidei*, it may be that Benedict was at once connecting the Church to its memory while also acknowledging Balthasar's work for the Church and its influence on him regarding this theme. Both Balthasar and Benedict discuss the notion of faith and what faith opens to the believer in terms of illumination of knowledge. The two, however, tackle the topics in different ways: Balthasar's theological considerations are undertaken in dialogue with, or at least in response to, the concerns of philosophy, while Benedict, writing a document for the faithful, focuses on the Judeo-Christian notion of faith, why it is reasonable, and why it can be perceived as a light and not darkness. Benedict's considerations reflect the signature themes of his prepapal writings in *Lumen Fidei*'s theological emphasis, particularly with regard to the role of relationship and the desire to articulate the meaning of faith to the world today. Balthasar's statement on faith draws on Paul's letters to early Christian communities, in which faith is much more than a worldly knowledge of measurable, verifiable facts and figures, that through the Spirit faith opens a new dimension to humanity. As such, it reflects Ratzinger's own vision of faith:

> Paul constantly refers to the knowledge of salvation which he takes for granted in those he addresses: they know what Paul has proclaimed to them as certain truth, but they also know what knowledge of faith the Spirit opens up on them. The latter knowledge possesses the same certainty which Christian hope has for Paul, a certainty based not on the human understanding's own power of conviction, but on the manifest evidence of divine truth. In other words, this certainty is founded not on having grasped, but on having been grasped.[90]

Another striking incidence of Balthasar's influence on Ratzinger's thought is seen here in *Lumen Fidei*, where Benedict writes of truth possessing the believer and not the believer possessing truth.[91] This is

---

90. Balthasar, *Glory of the Lord*, 1:131–218, at 134.

a perspective that Ratzinger and Balthasar share, the latter of whom argues that there is a possessive intent in those who seek to verify revelation through scientific truth, that they are "enmeshed in an insoluble dilemma" where faith is negated by rationalistic certainty.[92] Ratzinger, addressing the same theme from a different angle, seeks to demonstrate that faith and reason are *complementary*, not contradictory. Ratzinger and Balthasar both reject the limitation of the modern scientific approach, and instead speak of the light of being, that Christ is the "very appearance of Being itself," and that "it is the light of being that enables us to know all existent, since anything we know can be known only in the light of being and from the view point of Being."[93] This light of being is not passively received but actively received by critical reason. This critique of faith is what we will consider presently.

Theology as a Critique of Faith and Revelation through Reason

While theology and faith are distinct, for Ratzinger theology is contingent upon and presupposes faith. Theology is a critical exercise that develops out of faith: "Theology is born when the arbitrary judgement of reason encounters a limit, in that we discover something which we have not excogitated ourselves but which has been revealed to us."[94] Theology interprets and critiques faith; it is not human thought about God, but human thought about God's self-revelation: theology interprets God's Word, which has been revealed to humanity. In this process, theology seeks to understand the foundations and content of Christian faith and does so by inquiring about truth itself. What Ratzinger means by truth is knowledge

---

91. *Lumen Fidei*, no. 34.
92. Balthasar, *Glory of the Lord*, 1:173.
93. See ibid., 1:164; and Ratzinger, "Freedom and Constraint in the Church," in *Church, Ecumenism, and Politics*, 191.
94. Ratzinger, *Nature and Mission*, 8.

of our own being, our origins, and our future. This knowledge, for Ratzinger, requires faith to be truly perceived.[95] Here there is a symmetric relationship between faith and truth, each illuminating the other. Faith opens up the horizon of truth, and truth places faith in its proper contexts; the link between faith and truth opens humanity to its capability of perceiving and engaging with truth and to the reasonableness of reality. Ultimately, for Ratzinger, "theology is pondering what God has said and thought before us."[96] But more than this, theology is pondering what God has done in God's self-giving, God's self-gift. In this way theology is determined by its object.

Four key aspects to Ratzinger's theological approach can be identified. First, revelation—as God's self-giving act—grounds all Christian thought and speech. Second, Christology—the person of Jesus Christ and the God revealed in Christ—is the matrix for theological epistemology. Third, that an ad hoc relationship to Greek philosophy, most notably its intellectual and contemplative dimensions, provides a set of tools that can be appropriated with discernment in the process of theological reflection and construction. And, fourth, the early church identified that the One of Greek philosophy, the God that humanity had deduced, was one and the same God who God had self-revealed in Jesus Christ.

Having previously discussed the first and second aspects, it is necessary to consider the third and fourth in more detail. The theological activity of reflection is a specifically Christian activity that arose out of a synthesis of biblical faith and Greek rationality, and it is the combination of the two that Ratzinger maintains produced historical Christianity. The importance of this, from Ratzinger's perspective, is that Greek rationality is the search for the truth about

---

95. Ibid., 56.
96. Ibid., 104.

being itself. The intricate nature of the early symbiotic relationship between theological inquiry and contemplation—or Greek rationality—can be seen in Ratzinger's description of the development of eschatology: "It means the effort of thinking through the inner logic of the Christian dogmas about eternal life, probing this logic from the inner unity of the whole of the Christian message about God, world and man, and thus bringing its content to bear on human thinking in a meaningful way. This quest for the logic of faith allowed the Church Fathers to call the faith a philosophy, in the sense of a meaningful overview of reality."[97]

Early Christian thinkers drew deeply from the Greek philosophical and contemplative tradition—its method and manner of searching for the unity of meaning in being and reality, and its quest for wisdom—and applied that to the content of biblical faith in attempting to express *a meaningful overview of reality* and to articulate the unity of Christ's message with the tradition of Jewish-Christian faith. Here, Ratzinger suggests that Greek rationality created a dynamic in which questioning and logic pushed the boundaries of thought in relation to the entirety of the Judeo-Christian tradition to release the meaning of the totality of God's Word. In this, an organic development of thought arises from reflection on God's self-revelation.

Philosophical methodology concretizes the testimony of the New Testament so that it does not get lost within the meaning of other contemporary religions. The true nature of biblical faith is drawn out and anchored in the real through philosophical terminology, such that philosophy clarifies "beyond the possibility of misunderstanding, the belief that is the essence of Christianity."[98] Ratzinger rejects the idea that philosophy distorts authentic theology[99] and maintains that

---

97. Ratzinger, "Eschatology and Utopia," in *Church, Ecumenism, and Politics*, 224–25.
98. Ratzinger, *Principles of Catholic Theology*, 114–15.

such criticism of theology is "very ancient" and can be found in Tertullian.[100] Against this he argues that, in their manner of thought, Plato and Aristotle did access the origin—the truth and ground of all being—such that "a certain aspect of reality, a dimension of being, is caught as in a mirror."[101] Ratzinger's interpretation of this synchronicity between the early Christian theological tradition and Greek philosophy harmonizes with Yves Congar's analysis of the origin and evolution of tradition. Congar argues in *Tradition and Traditions* that the fathers, particularly the Cappadocians, borrowed freely from the culturally available tools to explain, demonstrate, and defend revelation and the unique features of Christian teaching, yet "without mixing" Christian faith and philosophy.[102] Biblical faith is not led astray by philosophy but requires it to become what it truly is in fullness.[103]

Christianity's equation of the God of Jesus Christ and the God of the philosophers, that the two are one, for Ratzinger means that the

---

99. Ratzinger, *Eschatology*, 257, 269.
100. Ratzinger, *Nature and Mission*, 18.
101. Ratzinger, *Eschatology*, 257, 24.
102. Congar, *Tradition and Traditions*, 43.
103. Greek philosophy and rationality, for Ratzinger, is not an intellectual construction the Greeks made, devoid of the real and true; rather, through its insistence upon and search for the truth it opened a window onto the real and true. The dispute on the role of Greek philosophy within the development of Christianity highlights that the work of articulating the precise meaning of our thought in words, concepts, grammar, and phrases is a critical work of a scholar. I think it is a much underestimated skill and a task whose role is not fully acknowledged in the process of intellectual reflections. Finding or developing the right words, concepts, terms, and phrases—in other words, the language and grammar—to articulate the meaning of what is trying to be expressed is a precondition for the scholar to appropriately and fully express what they are trying to communicate. Greek philosophy offered fertile ground for the Fathers to appropriate in support of their own struggle to articulate the meaningful overview of reality of God's self-revelation in Jesus Christ. Whether Enlightenment thought offers a coherent and meaningful overview of reality to match and parallel Greek rationality and thought remains to be seen. Answering the critique Ratzinger himself makes of the Enlightenment's idea of autonomous reason, that rationality cannot arise from what is irrational, is an important aspect of that assessment, for the dynamism produced by autonomous reason in relation to the Enlightenment can be viewed as a direct alternative to the dynamism of Greek philosophy and rationality for theology.

God of Jesus Christ reveals the fullness of the divine which the human mind deduced to be pure thought. Through God's self-revelation it becomes clear that the divine is not simply pure thought (creative reason, *logos*), but is thought *and* love. And because it is love, it is has given what has been thought its own freedom such that it is being thought but also "is true being itself." In this, Christianity asserts the primacy of reason, of rationality, over irrationality as the origin and grounds of all being: reason and love are of the same source. This also means that faith and reason, too, are compatible aspects of reality[104] that opened humanity to something greater. As we saw earlier, Christian faith, upon reflection on revelation, understood that God was relationality, person. This movement of thought from an enclosed, self-contemplating being-thought to a relational being-thought that is love, and because it is love provides thought the freedom of its own being, is evident in the movement from the notions of the individual as a reproduction of the universal to the uniqueness and unrepeatable person. It is the primacy of the person in the particular and of freedom, Ratzinger contends, that distinguishes Christianity from idealism. The minimum, the particular—the person—"is something supreme and real."[105] Ratzinger argues this passage of thought "contains the whole span of the transition from antiquity to Christianity, from Platonism to faith."[106] There are profound implications for Ratzinger of this reality: it means that freedom is the supreme factor in the world. More than that, freedom means incalculability, which in turn means that the world cannot ultimately be decoded through mathematical logic let alone is cosmic necessity. The incalculability aspect of freedom points to something that theology, and thought in general, has yet to consider, that the

---

104. Joseph Ratzinger, "Theology and Church Politics," in *Church, Ecumenism, and Politics*, 148–50.
105. Joseph Ratzinger, *Introduction to Christianity* trans. JR Foster (San Francisco: Ignatius Press, 2004), 158-61.
106. Ibid., 137–61, at 160.

trajectory of this aspect indicates an ever-possible "something more." Freedom, however, brings with it the risk of evil, the mystery of the demonic. Ratzinger's response is that freedom and love are the "greater light."[107] And it is this greater light of freedom and love in response to God that is the Christian vision, a vision that can be described as person in freedom; a vision that the Church's development of thought within tradition perceived. So Ratzinger's theological thinking is very far from being a failed "'ordered' and ethereal Neo-platonic/Augustinian worldview" as Anthony J. Godzieba argued shortly after Ratzinger's resignation from the papacy.[108] What we see here is the very specifically Christian nature of Ratzinger's thinking which, certainly draws on the God of the philosophers, but transcends and transforms the limitedness of their discovery through the God who is love. In retrieving these critical aspects of Christian thought, Ratzinger has protected, or simply reminded the Church of the great breakthrough that God's self-revelation in Jesus Christ gifted to us: person is the unique, supreme relational reality not an unconnected individual atom. The human being as person in relation to the Other and others transcends the determinism of nature. In the freedom and creativity of love and reason the unlimitedness of the creative potential of the human being stands forth. The concreteness of this unlimited potential is very much evident in the female and male lines in the Bible and is open to each human person.[109]

---

107. Ibid.
108. Anthony J. Gadzieba, "From the Editor," *Horizon* Volume 40, No. 1 (June 2013), v.
109. I develop the implications of these thoughts further in my paper "The Incalculability of Freedom: A Consideration of Horkheimer and Adorno's critique of Enlightenment in relation to Ratzinger's Notion of Freedom as the Fundamental Structure of the World" at the 3rd Ratzinger Symposium, Christianity, Modernity, and Freedom, Maynooth, 20th of June 2015.

Tradition through the Church

As faith is ecclesial, so, too, is theology.[110] Just as there is no theology without faith and there is no faith without the Church, theology is brought into being and exists only through faith and the Church. As Ratzinger puts it, faith and the Church are theology's "inner foundation and its immediate wellspring."[111] Theology is undertaken by the Church and not the individual[112] because, to Ratzinger's thinking, individual theologians do not stand alone; rather, they stand with and are connected to all the generations of the Church.[113] It is in this way that the Holy Spirit leads the Church "in remembrance" to understand what was not previously grasped. In this we hear an echo of Balthasar's insistence that development of dogma can only occur based on "the model of the pneumatic" and is demonstrable in pneumatic existence. For Balthasar—and Ratzinger would concur—the totality of the reality of faith is something that the believer moves into such that there is a "progressive realisation of that reality."[114] The role of the theologian as a consequence is, for Ratzinger, "to serve the knowledge of the truth of revelation" and in that way serve the unity of the Church.[115] This points to the integral role tradition plays in his notion of theology and for theologians. In Ratzinger's view, the acceptance of tradition is an essential part of theology's interpretation of God's Word and the development and maintenance of the Church's authentic understanding of it. Tradition, Ratzinger contends, is a river from which the Church can draw to renew herself over and over again.

---

110. Ratzinger, *Nature and Mission*, 105; and idem, *Eschatology*, 244.
111. Ratzinger, *Nature and Mission*, 61.
112. Ratzinger and Messori, *Ratzinger Report*, 71.
113. Joseph Ratzinger, *Called to Communion: Understanding the Church Today*, trans. Adrian Walker (San Francisco: Ignatius, 1996), 99.
114. Balthasar, *Glory of the Lord*, 1:229, 239.
115. Ratzinger, *Nature and Mission*, 9.

Tradition is about the unity of the past, present, and future. It is, in fact, the continual transmission of memory through time, which unites, in a transcendent and indivisible way, the people and communities throughout Christian history. Tradition as memory is historical connectivity, what Ratzinger refers to as the "transtemporal relationship of person to person."[116] The individual I is no longer simply an individual, but in connection with other individuals in time. The individual I sits within the context produced by that connectivity, and in this way accesses something more than the individual I can, and does so through all other I's. In doing so the individual I, in conjunction with all other Is become humanity. The movement and connectivity of history allow humanity to be truly human. In this unity and connectivity of the movement of past, present, and future, in which memory is the context, history realizes itself in humanity.

This transtemporal relationship is created by the communicability that speech allows, in which, as Ratzinger puts it, a sharing-with can occur. Speech, then, is the means and the context of tradition, such that memory and speech are the model of the relationship between tradition and time. The unity created by memory occurs through the communication of the past to the present, which makes it accessible for the future. This memory consists of two parallel aspects: first, faithful preservation of the past; and, second, understanding this past in a new way through present experiences. This allows one to advance into the future because it enables one to give expression to the reality that tradition is "continually in the process of formation" and that the purification of tradition occurs in that ongoing history.[117] In this framework, tradition means continuity through memory passed from person to person, which allows for, on the one hand, a

---

116. Ratzinger, *Principles of Catholic Theology*, 87.
117. Ibid., 88.

continuation of that memory as well as, on the other, a renewal of the understanding of that memory. The connection among the persons who carry this memory is the connecting tissue of tradition, which to Ratzinger's mind means tradition is not, nor becomes, abstract or an abstraction. Tradition is tradition through persons.

Tradition, Ratzinger maintains, requires a bearer or subject because history requires a linguistic, or communicable, community. The Church, in which the many are transformed through faith to become one subject, is the one subject with the one common heritage. It has been noted above that tradition is a fundamental aspect of history, which itself provides for the humanness of humanity. But because humanness is, as original sin describes, alienated from itself by the forces of the antihuman, Ratzinger argues that tradition must be guarded against traditions: Ratzinger insists that behind traditions there is *tradition*. As traditions build up over time, which are not necessarily part of tradition, the Church must let herself be pruned of traditions to reveal tradition: what is accidental and temporary must be removed so that what is fundamental is protected.[118]

This pruning of tradition to reveal what is fundamental necessitates that theology reject two approaches which would destroy tradition. The first is a rejection of or an emancipation from tradition; the second is traditionalism. Ratzinger argues instead that reason *and* tradition are required for this pruning process in which both faithfulness to and criticism of tradition occurs. Ratzinger's idea of Church reform indicates what this pruning would entail: neither new structures are needed nor a remodeling of the Church. Rather, reform is about clearing away subsidiary constructs so that the pure light from above is let into the Church. Reform means that we clear away the dross, the excess marble,[119] and make room for the Holy Spirit

---

118. Ibid., 95.

to work. So the continual growth of tradition is a continual pruning of casuistical, accidental traditions through the interplay of tradition and reason. This idea of tradition refined of cauistical traditions is a response to an omission he identifies in *Dei Verbum*. He sees it as "unfortunate" that the possibility of "a distorting tradition," where Scripture is the element through which tradition is critiqued, was not mentioned. Had there been, he maintains that a "real achievement in theological examination" could have occurred in relation to an important aspect of the "problem of tradition."[120] Ratzinger's solution to this problem is that distorting traditions are critiqued by the tradition of Jesus to protect and reveal tradition. Jesus, Ratzinger maintains, provides the Church access to the center of tradition, which he describes as "a breakthrough to what was in the beginning." What Jesus reveals is that *God is*—the simple, ancient creed of Israel. Jesus reveals tradition through his relationship to the Father and that relationship, as we saw, manifests itself in his communion in conversation, through prayer, with the Father. Seeing tradition as Jesus did the Church, in its role as the historical bearer of that tradition, opens the possibility of participation in the tradition of Jesus. Without the Church, it can only be private memory.[121] Ratzinger contends that

> Salvation comes, not from the destruction of tradition or the archaeological neutralization of tradition, but only when the Church, the bearer of tradition, penetrates to its true centre, to the life at the heart of tradition, to the community with God, the Father of Jesus Christ, that

---

119. Ratzinger, *Called to Communion*, 142. Ratzinger states in this regard that: "Reform is ever-renewed *ablatio*—removal whose purpose is to allow the *noblis forma*, the countenance of the bride, and with it the Bridegroom himself, the living Lord, to appear."
120. Joseph Ratzinger, "Dogmatic Constitution on Divine Revelation," in *Commentaries on the Documents of Vatican II*, vol. 3, Herbert Vorgrimler, gen. ed. (London: Burns & Oates, 1969), 155–98, at 193.
121. Ratzinger, *Principles of Catholic Theology*, 89–101. The influence of Josef Pieper, who plays an important role in his notion of love, is evident in this view of tradition and traditions.

is revealed only through faith and prayer. Only when this occurs can there be that true progress that leads to the goal of history: to the God-man who is humanity's humanization.[122]

It is in the classical catechesis, Ratzinger argues, that the Church finds what is unchangeable: the confession of faith of the creeds, the liturgy, the Our Father, and the moral teachings of the Church based on the Ten Commandments and the Sermon on the Mount. This unchangeability of the Church sits in parallel to the changeability of the members of the body of Christ as generations pass. The Church as Christ's body remains always herself just as a human being progresses through the stages of time while always remaining oneself.[123]

Here, Ratzinger is positively aligned with Yves Congar's understanding of tradition and reception. Congar, in his historical assessment of the development of tradition in the New Testament, as well as in the apostolic and post-apostolic eras, maintains that such development was the necessary method of transmission, from generation to generation, of what was received, something that did not originate from those who receive. The body of truths, and a particular understanding of God's plan of salvation, are the *deposit* that tradition carries. The transmission of that deposit is entrusted to the Church. Congar argues that tradition in this period combined a recollection and a deepening of insight through the activity of the Spirit in the Church. This means that apostolic tradition is historical and pneumatic or charismatic: that is, the content is historical while the development of the comprehension of that content by the Church is pneumatic and charismatic. As Congar puts it: "The tradition of the apostles is simultaneously unchanging and timely, recollection of events and unfolding of their significance, conformity to what has been given or done once and for all, and the permanently present

---

122. Ibid., 101.
123. Ibid., 131–32.

and dynamic reality of this thing given or done once and for all."[124] Congar admits that the idea of tradition is not explicit in the Fathers but is an idea that is integral to their thought. It contains three dimensions: a deposit handed on, a living teaching authority, and transmission by succession.[125] Contained in the Fathers' implicit notion of tradition is the unity of Scripture, tradition, and the Church.[126] The tradition of the Church, as Congar sees it, is the interpretation of Scripture by the Church in which Scripture and tradition are two parallel, complementary sources of revelation.[127]

In their constructive work, Ratzinger and Congar both draw on similar sources—particularly what Congar refers to as the rediscovery of tradition in the nineteenth century, Möhler, the Tübingen school with the influence of Passaglia, Franzelin, Scheeben as well as Newman, and the following movement in the twentieth century.[128] Ratzinger, indeed, refers to the "dynamic and organic" idea of tradition of the Catholic Tübingen school of the nineteenth century that Congar sums up in *Tradition and Traditions*. Ratzinger argues that this played a vital role in the positive development of *Dei Verbum* at Vatican II, in that it "extended the field of vision" and "led to a new level" of what initially was, to his mind, a conservative document.[129] Neither Ratzinger nor Congar is interested in one particular theologian's or one historical era's notion of tradition; rather, their interest is, and they seek, the authentic nature of tradition. For them, the tradition borne by the Church is normative and the fathers hold an essential determinative place, which provides the criteria to assess authentic tradition, not in the sense of an audit but in the sense

---

124. Congar, *Tradition and Traditions*, 1–87, at 19.
125. Ibid., 24, 34–35.
126. Ibid., 37–38.
127. Ibid., 38, 64.
128. Ibid., 394.
129. Ratzinger, "Dogmatic Constitution," 157n7; 184n9.

of compatibility and coherence. It could be argued that authentic tradition for Ratzinger and Congar would mean tradition that is "in tune" with the symphony of the fathers and Scripture. This would not mean that the fathers hold the totality of tradition, but an organic development of thought, like the seed and the flower.

Their unity on tradition is based on their acceptance of the Church's transmitted tradition; however, each engages tradition in response to specific challenges of their particular eras of writing: pre– and post–Vatican II. Congar articulates the accepted Catholic position on tradition as against the Protestant position, which is reflected in his extensive consideration of the issues of the relationship between Scripture and tradition, the sufficiency of Scripture and *sola Scriptura*. Ratzinger, on the other hand, in the post–Vatican II era, articulates the orthodox Catholic position on tradition against trends in Catholic theology that moved away from the acceptance of tradition as an elementary aspect of that theology. This is reflected in the recurring theme of the role of Greek philosophy and rationality in the historical development of Christianity in Ratzinger's considerations on tradition. What can be said is that Ratzinger articulates the Congar view of tradition in the post–Vatican II environment, which itself is, to all intents and purposes, the apostolic and post-apostolic notion of tradition. Moreover, this paradigm shift between a pre–Vatican II thought in relation to Protestantism and post–Vatican II thought in relation to Catholic thought itself reflects the shift in Catholic thought in general.

Congar, like Ratzinger, rejects the idea of the Church's tradition as a man-made structure and insists that through the living, unchanging principle of the relation between Christ and the Spirit the Church's tradition is continually renewed and fertile.[130] This living aspect of

---

130. Congar, *Tradition and Traditions*, 264–65.

the Church's tradition allows for the continual development of reflection. This means, for Congar, that tradition allows for the transmission of the deposit of the faith, but there is a development in parallel that is guided by the living principle.[131] It is Congar's view that a "necessary dialogue needs to be maintained" between Scripture and tradition, for, on the one hand, they mutually complete and support each other, while, on the other hand, Scripture is in need of interpretation which is "in harmony with the *sensus Ecclesiae*."[132] Congar, as per his title, *Tradition and Traditions*, discusses tradition and the traditions within that one tradition. He argues that the charisms of the *ecclesia*, as expressed by the magisterium, clarifies tradition in three ways: first, by discerning the authentic elements of tradition that have been carried through history; second, by identifying those elements with its normative value for Christian faith. In this way, Congar says, the material elements of historical tradition are turned into the formal elements of normative tradition in a process he refers to as active tradition. The third way is through an authentic interpretation of the content transmitted. The guardian of this authentic interpretation is the *ecclesia* as a whole, with and under the magisterium.[133] Congar maintains that implicitly in Scripture the truths of salvation are contained, so that he can say in concert with the Fathers that "unwritten tradition consists dogmatically in a true interpretation of Scripture."[134] So it is not a case of tradition carrying anything that is not congruent with Scripture; rather, tradition draws out the true meaning of Scripture in a harmony.

Congar sought to give precise guidelines for what tradition is and how the Church validates the traditions included in tradition. He

---

131. Ibid., 266
132. Ibid., 295
133. Ibid., 302–3.
134. Ibid., 305.

distinguishes, as a point of clarification, apostolic and ecclesiastical tradition, where apostolic tradition is that which the apostles received directly and immediately, while the ecclesiastical tradition receives and is the ongoing witness to apostolic tradition.[135] Ratzinger takes a somewhat different approach. For Ratzinger, Jesus validates tradition and this Jesus tradition must be protected from traditions. In doing so, Ratzinger offers an organic approach to validating tradition by making what is normative for tradition dependent on Jesus and the Jesus tradition. It is through this lens that the arbitrary traditions that have built up over time can be pruned and *tradition* can be revealed. The manner of that pruning is carried out through the classical forms of the Church's confession of faith mentioned above: the creeds, the liturgy, the Our Father, and the moral teachings of the Church based on the Ten Commandments and the Sermon on the Mount—in harmony with what Congar referred to as the *sensus Ecclesiae*. Ratzinger's organic approach is open to validating tradition at any point in the past, present, or future. And this provides a dynamic approach to authenticating tradition, which operates in parallel to the movement of the Spirit in continually deepening the Church's comprehension of the revelation and the deposit of the faith.

Ratzinger and Congar exhibit significant convergence of thought on the Holy Spirit's activity in the Church. Ratzinger refers to the pneumatic character or dimension of the idea of tradition in which the Christ event is not simply a historical event but remains present through the Spirit who reminds the Church of God's activity in his self-Revelation, and in and through that the Church remembers not only the inner significance of those events, but also assimilates and experiences that as a present event.[136] This is not simply a

---

135. Ibid., 300–304.
136. Ratzinger, "Dogmatic Constitution," 189–90.

remembering of something static; rather, at the heart of Ratzinger's thinking on the idea of tradition is the reality of an ever-renewed appropriation of tradition by the Church in fidelity with the Spirit.[137] From Congar's perspective, the Spirit's work in tradition is in "actualising and interiorising" the once-and-for-all words and deeds of Jesus Christ in the Church and the hearts of its members. This activity is not independent of Christ; rather, the Spirit carries out the work of Christ, and in that way "ceaselessly acts to make his Gospel ever new, in continuity with the form he gave it once and for all."[138] Based on Ratzinger's work on Bonaventure, Congar asserts that revelation is fully itself when it is given to someone and received by that *living* person.[139] The living nature of tradition means tradition is not some material object, but is "the active presence of revelation in a living subject, by the power of the Holy Spirit, represents what is yet unfulfilled in progress, ceaselessly requiring fulfillment in the Word of God."

The living, active nature of tradition fundamental to both Ratzinger and Congar is that aspect which the Spirit provides, enabling the Church to express and comprehend its faith in Jesus Christ in every generation but also to develop its interpretation, and express it in the present, in harmony with the original deposit of faith. Congar maintains in relation to Scripture and tradition that

> Some kind of development is necessarily entailed: at least, as an unfolding or an explanation. The Church is commissioned to proclaim and to fulfill the plan of the covenant established in Jesus Christ in an earthly context. The Church is both transmission and life, both repetition and reissuing, a response given on the basis of the one and only text to the ever new questions asked by time. It is the making present in personal and world history of the saving plan made in Jesus

---

137. Ibid., 165.
138. Congar, *Tradition and Traditions*, 342–43.
139. Ibid., 401.

> Christ, and it requires a future fulfillment. The Holy Spirit bears witness to the Church, that what it preaches is indeed the content of the mission it receives to proclaim the Gospel. He enlightens the Church about the true content of the economy of salvation and this activity cannot thwart in any way what God has already done.[140]

For Congar, on the one hand, there is the faith received, while on the other, there is an ongoing development of interpretation and expression of that faith. Scripture and tradition are always to be "combined and referred to each other."[141] They are not rivals but complementary modes of expression, or states of knowledge, in differing forms, of the same revelation. Nevertheless, Scripture, which is fixed in its "absolute sovereignty" due to its divine origin, governs tradition and the Church in the manner that tradition and the Church does not do to Scripture.[142] The unity of approach seen in Ratzinger and Congar's notion of tradition enables us to say that Church and tradition receive what is transmitted from the apostles and the fathers and, guided by the Holy Spirit's activity in the Church, expresses it for that era and develops its understanding, while never altering the deposit of faith received. Tradition, for Congar, and we can also say for Ratzinger, grows because it is alive, and that life is given by the Holy Spirit who also protects the Church's growth of comprehension against arbitrary development and expression.

The Historical Nature of Christianity

The historical nature of Christianity is integral to Ratzinger's notion of faith, theology, and tradition: the events of the incarnation and the crucifixion and resurrection truly happened within history and the Church lives from these events. Reconciling the ontological aspects

---

140. Ibid., 402. Congar maintains that the liturgy is the primary earthly context through which the Church is to proclaim Jesus and his plan of salvation.
141. Ibid., 414.
142. Ibid., 422.

of these events and their historical nature into a unity is what Ratzinger's idea of salvation history seeks. Or, in other words, through Christ's incarnation and resurrection the union of being and history, between ontological and historical nature, occurs. Ratzinger's approach strives to heal the idea that the ontological, which expresses continuity, is in opposition to or is opposed to history, which expresses discontinuity. In that process he seeks to bring the ontological incarnation together with the historical crucifixion. Ratzinger acknowledges that where Christian faith provides form and freedom to a human beings' life, it is accepted as salvation. Where it is experienced as alienation, however, the idea that history does not lead to being arises, which generates crisis and the search for a new way.[143]

Christian historical consciousness, anchored in Jesus' message of a new beginning which is at the same time the end of all history, is characterized by a personalization or individualization, on the one hand, and a universalization, on the other. The Pauline notion of Jesus as the last Adam, integral to Ratzinger's theological thinking, structures his thinking on salvation history. Jesus manifests what is truly human or, as Ratzinger puts it, man's hidden nature, and this relates to the whole of humanity: that universal applies to each particular human being. In bringing ontology together with history, Christianity reveals the creatureliness of humanity's origin in creative freedom. This means that "the temporality of being is the mode of its self-fulfillment . . . that time has its unity in the *Creator Spiritus* and because it is sequential, is still a continuity of being by way of succession."[144] This points to the notion that Jesus Christ is Christianity's expression of freedom and hence the form of freedom for each particular human being. It is by going out of oneself that one

---

143. Ratzinger, *Principles of Catholic Theology*, 153–58.
144. Ibid., 162.

finds freedom, which is intrinsically linked to love and redemption. As Ratzinger puts it, "The tension between ontology and history has its foundations in the tension within human nature itself." And he argues that the unity of the two is to be found in the mystery of God, which is freedom.[145] Salvation history is defined for Ratzinger by the fact that Christian theology is at its core a theology of resurrection. What this means is that God's power, God's actions, have overcome the power of death and in that way offers a new hope in history. The resurrection is, as Ratzinger puts it, *the* eschatological action of God. The late Judaic expectation was that eschatology lay at the end of history, but, Ratzinger maintains, in Jesus' resurrection this was brought into the middle of history. The resurrection, which includes the cross as the ultimate Passover, points for Ratzinger to the whole of history being an exodus history.[146]

Ratzinger's notion of salvation history is structured around the meaning of the incarnation and resurrection both for God and humanity: Christ brings being and time together. Salvation history ultimately is about the meaning of the God-man's being in time, which itself reveals the true nature of the human being. God's action—God's power—makes this salvation history and points humanity to its true nature, its true origin, and its ultimate future. The union of the ontological and historical in Jesus is the mystery of salvation in human history. This reflects Congar's historical assessment that tradition is the "manifestation, *in the time of human history*, of the mystery of salvation" and that mystery, proclaimed in the Old Covenant, was given in its fullness in Jesus Christ.[147]

This connects, in some measure, to Balthasar's theology of history.[148] For Balthasar, how Christ stands in time is explicated

---

145. Ibid., 170–71.
146. Ibid., 184–90.
147. Congar, *Tradition and Traditions*, 42–43.

through how Christ stands in relation to world history and man. There are two aspects of this. First, history, including salvation history, is a necessary presupposition to the historical Jesus, but the historical Jesus also is a necessary presupposition that makes history possible, including salvation history. In this, history is related to Christ as promise to fulfillment. Second, the norm of each man and every history is revealed through the fulfillment of Christ. This norm relates to Christ's universal relation to everything and as a quality that norm generates for the Christian, the Church, humankind, and history.[149] Balthasar posits that "It was in view of him that the venture of having any such thing as a world and a world history could be made at all; in view of him and his Church that such a thing as the creation of man and woman could take place (Eph. v 31-2); in view of him and his Mother that the expulsion of sinners from paradise could be justified (Gen. iii 15)."[150]

It is Christ's existence, his receptivity to everything from the Father, that time and temporality receive their meaning and through which eternity can be glimpsed and form the basis of Christian existence: believing and hoping love. In that way, Jesus brings the eternal into time, which is itself the meaning of following Christ: Jesus' existence speaks of the Father and provides the meaning of all existence.[151] And it is in such a context that meaning arises for man in that through faith and prayer he is "broken open" toward God, and it is in that attitude that the grace of mission "provides the full and overflowing content of meaning for each successive historical now."

---

148. Hans Urs von Balthasar, *A Theology of History* (London: Sheed & Ward, 1965 [1959]).
149. Ibid., 20–21. Balthasar considers the theology of history with regards to four specific themes: Christ's mode of time; the inclusion of history within the life of Christ; the person of Christ as the norm of history; and history under the norm of Christ.
150. Ibid., 62.
151. Ibid., 28–29, 40, 42, 49, 71.

In that way, the Church and each Christian's relationship with Christ, like his with the Father, is one of "conception and femininity."[152]

In considering history under the norm of Christ, who is the center of history, Balthasar sees that the fullness of time has been attained, and with it, the end of ages prior to the "transition to eternal life." The relationship between sacred and secular history then comes into view, which is not, according to Balthasar, a convergence or harmonization of the two, even if there is an indivisible connection between the two that will be perceived at the last judgment. Secular history, through God's using it to attain the goal of incarnation, is permanently marked by that grace. So there are two movements in Balthasar's theology of history: God's action and human history. The meaning of history is not imposed from above but emerges from the union of the two.[153] Ultimately, for Balthasar, the theology of history is formed not in the battle between the two cities of Jerusalem and Babylon, but in the deeper, interior battle within the human being.

Ratzinger underscores continuity in the reception of history in the Church's tradition. This does not mean, however, a lack of development or innovation; that is part of the ongoing procession of comprehension in transmission. Yet, where others argue that change through the course of different eras of history is preeminent and should be recognized in the Church's thought and doctrine, for Ratzinger, reception history unfolds the capacity of the Church to *deepen* its comprehension of revelation through the guidance of the Spirit within the particularities and variegated contexts of intellectual and cultural history. In interpreting these historical dimensions, Ratzinger engages with the specific historical and theological issues, and these determine his response in addressing related problems or disputes. Ratzinger's view is that in acknowledging the historicity of

---

152. Ibid., 118.
153. Ibid., 123–36.

Christianity and the contextually conditioned nature of our thinking, the scholar and Christian converse with and become embedded in the wider history of the Church.[154] In that way, historical consciousness—and constructive theology—are not focused on a delineation between historical eras. Rather, they focus on the integration of each era with all other eras, which generates connection to the memory that the Church's tradition bears. Thereby the Church avoids the trap of an analytical discussion and abstract idea of history, which itself distorts history, and hence Christianity.[155]

Vatican II's Place in the Church's Tradition

Ratzinger's understanding of tradition, as outlined above, also determines his interpretation of Vatican II. Theological debate on Vatican II centers on the issue as to whether it was a rupture with the past or in continuity with it. Ratzinger maintains that it was in continuity with all previous church councils and tradition

---

154. Ratzinger, *Principles of Catholic Theology*, 152.
155. There is, as Rausch rightly identified, a particular structure to Ratzinger's theological thinking that influences his engagement with modern discourse. Rausch's assessment is accurate as to the structure but not to the impact of that structure. It is not a closed system but a system open to each generation of theologians: memory connects the Church of today with that of yesterday and tomorrow. That openness is not an openness to replace what has gone before with the historical concerns of a particular era but an openness to contribute to the already existing insight and comprehension of the Church's tradition. It means that in Ratzinger's thought the concerns and influence of any era or any theologian is always subordinate to that overall structure. Plato and Augustine each influence aspects of his thinking but each remain secondary, indeed relativized, to the interrelated structure of his theological framework: faith, theology and tradition, and the Christian categories of thought, relationship, and relatedness. Each influence draws his attention to certain aspects of theological concern, but his acceptance of the God of Jesus Christ as the truth and his embrace of the Church's tradition is the prism through which he engages with those issues. This reflects Congar's thinking that the most creative and the most passive members of the Church are subject to tradition (Congar, *Tradition and Traditions*, 234). Ratzinger's engagement with contemporary concerns is carried out in two ways. First, he identifies areas that require further development to enable discourse to fruitfully continue within tradition. Second, he articulates tradition in light of the concerns of the modern era and its specific challenges. In this development of thought and articulation of tradition, faith in revelation and the ecclesial nature of faith is the power and dynamism that provides the energy to his theological thinking.

itself. Ratzinger held a unique position in the Church in relation to Vatican II due to his participation in the council—he was chief theological adviser during the council to Cardinal Frings of Cologne—and the Church positions he has held since the close of the Council: bishop, prefect of the Congregation for the Doctrine of the Faith, pope, and finally pope emeritus. In viewing Vatican II through the lens of continuity with tradition he argues that its reception was far from unique in that "nearly all councils have seemed to destroy equilibrium, to create crisis."[156] But he also sees the Council as embedded in the zeitgeist of the time, an era in which turbulence affected society across the board. So, Vatican II was simultaneously a reflection of that turbulence and to a certain extent a contributor to that turbulence, given its effects on the Catholic community. He identifies the positive effects of the Council as having achieved five specific things: the integration into the Church of the doctrine of primacy, the hierarchy into the Body of Christ and Mariology into faith; fully acknowledging the biblical word; making the liturgy accessible; and making strides toward Christian unity.[157]

It is his view that the Second Vatican Council was ahead of its time and that it was only after the student revolts of 1968 did it seem to lag behind the times.[158] He believes that the documents of the Vatican Council have been misunderstood and that a true interpretation of the Council's documents has yet to occur. To do this, the Church must return to the documents and explore them afresh, [159] reading them as a whole and neither in isolation from each other, against each other, or as a prelude to something more.[160] Only in that way will the authentic reception of Vatican II occur.[161] This is reflected

---

156. Ratzinger, *Principles of Catholic Theology*, 369–71.
157. Ibid.
158. Ratzinger and Messori, *Ratzinger Report*, 34.
159. Ibid., 31.
160. Ratzinger, *Principles of Catholic Theology*, 390.

in his argument that one of the problems that arose after the Vatican II, which led him to co-found the journal *Communio*, was that it seemed that being relevant had become more important in theology than stating and exploring the truth. Ultimately, the historical value of Vatican II, Ratzinger argues, depends on "those who transform its words into the life of the Church."[162] For Ratzinger, Vatican II is an integral aspect of tradition and can only be truly understood as an aspect of the continuing tradition of the Church. It is not about this generation but about all the generations of the Church, and a particular era or generation is not free to impose its unique ideas on the Church. Connecting Vatican II to the memory of all previous councils and the tradition of the Church, guided by the Holy Spirit, is the manner in which Ratzinger believes interpretation of Vatican II should proceed. Building on Ratzinger's approach one could say that in following *the Way* of Jesus Christ (Acts 9:2, 19:23) the journey of the Church has brought it to many ports of call, or councils, and Vatican II is not a point or ports of departure but one of the latest ports of call for the Church, and no doubt there will be many more to come.

Vatican II as rupture or discontinuity was recently restated by the editors of *Concilium*, in an edition marking the fiftieth anniversary of the opening of the council. The editors, Silvia Scatena, Dennis Gira, Jon Sobrino, and Maria Clara Bingermer, argue that Vatican II was a significant "turning point, and one which has irrevocably changed the Church's consciousness from what went before." Due to what they maintain as current widespread trends of reductionism and denial of the scope of a council that "changed the face of the Catholic Church," they wish to stress "the Council's epoch-making value and ground-breaking nature within and between generations."

---

161. Joseph Ratzinger, "*Communio*: A Program," *Communio* 19, no. 3 (1992): 436–49.
162. Ratzinger, *Principles of Catholic Theology*, 378.

They include Benedict XVI's papacy as part of the trends they are seeking to combat, arguing that the acts of his papacy—specifying his 2005 speech on the fortieth anniversary of Vatican II and the July 2007 *motu proprio* "Summorum Pontificum" on liturgy—and his hermeneutics have gone hand in hand with recent reductionism and anticonciliar revanchism.[163]

In the same edition of *Concilium,* John W. O'Malley argues, with a different emphasis, that a dramatic change in Benedict VXI's approach to Vatican II occurred in his Christmas address to the Curia on December 22, 2005, which marked the fortieth anniversary of the closing of Vatican II. O'Malley maintains that his hermeneutic of continuity was replaced by a hermeneutic of reform.[164] This is an argument that has gained currency and which James Corkery put forward in his 2009 book, *Joseph Ratzinger's Theological Ideas.* Corkery argues that a change of style is a forerunner of real change,[165] and he contends that Ratzinger, as Pope Benedict XVI, in that address acknowledged, albeit in a nuanced way, discontinuity at Vatican II. He quotes Benedict as stating: "It is clear that in all these sectors, which all together form a single problem, some kind of discontinuity might emerge. Indeed, a discontinuity had been revealed but in which, after the various distinctions between concrete historical situations and their requirements had been made, the continuity of principles proved not to have been abandoned. It is easy to miss this fact at first glance."[166]

Corkery sees this as an acknowledgment of discontinuity, notwithstanding Benedict's clear assertion of the primacy of continuity. Corkery and O'Malley, to my mind, argue too much

---

163. Editorial, *Vatican II Begins: Fifty Years After,* issue of *Concilium* (2012/13), 7–8.
164. John W. O'Malley, "*Ressourcement* and Reform at Vatican II," in ibid., 53, 47–53.
165. Corkery, *Joseph Ratzinger's Theological Ideas,* 141–42.
166. Ibid., 130.

here. In Ratzinger's own theological approach the specific detail under consideration, whether that is a scriptural text or a church council or a document, as will be seen most clearly with Mary in relation to salvation history and Christianity in general, should, and can only, be understood as part of the whole of Scripture and tradition. Benedict's reference to discontinuity at Vatican II is a genuine reflection on the historical realities and conditions under which the council met, but it is also only a part of the totality of Ratzinger's/Benedict's reading of the council. Thus, such a statement on Vatican II should be read in relation to his larger interpretation of the council and his understanding of tradition. As we have seen, Ratzinger sees in Vatican II a continuity with all previous church councils, while, at the same time, asserting that a vigorous analysis of the proceedings and contexts must be deployed as a theological measure to protect against arbitrary traditions. Such ongoing reform or pruning is integral to that continuity. Thus, Ratzinger does not see in Vatican II *dramatic change*, or discontinuity of a substantive, dogmatic nature. Rather, Vatican II is connected to the memory of the Church in which tradition and reason work together in an organic process of interpretation concomitant with recognition of the deeply historical and contextual natures of such events and processes. Just as in every era, the Church in the post–Vatican II environment is called to express a renewed appropriation of tradition in fidelity to the Spirit.

It is worth noting that the 1999 Joint Declaration on the Doctrine of Justification by the Lutheran World Federation and the Catholic Church[167] is absent from theological discourse on the council's

---

167. "The Joint Declaration on the Doctrine of Justification by the Lutheran World Federation and the Catholic Church" (1999), http://www.vatican.va/roman_curia/pontifical_councils/chrstuni/documents/rc_pc_chrstuni_doc_31101999_cath-luth-joint-declaration_en.html. In particular, paragraph 40 states: "The understanding of the doctrine of justification set forth in this Declaration shows that a consensus in basic truths of the doctrine of justification exists between

rupture–continuity paradigm. It would be valuable to include it in the ongoing discussion of that paradigm at Vatican II, as it brings something quite new and different to that discussion, an attempt at coming together again, a healing, which needs to be addressed in the various arguments. This Declaration's position still stands from the Catholic perspective even if the German Evangelical church's position paper marking the five-hundredth anniversary of the Reformation, "Justification and Liberty" (May 2014), does not explicitly mention it. Equally, a new challenge to the widely held negative view in Catholic theological circles of pre–Vatican II theology and the argument for rupture at Vatican II has inadvertently arisen from the appointment of Justin Welby as Archbishop of Canterbury, in November 2012. In an interview in *The Guardian* in July 2012, following his appointment as a member of the Parliamentary Commission on Banking Standards in the UK, Welby makes clear that his major concern is the common good and that Leo XIII's 1891 Letter *Rerum Novarum* is the greatest influence on his moral thinking.[168] It is truly striking that the recently appointed leader of the Church of England draws inspiration for addressing today's moral challenges from an era that is now rejected by many Catholic theologians. This points to the urgent need to consider Vatican II beyond the very limiting constraints of the rupture–continuity paradigm, something that creates an inappropriate zero-sum game of winners and losers. By placing Vatican II within the river of tradition, that zero-sum game is

---

Lutherans and Catholics. In light of this consensus the remaining differences of language, theological elaboration, and emphasis in the understanding of justification described in paras. 18 to 39 are acceptable. Therefore the Lutheran and the Catholic explications of justification are in their difference open to one another and do not destroy the consensus regarding the basic truths."

168. Giles Fraser, "The Saturday interview: Justin Welby, Bishop of Durham." *The Guardian*, July 21, 2012. http://www.guardian.co.uk/world/2012/jul/21/bishop-durham-justin-welby-interview.

negated, while the continual development of the Church's comprehension of revelation, with an ongoing critique of it through reason, is facilitated.

The Place and Role of Dissent in Theology and Tradition

Ratzinger's attitude to dissent by theologians can be understood in light of the comments he made in relation to the Hubertus Halbfas case of the late 1960s, which occurred while Ratzinger was still a professor. Halbfas in 1968 published *Fundamentals of Catechetics: Speech and Experience in Religious Instruction*, in which he argued, based on the implications he identified in exegetical sciences including modern biblical criticism, that articles of the faith such as the resurrection the Church developed over time—in other words, they were not historical. He also asserted, in relation to Christian missionary activity, that conversion was not the aim; rather, missionaries were to help make the Hindu a better Hindu and the Buddhist a better Buddhist. The result was that the German bishops' conference issued a formal condemnation, and the teaching job Halbfas was offered in Bonn was vetoed by the See of Cologne.[169] John Allen records that "Ratzinger told him [Halbfas] that one certainly has the right to take the position he did in his book, but then one should not do so as a Catholic theologian."[170]

For Ratzinger, it is not dissent as such that is the issue, but the assertion of something that is incongruent with Scripture and tradition as being Catholic theology. What is important to him is the clear articulation of orthodox Catholic theology. Ratzinger sees that a theory that seeks to be identified and accepted as Christian or

---

169. John L. Allen Jr., *Cardinal Ratzinger: The Vatican's Enforcer of the Faith* (New York: Continuum, 2002), 221–24.
170. Ibid., 223. Similarly, with respect to Hans Küng's views on the origin of the Church, Allen records Ratzinger saying, "If I believed that, I couldn't say the creed."

Catholic theology must accept the historical identity which makes Christian and Catholic theology meaningful. This is an a priori acknowledgment and acceptance of the historical development of Christian faith and Catholic theology, something he calls a trademark. The application of contemporary concerns and scientific methodologies in an inappropriate manner to faith, which then supposedly debunk theology and tradition, is what he particularly has in mind. In his view, the task of theology is to explore the truth of revelation, which is a service to the Church. He states in this regard that "Everyone is free—within the framework of the responsibility of conscience before the truth—to think whatever this responsibility permits him to think or to say. But not everyone is free to assert that what he says represents Catholic theology."[171]

This explains succinctly Ratzinger's method of operation as a theologian, prefect, and pope: the protection and accurate articulation of Catholic theology. It means that he does leave room for theologians to develop theological ideas so long as those ideas are not framed or labeled as Catholic theology where they diverge from it. By sticking to the essentials of faith and theology, Ratzinger has sought to protect authentic Christian faith against well-meaning theological trends that, to his mind, endanger the fundamentals of Christianity. The question is, of course, did Ratzinger impose his own view of Catholic theology on the community of theologians and Church in general? Given his insistence on tradition as memory connecting all eras of the Church as a fundamental aspect of theology, the approach he offered as prefect and pope was not his; rather, it is the tradition of the Church, which incorporates all previous generations of the Church. So it is not reasonable to say that his approach is subjective in the sense of imposing his own ideas of

---

171. Ratzinger, *Nature and Mission*, 8.

theology; the tradition of the Church is distinct from his theological ideas and thought even if, as we have seen, he came to embrace it thoroughly. What would be subjective is if he were pointing to a specific era of theology or a narrow list of specific theologians, which he is not; rather, he is pointing to the river of tradition congruent with Scripture. His view of his role as prefect and pope is that he is to guard the memory of the Church. This does not fully address the question as to what is authentic Catholic tradition and theology, how it is identified and developed, and we will return to that topic presently.

But first, we must look at Ratzinger's concept of conscience to explore how theological dissent fits within the parameters of conscience he identifies.[172] Vincent Twomey argues that the concept of conscience is fundamental to Ratzinger's theology, stating: "Conscience, it seems to me, might well be a key concept to understanding both the personality of the man and his theology. More accurately, it is the link between both."[173] In Twomey's reading, Ratzinger regards the mystery of conscience as "the powerless limiting the exercise of power."[174] This means that in situations where abuse of power occurs, suffering by those of

---

172. Interestingly, both Ratzinger and Kant refer to conscience when discussing theological dissent. Immanuel Kant had argued in his *An Answer to the Question: 'What is Enlightenment?,'* in 1784, that there is a distinction between the role and scope of the theologian as clergyman and as scholar. As he puts it: "A clergyman is bound to instruct his pupils and his congregation in accordance with the doctrines of the church he serves, for he was employed by it on that condition. But as a scholar, he is completely free as well as obliged to impart to the public all his carefully considered, well-intentioned thoughts on the mistaken aspect of those doctrines, and to offer suggestions for better arrangement of religious and ecclesiastical affairs. And there is nothing in this which need trouble the conscience." Kant, *An Answer to the Question: 'What is Enlightenment?,'* trans. H. B. Nisbet (London: Penguin, 2009), 6.
173. D. Vincent Twomey, *Pope Benedict XVI: Conscience of our Age* (San Francisco: Ignatius, 2007), 22. He bases this discussion of Ratzinger on conscience on Ratzinger's *Wahrheit, Werte, Macht: Prufsteine de pluralistischen Gesellshaft* (Freiburg im Breisgau: Herder, 1993).
174. Twomey, *Pope Benedict XVI*, 109–10. As Twomey puts it, in reference to Ratzinger's essay "Conscience and Truth" (see n.176, below): "In it, it seems to me, he cuts the Gordian knot at the heart of the contemporary crisis, in the Church and in the world, which could be summed up as the triumph of subjectivity, the denial of man's capacity for truth and, so, for God."

conscience is the only way to overcome the injustice. It is reasonable to mention that theologians who have been subject to inquiry by the Congregation for the Doctrine of Faith would identify with the powerless–power paradigm that is referred to here. Twomey argues that Ratzinger recovers the ontological level of conscience, *synderesis*, of the Middle Ages. This notion of conscience stands in contrast to two other notions that Ratzinger maintains are contradictory and perverse notions of conscience: erroneous conscience and an infallible conscience.[175] Both are the result of subjectivity, which reduces morality to personal preference. *Erroneous conscience* here refers to the attitude that "it does not matter what one does provided that one is sincerely convinced it is right." And *infallible conscience* "affirms that conscience cannot err, that what you think is right is in fact right."[176] For Twomey, the value in Ratzinger's thoughts on conscience lies in his assertion that man as the image and likeness of God, who is "capable of truth," has recovered the *objective* nature of conscience and morality—"the ontological level"—from a subjective notion. It is also a reminder that the Church is the place that awakens conscience. Twomey does argue, however, that Ratzinger's theology of conscience, although it contains the seeds of potential, requires further theological development to bear fruit. Specifically, Twomey identifies that the relationship between the teaching authority of the Church, among others such as moral authorities in education, and our "primordial conscience" need "to be teased out further." Nonetheless, he believes Ratzinger's thought on conscience "is a major contribution to moral theology."[177]

---

175. Ibid., 121–26.
176. Ibid., 123. Twomey points out that Ratzinger responds to this situation by identifying two levels of ontological conscience: first is memory of the good that is implanted in human beings; second is the act of judgment in a particular situation, which is always unique. In addition, Ratzinger mentions the grace of God's forgiveness once we recognize our guilt.
177. Ibid., 127–30, 132–37.

Although Ratzinger draws on the Church's tradition on conscience, when addressing issues related to Enlightenment concerns such as freedom, subjectivity, and truth he turns to John Henry Newman's response to liberalism and Christian subjectivity. Drawing on Newman, Ratzinger insists that the issues of subjectivity and authority are at the core of the problem of conscience in the modern era. Subjectivity becomes disorientated without truth, which is the measure of conscience. Indeed, it is the absence of truth that gives rise to the primacy of the measure of progress in the modern era. To ensure that subjectivity is orientated correctly in relation to authority, and authority to subjectivity, Ratzinger, via Newman, argues that it is truth that holds them together. Truth provides the correct orientation between subjectivity and authority so that each has its proper place and neither is negated to the exclusion of the other. The truth of God which is the truth of humanity means that conscience in humanity is arbitrated by the human being in relation to God and never arbitrated by the subjective self in itself in isolation from God: there is objective truth. Ratzinger as a result argues that "Conscience signifies the perceptible and commanding presence of the voice of truth in the subject itself. Conscience means the abolition of mere subjectivity when man's intimate interior sphere is touched by the truth that comes from God."[178] Although he refers to the Platonic *anamnesis* to express the nature of conscience, it is from Paul, Basil, and Augustine that he draws the Christian content and context to articulate what he specifically means by conscience. Anamnesis, according to Ratzinger, is "primal remembrance of the good and the true," of our origin in God and image of God. This makes possible an internal recognition of the voice of that origin.[179] That

---

178. Joseph Ratzinger, "If You Want Peace . . . : Conscience and Truth," in *Values in a Time of Upheaval*, trans. Brian McNeil (New York: Crossroad/San Francisco: Ignatius, 2006), 86.
179. Ibid., 90–95.

voice is the law Paul recognized that the Gentiles knew as well: we can hear the voice of God in the core of our being (Rom. 2:1-16). Conscience, for Ratzinger, means "acknowledging that man—oneself and the other—is a creation and respecting the Creator in himself." The Creator–creature paradigm, truth and subject, is the structure of conscience; the subject is never a subject in isolation but always orientated to the Creator, the truth. Ratzinger readily acknowledges that conscience must be continually purified to prevent distortions arising from a superego or a subjective self-will that would distort conscience. However, the vulnerability of conscience, the danger that conscience can and is misused, is not a reason to diminish or shy away from it. For it is this paradigm of conscience that defines the limits and proper direction of all power so that he can say, "perseverance in the powerlessness of conscience is the fundamental prerequisite and core component of all real control of power."[180]

With this overview of Ratzinger's thinking on conscience we can explore the issue of theological dissent in relation to conscience. To do so, we need to consider two aspects of the notion of conscience: conscience in relation to the state and conscience in relation to the Church. In relation to the first, the objective notion of conscience, for Ratzinger, is guaranteed by the Church's separate role in society to that of the state. Indeed, he identifies the duality of Church and state as a specifically Christian paradigm arising from Jesus' command to give to Caesar what is Caesar's and God what is God's. It is this paradigm that underpins the Western notion of freedom. Importantly, Ratzinger argues, it ensures that the state is not the totality of things. Totalitarianism results where there is no publicly recognized authority of conscience that can place a check on the state's authority when it assumes sole authority for all aspects of life,

---

180. Ratzinger, "Conscience in its Time," in *Church, Ecumenism, and Politics*, 164.

including morality. Indeed, this duality of separate political and sacral authority, for Ratzinger, is essential to avoid totalitarianism by either Church or state.[181] To maintain the duality, Ratzinger argues, the Church must reject any attempt to render Christianity as a private belief or opinion. Rather, the Church must continue in its claim to speak of truth and moral values that are universally applicable.[182] The state pursues policies and activities in response to the environment in which it finds itself and the specific challenges it encounters. The underpinning dynamic may or may not be a Godward perspective, and may simply be a functional response to problems whose criteria are efficiency, progress, and growth. The duality of Church and state that Ratzinger insists upon is necessary for the church to witness to the Godward perspective of humanity and the world in light of functional responses.

In relation to the Church and theological dissent, Ratzinger argues that the faithful have a fundamental right to receive the faith of the Church and celebrate the liturgy of the faith, and not be subject to private opinions of theologians. Ratzinger's primary concern here is not to close out critical theological refinement but to ensure that the faith of the Church as expressed in the creeds and the liturgy—the expression of faith from the earliest times of the Church—is protected from inappropriate intellectualizing, which may be blinded by its incapability to integrate the fullness and potential of faith—God's power over matter (Father Almighty)—into critical theological reflections. For example, the precritical–critical paradigm is about the place of faith in theology and the world. It may usher in an acceptance of the primacy of reason in theology and the relegation of faith to a naïveté or lesser intellectual level, which is highly

---

181. Ratzinger, "Biblical Aspects of the Theme of Faith and Politics," in *Church, Ecumenism, and Politics*, 144; and idem., "Theology and Church Politics," in ibid., 157.
182. Ratzinger, "Biblical Aspects"; idem, "Theology and Church Politics"; and idem, "A Christian Orientation in a Pluralistic Democracy?" in *Church, Ecumenism, and Politics*, 193–208, at 206–7.

dangerous. The moment we view ourselves more intelligent than others we become blind; that blindness transforms our intelligence into arrogance and makes us stupid. It is entirely reasonable for the Church's magisterium to protect the Church's faith. This is not about theologians, but about the faith that is the pearl of life. For Ratzinger, all other freedoms in the Church are ordered to that fundamental freedom of receiving the faith of the Church, because through faith and the sacraments we have the opportunity to participate in divine being.[183] So, while Ratzinger believes that the theologian has a duty to follow their conscience *before truth*, which involves a full notion of conscience that goes beyond subjectivity, the Church, in parallel, has a duty to safeguard the Church's faith for the current and future members of Christ's body. The model of conscience, where the Church is a duality with the state, is different from that of the Church and the theologian. The Church witnesses to the truth in its moral and social teachings in relation to the policies and activities of the state. In parallel, the Church witnesses to and expresses faith in Jesus Christ, a witness, as we have seen, vivified by the Spirit, which enables the Church to both express that witness for each era and time and to continually deepen its understanding of that faith. The theologian is not in a duality with the Church, as if a separate entity, but is in total relationality with the Church and with Christ, while never being subsumed and always remaining an I. Freedom in the Church arises not from a duality of Church and theologian, but from participation in divine being.

While acknowledging the differences, it is reasonable to explore the dissenting theologian in relation to conscience before the truth through Ratzinger's model of the duality of Church and state. What can be said, first, is that each theologian, as does each Christian, has

---

183. Ratzinger, "Freedom and Constraint," 191.

the duty to witness to the truth in every circumstance whether in relation to the Church or the state, and this will result in suffering. Second, where authority in the Church is misused, the paradigm of conscience Ratzinger identifies between the Church and state does apply; the failings of Church authorities related to sexual abuse by priests and religious would certainly fall into this category. Where dissent is on specifically theological issues, however, the paradigm of abuse of power and position does not apply unless theological ideas disconnected from the continuing development of the tradition of the Church are imposed on the Church. From Ratzinger's perspective, theological issues are about truth, the truth of the faith of the tradition of the Church. Based on our considerations heretofore, what can be said is that theological dissent is not dissent in relation to the magisterium but the Church's development of tradition. The magisterium's role is to protect the Church's tradition and to allow for its continuing development through a deepening of the comprehension of that transmitted tradition in the guidance of the Spirit. Theological disputes are then to be resolved in the development of the tradition of the Church in continuity with the deposit of faith. This means the Church's tradition is transmitted while also critiqued by reason and purified by the tradition of Jesus. Resolution of issues of dissent cannot descend into an individual's view(s) against that of the Church's memory. Instead, it is in and through the development and deepening of the Church's comprehension of tradition that issues of dispute should be addressed, and this by necessity includes tradition being protected from and pruned of casuistical arbitrary traditions in the guidance of the Spirit. The theologian dissenting in conscience before the truth does so in relation to the Church's tradition, which expresses orthodox Catholic faith and theology, and only through the suffering that such dissent entails can the truth of the dissent be perceived and come to light in the fullness of time.

The reader may think, that's all well and good, but what is authentic orthodox Christianity, orthodox Catholicism? How is it determined? What is the criteria to be applied? This is the underlying issue for most of what already has been discussed, not just for this immediate section but for all the previous sections. The question, in many ways, is really about authentic tradition, and specifically how tradition can and should develop the Church's deepening comprehension of God's self-revelation. We've already seen that Ratzinger's approach is anchored in Scripture, the fathers, and the Church's tradition. Crucially, tradition does not stop at the fathers or Scholasticism—it never stops, nor can it be identified with one era, ancient or recent; tradition is of all eras of the Church. Tradition is always ongoing, which makes the question about the criteria for assessing appropriate congruent evolution of tradition supremely important.

From Ratzinger's perspective, four criteria can be identified. First and foremost is congruency with Scripture, the Church's confession of faith, the creed, and liturgy. Second is continuity with the memory of the Church, which is open to ongoing refinement and pruning; a rupture or discontinuity with the memory of the Church is a negation of tradition. This opens the Church to surprise, just as Ratzinger did with his resignation from the papacy. Within tradition, much under the surface awaits to be drawn out in a manner consistent with points one and two. Ratzinger reached back into the Church's tradition and to canon law to renew and rejuvenate the Church. The Church is called to repeat that process as it responds to ever-new challenges. The third criteria is critique or, in other words, critical engagement through reason of tradition. It is not simply about passively carrying whatever the current has happened to pick up along the way. Each aspect is open to critical examination. For example, Ratzinger, when Pope Benedict XVI, in his book on the infancy narratives rejects Augustine's argument, which tradition has taken up, that Mary had taken a vow of virginity and entered marriage in order to have a protector for that virginity. He rejects this explanation as "quite foreign" and "inconceivable" in the Judaism of Jesus' time.[184] We see here an example of Ratzinger using history to interpret history and to protect tradition from traditions. Something that is part of tradition but which the historical evidence is incompatible is rejected. Historical evidence, as distinct from theory determined by presuppositions, is a tool used to protect tradition from traditions. Fourth, the role of the Spirit in guiding the Church in the memory of the Lord must be accounted for and discerned. Discerning the movement of the Spirit, what is from God and what is not, is the critical element. The Church cannot do better when attempting to discern the movement of the Spirit than taking on board Rabbi Gamaliel's advice to the Jewish community when discerning the early Christian movement: "If this enterprise, this movement of theirs, is of human origin it will break up of its own accord; but if it does in fact come from God you will not only be unable to destroy them, but you might find yourselves fighting against God" (Acts 5:38-39). The test of time and how an idea, an approach, survives and responds to the vagaries of time and the passing on to others is critical to this spiritual discernment. This is a point we will return to in the next chapter. While each of these four criteria requires interpretation and defies a simple list of items that could be checked off, importantly, the four criteria work together as a whole, not in isolation from each other, in the assessment of the appropriate evolution and development of tradition. There is not

---

184. Joseph Ratzinger, *Jesus of Nazareth: The Infancy Narratives*, trans. Philip J. Whitmore (New York: Image, 2012), 34–35.

one methodology than can discern authentic Christian orthodoxy and tradition, but as always with Ratzinger, a nuanced synthesis of multiple strands that, when woven together, create a strong rope to hold tradition as one and protect tradition from traditions.

There is one aspect of the development and refinement of tradition in Ratzinger's thought that awaits development. In his commentary on *Dei Verbum*, as we saw, he does regret that a methodology to refine accidental or cauistical traditions from tradition was not developed in that document. As we saw, he sees the tradition of Jesus as a mechanism to prune accidental and cauistical traditions; this process does not sufficiently address the gap he identified. What would be truly valuable is if, in his retirement, the pope emeritus would take up this issue that he identified in his Commentary on Dei Verbum in 1968 as a gap in the output of Vatican II, and, prioritizing clarity as regards criteria without being proscriptive, he would develop a transparent approach to both the refinement of accidental or cauistical traditions and the development of authentic Christian theology and tradition. To avoid inappropriate engagement in Church matters and to maintain full obedience to his successor(s), such a document would not be published until after his death: a pope emeritus's role is to pray for and with the Church.

Authentic, orthodox Christianity in continuity with the tradition of the Church is Ratzinger's goal. He wants to avoid subjectivity on the part of an individual theologian or a theological era from displacing the objective truth of the faith of the God of Jesus Christ. To that end, caution is always advisable. When developing and refining tradition I would argue that the Church should follow in the footsteps of Lossky, Ratzinger, and Williams in their efforts at continuing the elucidation of person in the divine and the human. Perhaps, at a minimum, the principle should be adopted that one generation or era proposes a development, a second considers that proposal in all its dimensions, and a third or later generation or era, if appropriate, determines the appropriate place of the proposal in the Church's faith and tradition. A level of built-in objectivity is included in such an approach in the sense that the subjective aspect is mediated through successive generations or eras. I would also argue that the Church must be on the lookout for lever arguments, arguments devised to discredit or dislodge certain aspects of theology or tradition that are no longer appealing or are barriers in the way of asserting ideas that resonate with themes associated with modernity. Subjective ideas that are incapable of passing the test of each era of the Church's tradition should be rejected. We, too, as individual theologians, also must be on guard against constructing a theology in reaction against aspects of tradition we do not believe are truly part of *tradition*. Our theological approach must remain an organic development of God's self-revelation based on core principles, which then are used to engage with those aspects of tradition that we feel are not tradition while always striving to first understand and then to be understood. The aim must be refinement and development, not a reaction against and a wholesale replacement where I or my generation have uniquely managed to understand the true meaning of Christianity. All in all, authentic, orthodox Christianity ultimately refers to the Father through the Son and in the Holy Spirit. This is the starting point and end point, and it is through this paradigm that Christian faith and theology must be measured. As we will see in in the following chapters, however, this does not close out development, creativity, and innovation of Christian theology from *within* tradition. The task is to go back to tradition and retrieve aspects that have not been given sufficient attention and renew, in congruence with Scripture, interpretation by including these "forgotten" or "hidden" aspects. From the earliest time the Church has robustly debated what authentic orthodox Christianity is, and leaders have forcefully asserted what is alien or incompatible with it: Acts, Paul's and John's letters, and the letter to the Hebrews, as well as the fathers, all demonstrate that. No individual theologian should shy away from that continuing robust debate, for the worst that could happen to the Church is that the faith of the Church, and the Church itself, is no longer something worthy of struggle.

Innovation within the Tradition of the Church

Ratzinger's insistence on authentic tradition that remains in continuity with tradition as exemplified by the fathers and on objective truth can make him appear to be not only orientated to, but simply wanting to blindly repeat, the past. But a deeper consideration of Ratzinger's theological thought points to something else, that is the desire to share the faith in the God of Jesus Christ. This is the animating principle and chief importance of his life's work: it can be understood as a response to his belief in Christianity as the truth and how that truth transforms the experience of reality for humanity. He remarks that, "For what I really have at heart is keeping this precious treasure, the faith, with its power to enlighten, from being lost."[185] His theological writings, therefore, are an attempt to preserve the Christian faith and are, for him, "a genuine, honest, intellectual attempt to understand the world and man."[186] So we can say that Ratzinger's life's work is twofold, but complementary in nature: to protect the Christian faith and to seek to understand humanity and the world through this faith. This driving feature—that Christ is the revelation of God *and* humanity, and that this fundamentally constitutes a new way of being and relation to the world—means, for Ratzinger, that we are all caught up in a single story and that "we

---

185. Joseph Ratzinger, *Salt of the Earth: The Church at the End of the Millennium: A Conversation with Peter Seewald*, trans. Adrian Walker (San Francisco: Ignatius, 1997), 113.
186. Ibid., 97.

are all a part of a single history that is in many different fashions on the way towards God."[187] A certain similarity is evident here with Karl Barth. Ratzinger's longstanding interest in Barth is demonstrated by the fact that in February 1967, when a professor, he brought his students to Basel in Switzerland to meet with Barth. This was part of the nascent *Schülerkreis* of Ratzinger's doctoral students, which at that time met with theologians outside of their faculty. The topic of the discussion was Vatican II's document on the interpretation of Scripture, *Dei Verbum*, which Ratzinger played a role in developing and which Barth considered to be important.[188] Although it cannot be undertaken here a greater exploration of Ratzinger's engagement with Barth would be highly valuable and very welcome.

At this stage it is reasonable to ask, is it actually possible to talk about *the theology* of Joseph Ratzinger? The answer would have to be no. Indeed, the strength of Ratzinger's work is that he has not developed a theology that could be viewed as uniquely his, separate from a contribution to the continuous development of the church's understanding of revelation. He is a theologian who draws from the river of tradition and seeks to evolve and deepen the Church's comprehension of that tradition. As well, in accordance with his relational thinking and the Pauline structure of the framework of tradition, his theological signature is that of innovation within the tradition of the Church.

Ratzinger's thinking focuses on the core issues, cutting through the fog of time, of ideas and thoughts, hopes and dreams. He synthesizes and sums up what is already there. He separates the wheat from

---

187. Joseph Ratzinger, *Truth and Tolerance: Christian Belief and World Religions*, trans. Henry Taylor (San Francisco: Ignatius, 2004), 44.
188. See Father Stephan Otto Horn's history of Ratzinger's *Schuelerkreis*: "It Cardinale Ratzinger e i suoi studenti," in *Alla Scolla della Verità. I settanti anni de Joseph Ratzinger*, ed. Joseph Clemens and Antonio Tarzia (Milan: San Paulo, 1997), 10. I would like to thank Rev. D. Vincent Twomey, professor emeritus of moral theology, Pontifical University, Maynooth, for bringing this book and article to my attention.

the chaff so that a coherent whole is produced. His clarity enables him to pinpoint the core issues and then articulate a response that builds upon the Church's theological framework. Since the end of Vatican II, he has confronted issues that, in his view, threaten the faith and he does so in the model of Paul, the fathers, and especially Augustine, who worked out the content of Christian faith in response to heresies: Arianism, Nestorianism, Docetism, Pelagianism, and the like. In this regard, Ratzinger's approach has always been to clarify a correct interpretation of the faith. This leads me to argue that had Ratzinger not taken the name Benedict he may very well have been Paul VII. He has even pointed to 2 Timothy 4:2-5 in 1997 as his standard:

> Preach the word, be urgent in season and out of season, convince, rebuke and exhort, be unfailing in patience and in teaching. For the time is coming when people will not endure sound teaching, but, having itchy ears, they will accumulate for themselves teachers to suit their own likings, and will turn away from listening to the truth and wander into myths. As for you, always be steady, endure suffering, do the work of an evangelist, fulfill your ministry.[189]

Ratzinger's approach has been Pauline: robust, uncompromising, and willing to undertake the unpopular task of confronting misinterpretations and to identify an orthodox interpretation of the Christian faith. In this, his emphasis as a theologian is to articulate clearly and clarify *Christian* theology, rather than necessarily Catholic theology. An example of this concern can be seen in his work with the Lutheran Church on the 1999 Joint Declaration on the Doctrine of Justification by the Lutheran World Federation and the Catholic Church.[190] His works *Introduction to Christianity* and *Eschatology*,

---

189. Ratzinger, *Salt of the Earth*, 114.
190. "The Joint Declaration on the Doctrine of Justification by the Lutheran World Federation and the Catholic Church."

among many others, also demonstrate this concern for Christian theology.

When Ratzinger defends the Christian faith, it is its reasonableness that is important to him. With this approach, he has pursued answers to the big questions of his time: What is Christianity? What is theology? What does Christianity tells us about salvation? Who is Jesus Christ? How should faith and reason interact? What is truth? and What is freedom? Because he is interested in the wider perspective he has been able to confront the larger failings of the Church and of society. But this also means that lesser, though important, issues are overshadowed, and the perception can arise that these questions are not of importance, or that Christianity remains an academic, abstract affair. On the other hand, with his wider perspective, Ratzinger has developed the intellectual capital to articulate responses to the challenges that face Christianity and the world today. The intellectual underpinning of Christian faith and articulating it in an accessible and concise manner is of utmost importance if the faith is to answer the challenges of the secular world. Ratzinger has greatly contributed to this task.

Ratzinger does not borrow wholesale from any of his influences. His is more of an *à la carte* approach. So, if he is seen as part of the staunch conservative wing of the Church, he is, in fact, a highly independent, innovative, and nuanced thinker. Ratzinger is very much his own man intellectually, and, this in many ways is hidden, due to his leadership roles in the Church and as pope. It can be argued that Ratzinger's silence on issues related to Church teachings and positions should not necessarily be taken as acceptance or agreement. In fact, the opposite may be more accurate. He is a politician in the best sense: he focuses exclusively on his aim and goal, which is the defense of fundamental tenets of the Christian faith. Where he sees issues with Church teachings he expends his intellectual energy on building an alternative option rather than criticizing the existing position.

Ratzinger's understanding of the papacy and the Church means that the innovative aspect of his theological thinking is not immediately obvious. His view is that the role of the prefect of the Congregation for the Doctrine of Faith, and of the pope, is to protect the memory of the Church, to protect the Church from arbitrary action.[191] In particular, he does not think that the pope is an instrument to call into existence a new Church, as if a new pope is like a newly elected prime minister or president reversing the decisions their predecessor took the day they are sworn in to office.[192] This theological understanding of the role of the pope meant that Ratzinger as pope acted for the Church and not in response to his own specific individual theological views or ideas.

For example, Ratzinger the theologian, as opposed to the prefect of the Congregation of the Doctrine of the Faith, does not appear to have commented significantly on *Humanae Vitae* (1968), for or against, prior to his election as pope. After his election, however, he articulated on numerous occasions the Church's position on contraception, and has been roundly condemned for this position. On the other hand, in the fourth book/interview, *Light of the World* (2010), he asserted that condoms can be used to protect life.[193] Whether this can be seen as a major shift in the Church's stance on the issue is unclear, particularly given the Vatican's clarifying statements on the matter in November 2012. The statement issued by Father Federico Lombardi declares: "the reasoning of the Pope certainly cannot be defined as a revolutionary change. Numerous

---

191. Ratzinger, "If You Want Peace . . . ," in *Values in a Time of Upheavals*, 95.
192. Ratzinger, *God and the World*, 377.
193. Benedict XVI, *Light of the World: The Pope, the World, and the Signs of the Times: A Conversation with Peter Seewald*, trans. Michael J. Miller and Adrian J. Walker (San Francisco: Ignatius, 2010), 118–19.

moral theologians and authoritative ecclesiastical figures have supported and support analogous positions; it is nevertheless true that we have not heard this with such clarity from the mouth of the Pope, even if it is in an informal and not magisterial form."[194]

What can be said is that his statement opened the door to debate on a matter that, up to then, appeared closed, and this desire for debate on the matter may indicate an element of unease with the Church's position and a belief that issues remain to be worked through more fully particularly in light of contemporary developments such as AIDS. It may also indicate that this has been Ratzinger's own individual view all along, and there is evidence to support this. Commenting on Ratzinger's *Zur Theologie de Ehe*, Francis Schüssler Fiorenza states that: "Reflections similar to those of Ratzinger's have led innumerable theologians to argue that the Catholic Church should change its traditional opposition to 'artificial means of birth control.'"[195]

What can be said is that Ratzinger has opened debate on aspects of the issue that he believes requires further exploration while leaving it to the church of subsequent generations to develop the Church's position on contested issues in the post–Vatican II era, particularly those upon which John Paul II pronounced, rather than imposing his own view. This is why there is a need to distinguish Ratzinger

---

194. Federico Lombardi, "The Pope Does Not Reform or Change the Church's Teaching," trans. Joseph G. Trabbic, http://www.zenit.org/article-31024?l=english. The quote continues, "With courage Benedict XVI thus offers us an important contribution of clarification and reflection on a question that has long been debated. It is an original contribution, because on one hand it maintains fidelity to moral principles and demonstrates lucidity in refuting an illusory path like that of the 'confidence is condoms'; on the other hand, however, it manifests a comprehensive and far-seeing vision, attentive to uncovering the small steps—even if only initial and still confused—of an often spiritually and culturally impoverished humanity, toward a more human and responsible exercise of sexuality." Ratzinger's desire for the Church to consider its position on condoms is evident here in this longer quotation. While anchored in moral principles, he sees a need for the Church to respond to the concrete situation of humanity.

195. Francis Schüssler Fiorenza, "Marriage," in *Systematic Theology: Roman Catholic Perspectives*, vol. 2, ed. Francis Schüssler Fiorenza and John P. Galvin (Minneapolis: Fortress Press, 1991), 305–46, at 341.

the theologian from his role as prefect and pope. The Church's position that he enforced may not necessarily have been completely congruent with his own personal theological viewpoint.

To understand Ratzinger as theologian, prefect, and pope, there is no better place to explore than his book *Eschatology* (1977), which he finished at the time he was appointed archbishop of Munich. Here, he describes clearly, as he saw it, the challenges facing the Christian faith. It is like a blueprint for his time as prefect and later as pope. Nichols would appear to be correct that Ratzinger's *Eschatology* is "heavy with consequence for his own future dealings with theologians elsewhere" (i.e., liberation theology).[196] Within *Eschatology*, he expounds his views on biblical interpretation and Christian salvation in detail, and these were the controversial issues during his time as prefect. Ratzinger's theological approach since Vatican II can be seen in comments he makes in *Introduction to Christianity*, where he observes that "The idea that one can do more constructive work in isolation than in fellowship with others is just as much an illusion as the notion of a Church of 'holy people' instead of a 'holy Church' that is holy because the Lord bestows holiness on her as a quite unmerited gift."[197] Ratzinger is very aware of the limitations of humanity in this endeavor and he does not view theology or the Church as pristine or perfect.

John Allen reports that the consensus among professional Catholic theologians is that Ratzinger's work will not be read in one hundred years' time apart from his commentaries on Vatican II.[198] That may or may not be the case, but what can be said is that Ratzinger has had a gravitational pull on the Catholic and wider Christianity

---

196. Aidan Nichols, OP, *The Thought of Pope Benedict XVI: An Introduction to the Theology of Joseph Ratzinger*, new ed. (London: Burns & Oates, 2007), 167.
197. Ratzinger, *Introduction to Christianity*, 344.
198. Allen, *Cardinal Ratzinger*, 102.

communities and on the secular world. Another German who had a paradigm-shifting impact on his world was Otto von Bismarck, the first German chancellor, who remade the map of Europe between 1860 and 1870. He observed: "Man cannot create the current of events. He can only float with it and steer."[199] In this regard, it may be argued that Ratzinger steered his Church and the wider world through the currents of major upheaval and did so, in his own unique way, through the compass of Jesus Christ.

---

199. A. J. P. Taylor, *Bismarck: The Man and the Statesman* (London: Penguin, 1955), 70.

2

The Female Line

Foundations and Methodology

Ratzinger's advocacy for "the female line in the Bible" is a new perspective that provides a theological grid for grappling with substantial questions, such as anthropology, salvation, Mariology, the Church, and biblical interpretation. This framework is rooted in a hermeneutics that grounds itself in the biblical stories and figures of the tradition and seeks to unfold theologically a view that encompasses the full weight of salvation history spanning both the Old and New Testaments. There is a twofold upshot to this: on the one hand, it offers a synthesized vision of the genealogical lines of salvation history—from Eve to Mary and Adam to Christ—and, on the other hand, it advances a constructive vision of a biblical and Marian ecclesiology that fills in a theological space left open at Vatican II. From Ratzinger's perspective, these are critically important tasks, for if Mary and the Church are ignored, the result is an inability to read the Bible in its totality; and if a biblical concept of the Church is abandoned, "we lose the place where the unity of the Bible's testimony is experienced."[1] Ratzinger's answer is that only by considering the whole can we comprehend the whole.[2] For him, the two Testaments are a unity, and Christ and the *ecclesia* are the hermeneutical center of the whole.[3] The female-line concept, then, reflects not just his concern to address the issues that feminist theology raises but also his wider concerns around biblical interpretation and the essential role the Church plays in that interpretation. In this chapter I will first look at the foundations of Ratzinger's idea of "The female line in the Bible," and then at the role that biblical interpretation, and Ratzinger's own specific approach to it, plays within the female line.

The Origin and Development of the Concept of the Female Line in the Bible

Ratzinger's female-line concept developed over a twenty-five-year period beginning in the early 1960s. Vatican II's reference to Mary as type of the church, his own theological evolution, and his response to post–Vatican II theological developments, particularly in relation to biblical interpretation and feminist theology, were all important contributing factors leading to his articulating this concept. The ideas included in Ratzinger's female-line concept, and the meaning of the women of the Old Testament and Mary for salvation history that this concept reveals, are preliminarily seen in his early writings on

---

1. Joseph Ratzinger, "The Sign of the Woman," introduction to Pope John Paul II, *Mary: God's Yes to Man: John Paul's Encyclical* Redemptoris Mater, trans. Lothar Krauth (San Francisco: Ignatius, 1988), 18.
2. Ibid., 19.
3. See Joseph Ratzinger, *Daughter Zion: Meditations on the Church's Marian Belief*, trans. John M. McDermott, S.J. (San Francisco: Ignatius, 1983), 31–33; and idem, "On the Position of Mariology and Marian Spirituality within the Totality of Faith and Theology," trans. Graham Harrison, in Helmut Moll, ed., *The Church and Women: A Compendium* (San Francisco: Ignatius, 1988), 75.

Mary and Mariology. But it was his adoption of a Church-centered Mariology that provided the hermeneutical framework in which the ideas could receive full expression. I will first explore the path of that twenty-five-year development.

An early example of Ratzinger's writings on Mary or Mariology is his homily on the visitation entitled "Maria Heimsuchung. Eine Homilie," published in 1962 in *Bibel und Leben*.[4] Here, Ratzinger compares Mary and Elizabeth's *faithful* reaction to the annunciation to Zachariah's unbelief, which prevents him from abandoning himself to God. We find in this article the seeds of the key tenets of his Mariology: Mary, in faith through grace, is the fulfillment of Israel's faith. His writings on Mariology that appeared in his commentaries on sessions two (1963) and three (1964) of Vatican II give further shape to this idea.[5]

The Vatican II documents, *Lumen Gentium* and *Dei Verbum*, are important for the development of his understanding of Mary and form the soil in which his idea of the female line sprouted. In his commentaries on sessions two and three, he maintains that the aim of the decision to include Mary in *Lumen Gentium* was to "preserve proportion" in the Church's teachings so that Mary stood with the Church and not with Christ.[6] In that way, Mary's role is clarified: Mary is not divine but human; Mary is not to be worshiped but venerated. The prior poor theological situation, as he viewed it, was replaced, through the inclusion of Mary in *Lumen Gentium*, by a scriptural Mariology where the events of salvation history are understood in the light of faith. An important aspect of this was

---

4. Joseph Ratzinger, "Maria Heimsuchung. Eine Homilie," *Bibel und Leben* 3 (1962): 138–40. This article was republished in 1974 in *Dogma und Verkündigung*, 411–14.
5. Joseph Ratzinger, *Theological Highlights of Vatican II*, trans. Gerard C. Thormann (New York: Paulist, 1966). The commentaries on the sessions were published in German after each session of the council and published in English by Paulist as one book in 1966.
6. Ibid., 140.

the discarding of inappropriate titles for Mary that had accrued over centuries, particularly "Mediatrix of all graces." However, he notes that the council fathers misunderstood the theological situation, which he referred to as "the problem of Mariology," and which led him to publish the 1965 article "Das Problem der Mariologie."[7]

In this article, as we saw in the previous chapter, Ratzinger argues for a scriptural Mary to counter the development of an inappropriate Mariology that occurred in the previous centuries. He refers to John XXIII's deep misgivings of some Marian devotions that misunderstand the place of Mary's in the teachings of the Church as well as to Pius XII's rejection, expressed to the International Congress at Lourdes, of definitions for Mary as Mediatrix and Co-Redemptrix. Ratzinger contends in this article that John XXIII's statements are a decisive point in Mariology: it is in the Bible that the teachings on Mary are to be found.[8] Ratzinger rejects the maximalist and minimalistic paradigm for thought on Mary and argues that Mariologists either neglect Scripture or use unscientific methods of interpretation. He argues instead for the paradigm of truth and untruth where scriptural exegesis occurs. He sees in the work of Vatican II the opportunity for *inner progress*, in which the expansion of the past would be refined and pruned of excess. Mary, who listens to God's word wordlessly, who dwells in God's holy word and allows herself to become so utterly immersed in it, is our model as Christians.

Ratzinger is extremely positive in his commentaries on Vatican II about the outcome of the debate on Mariology at the council. He believes that it opened up a better understanding of Mariology and the possibility that Christians could understand each other on this divisive issue. Three tenets of Mariology that subsequently developed into important aspects of his thinking on his concept of a female

---

7. Joseph Ratzinger, "Das Problem der Mariologie," *Theologische Revue* 61, no. 2 (1965): 74-82.
8. Ratzinger also points to Alois Muller, René Laurentin, and Bishop Rusch.

line are outlined in the commentaries. He identifies that Mary "sheds some light on the mystery of the Church," that she personifies the Church, and that she embodies Israel. As well, these tenets of his Mariology, facilitated by the discussion at Vatican II, evolved to become central elements of his larger theological vision and program.

Ratzinger refers to a line of women that culminates in Mary when discussing the incarnation in *Introduction to Christianity*.[9] Mary here is discussed in relation only to the incarnation, and the Church is discussed in relation to the Spirit. As the idea of the female develops and takes shape in subsequent writings, however, the backdrop evolves from the incarnation to the whole of salvation history and the Church. The notion of a "line" in reference to the women of the Bible is first evident in Ratzinger's book *Daughter Zion*, based on three lectures given in 1975.[10] This book does not refer to "the female line in the Bible" as such, but the roots of the concept are there. In *Daughter Zion*, a central insight comes to the surface around the connection between the women of the Old Testament and the history of Israel: the history of the women of the Old Testament is the history of God's people under the covenant. This history is the crucial thread—and culminates in—the New Testament story of Mary. Marian theology, as such, is grounded in a reception and recapitulation of the Old Testament narratives of the women of Israel. Ratzinger, in fact, identifies three genealogical strands of the Old Testament witness that converge and are recapitulated in the mystery of Mary: first, the great mothers of the Old Testament, particularly Sarah and Hannah; second, the daughter of Zion; and, third, the figure of Eve.[11] In this, Mary not only fulfills and completes

---

9. Joseph Ratzinger, *Introduction to Christianity*, 2d ed., trans. J. R. Foster (San Francisco: Ignatius, 2003), 272–80. In this seminal book, Ratzinger discusses the Church in relation to the Sprit rather than, as he will later, in relation to Mary.
10. Ratzinger, *Daughter Zion*, 9–29.
11. Ibid., 11–16.

the female line of the Old Testament, she links the Old and New Testaments together. As he states:

> [I]n a certain respect Mariology ties the knot joining Old and New [Testaments]. Mariology cannot be found apart from its union with the prophetic theology of the bridal people of God. . . . If Christ brings the marked distinction and break from the Old Testament, in the novelty of his words, his life, his passion, his cross, and his resurrection, Mary, through her silence and faith, incarnates the continuity.[12]

There is an organic hermeneutic and theological principle operative in this: the women of the Old Testament are fundamental to, and play constitutive roles in, salvation history. Thus, to understand salvation history, the meaning of this line of women, which is fulfilled in Mary, must be drawn out and read anew in the light of Christ.

"The female line in the Bible" appears explicitly for the first time in Ratzinger's introduction to John Paul II's Encyclical *Redemptoris Mater* (1988), entitled "The Sign of the Woman."[13] This develops and solidifies the initial insight of *Daughter Zion*. Ratzinger's introduction, written in a personal capacity to facilitate the reading and understanding of the papal document,[14] begins by addressing the specific methodology of John Paul II, which he describes as a "meditation" on the Bible. It is in this explanation of the methodology that Ratzinger articulates his thinking on the female line. As he puts it:

> [I]n the Old Testament, alongside the line from Adam through the Patriarchs down to the Servant of God, there appears another line from Eve through the Matriarchs to figures like Deborah, Esther, Ruth and finally to the personified Divine Wisdom. This line simply cannot be dismissed theologically, although it is unfinished and its message open-ended, incomplete—just like the Old Testament as such, which still

---

12. Ibid., 31–32.
13. Ratzinger, "Sign of the Woman," 17–18.
14. Ibid., 10.

awaits the New Testament and its answer. The line from Adam receives its full meaning in Christ. Similarly, the significance of the female line in its inseparable interaction with the Christological mystery is revealed in Mary and in the symbolism applied to the Church.[15]

There are four important constitutive features to Ratzinger's concept of the female line. First, there are two lines, male and female, in salvation history. Second, both of these lines have theological significance. Third, these lines are completed and fulfilled theologically in the New Testament by Christ and Mary, and through her the Church. And fourth, the two lines are synthesized and united in the christological mystery itself. The two lines—male and female—are complementary and requisite to one another, and both reveal concomitantly the nature of salvation history as the history of the God's intimate yet noncompetitive relationship with humanity. This reaches fullest fulfillment in the person of Christ—the mystery in which these truths converge. It is in this that the depth dimension of Scripture, interpretation, and the tradition of the Church comes most clearly to the surface—a way of reading and understanding Scripture with the Church, provoked by the simultaneous forces of an increased perception of the lasting theological value of tradition and the need for fresh articulation and reflection in light of contemporary concerns.

Influences and Context of the Development of the Female Line

Insights from feminist theology and biblical scholarship contributed significantly to awareness of the need for fresh, forward thinking and are a critical aspect for how Ratzinger enhanced and enriched the theological development of this pivotal constructive insight. Spurred in this way, Ratzinger's theological interpretation of salvation history

---

15. Ibid., 17–18.

brings the female line of the biblical narratives to the fore out of the depth of tradition *into the light of tradition* and provides a framework and grammar for articulating and reflecting on that reality. The female line gives voice to the women of Scripture and provides a crucial theological and hermeneutical lens through which the Church can deepen its comprehension of salvation history itself.

Widening the frame in this way, Ratzinger's vision provides counterbalance to certain trajectories of interpretation within the tradition. A standard version pivots around a singular focus on the male line of salvation history, tracing the history of faith from Adam to Christ, the second Adam; in conjunction with this is the underscoring of the theological fulfillment of the Old Testament—its supercession—in Christianity. It is this hermeneutical and theological context that, as Ratzinger recognizes, feminist theology perceives as providing an androcentric view of salvation and as such pushes against. Such an androcentric definition of salvation history, for instance, can be seen in *Dei Verbum*, which refers directly to neither Mary nor any other female of the Bible, apart from "our first parents" and thereby to Eve:

> God, who creates and conserves all things by his word (see Jn 1:3), provides constant evidence of himself in created realities (see Rom 1:19-20). Furthermore, wishing to open up the way to heavenly salvation, he manifested himself to our first parents from the very beginning. After the fall, he buoyed them up with the hope of salvation, by promising redemption (see Gen 3:15); and he has never ceased to take care of the human race, in order to give eternal life to all those who seek salvation by preserving in doing good (see Rom 2:6-7). In his own time, God called Abraham and made him into a great nation (see Gen 12:2). After the era of the patriarchs, he taught that this nation, through Moses and the prophets, to recognize him as the only living and true God, as a provident Father and just judge. He taught them, too to look for the promise of a Saviour. And so, throughout the ages, he prepared the way for the Gospel.

After God had spoken many times and in various ways through the prophets, "in these last days he has spoken to us by a Son" (Heb 1:1-2).[16]

Ratzinger—without erasing the crucial theological insight of christological recapitulation resident in the traditional pattern of interpretation—constructs a more inclusive and synchronic vision of salvation history; his interpretative paradigm of a female line, parallel to and concomitant with the male line, attempts to redress the critical imbalance that has persisted in theology, as reflected in the central document on biblical interpretation of Vatican II. What we see here is an example of what Ratzinger means by reason and tradition working together to defend and refine tradition. His correction consists of a fuller retrieval of the Christian understanding of salvation history, resurfacing the female line from within the tradition and identifying its essential role in the mystery of Christ. In doing so, Ratzinger attempts to create a contextual space of harmony of union between the riches of the tradition and the criticisms and desires raised by feminist theology. This is, in fact, a hallmark of Ratzinger's style as a reforming theology—a characteristic consistent to him not only before but subsequent to Vatican II and thereafter. Finding a critical open-meeting space on this issue does not warrant wholesale revision or criticism; he does not, for instance, criticize the document *Dei Verbum* or Christianity's apparent exclusivity. Rather, he approaches reform as a positive method, as the proposal of constructive solutions carried out by developing and refining the Church's theology through tradition in dialogue with modern situations.

Comparing Ratzinger's approach to that of others is instructive, as this demonstrates the innovative nature of his "female line in the

---

16. Dogmatic Constitution on Divine Revelation, *Dei Verbum*, November 18, 1965, in Austin Flannery, ed., *Vatican Council II: The Basic Sixteen Documents: Constitutions, Decrees, Declarations*, nos. 3 and 4 (Dublin: Dominican Publications, 1996), 97–115, at 98.

Bible." Hans Küng, in *Women in Christianity*, investigates the two-thousand-year history of women in Christianity. Küng admits that it was only at Vatican II that he became conscious of the question of the position of women in the Church.[17] This, it could be argued, is also the case with Ratzinger. However, they take different approaches to address this issue. In Küng's view, subordination is the chief problem that women have faced throughout the history of Christianity. As he puts it: "For most of the religions of the world women are a problem; from time immemorial they have been subordinate to men, second-class in the family, politics and business, with limited rights and even limited participation in worship. It is only in Christianity that equal rights for women is a great unfulfilled concern."[18]

In response to this unfulfilled promise, Küng examines the history of women in Christianity as a whole, so as to try to understand the present situation. He seeks to come to grips with the historical reasons for women being subordinate in Christianity, particularly in relation to the status and the functions of leadership available to women in the Church. Küng finds limited layers of openness and freedom in the earliest bands of the Jesus tradition, quickly snuffed out in practice over the course of centuries of development of ecclesial structures, hierarchies, and clerical bureaucracy. Ratzinger's approach, in contrast, while equally concerned with the pressing issue, is less framed by a focus on the negative trappings and failings of history and traditional interpretation. Rather, he seeks a positive theological and hermeneutical meeting point—retrieving Scripture and tradition, particularly around the female figures of the Bible, to situate the modern problem in the wider horizon of an understanding of salvation history and God's relationship with humanity.

---

17. Hans Küng, *Women in Christianity*, trans. John Bowden (London: Continuum, 2001), viii.
18. Ibid., vii.

Ratzinger's constructive position, though, is not devoid of historical focus on development around the issue. Nevertheless, he does not see it in terms of historical reification of prejudicial structures; rather, in concert with a program of retrieval, he plots the historical development of the female line in the tradition within the wider context of the Church's theological development of a doctrinal or dogmatic culture.[19] In particular, Ratzinger sees this in relation to early Christian developments in Scripture interpretation and doctrine that served as boundary markers for the early community. In this respect, he identifies three specific movements that the early Judeo-Christianity tradition rejected: the fertility cults, Gnosticism, and the *Solus Christus* movement. Based in part on the work of Louis Bouyer, Ratzinger contends that the roots of early Christian faith lie in the prophetic struggle with idolatry—a feature dramatically portrayed in the prophetic narratives of the Old Testament, and so very much a part of the early Christian ethos. That struggle with idolatry, particularly in the ancient Israelite context, according to Ratzinger, was often carried out as a contest with neighboring fertility religions, which celebrated fertility through ritual fornication with temple prostitutes;[20] as such, idolatry in the Old Testament is very often referred to as fornication. In contrast to this situation, Ratzinger is anxious to show that where fertility cults provided for a theology of prostitution, the faith of the Old Testament, as a "monogamous" relationship enacted through covenant, provides for a theology of communion and fidelity. Moreover, in relation to Gnosticism and the *Solus Christus*[21] movement, Ratzinger contends

---

19. See the work of Lewis Ayres on the question of theological culture, particularly around his work on pro-Nicene theological culture in the later third to fourth centuries of the early Church.
20. Ratzinger, *Daughter Zion*, 13–14. Ratzinger draws here on Louis Bouyer, *Women in the Church*, trans. Marilyn Teichert (San Francisco: Ignatius, 1979).
21. This movement accepts Christ as the only mediator between God and man, and is highly influential among Protestants, as well as the Catholic liturgical movement, which shaped

that both sought to eliminate everything female from the Bible's message.[22] Gnostic exegesis, he claims, identifies what is female as negative and worthless and inadmissible to the salvific message of the Bible. He highlights this negative understanding of the female in the *Gospel of the Egyptians* and the *Gospel of Thomas*.[23] So, for Ratzinger, Christianity's understanding of the female, of woman, is in strong contrast to Gnosticism's acceptance of prevailing attitudes toward the female in the Roman Empire—and thus he strongly resists attempts to reappropriate or revitalize such forms today.[24]

Here Ratzinger and Küng are in agreement, even if their views of early Christianity are at odds. Küng's position is that, through institutionalization, women were the losers in this period of the Church. However, Gnosticism, even though it appeared to be more open to women, did not offer women the equality and respect it offered to men. In Küng's view: "A warning must be issued here against any idealisation of Gnosticism at the expense of the community Church. Alongside the equal status for woman in practice and in the cult, in some texts there is also a marked devaluation of women, indeed a castigation of the feminine and a rejection of marriage. . . . Indeed, according to some texts the woman has to be made man in order to be able to enter the '*pleroma*.'"[25] There is no doubt that the Gnostic texts give the impression of respect for

---

Ratzinger's attitude to theology at the beginning. Ratzinger, *God and the World: Believing and Living in Our Time: A Conversation with Peter Seewald*, trans. Henry Taylor (San Francisco: Ignatius, 2000), 296.

22. Ratzinger, "Sign of the Woman," 17.
23. He cites, in particular, Logion 22 of Thomas and points to a similar text in Logion 37, 106, 46, 31.
24. In a footnote explanation, he states: "In view of the contemporary feminist discussion, it is important to be aware of the spiritual cultural background that underlies these texts; ancient Christianity took form against the confines of this background. This will help us recognise that Christianity in its organisation and its determination of canonical writings safeguarded what was unique and new in Jesus' teaching, in opposition to prevailing attitudes that, dressed in religion even claimed absolute status" (Ratzinger, "Sign of the Woman," 15n5).
25. Küng, *Women in Christianity*, 15.

women through the prominence of women in them, but, in fact, they do not respect women *as* women. For example, in "The Dialogue of the Saviour" in the *Gospels of Mary*, Judas asks Jesus how they should pray and he replies, "Pray in a place where there is no woman."[26] Another example is in "Pistis Sophia" in the *Gospels of Mary*, where it is recorded that "Peter stepped forward and said to Jesus, 'My master, we cannot endure this woman who gets in our way and does not let any of us speak, though she talks all the time.'"[27] The contrast to the four canonical Gospels is striking, where no such rejection of women or disrespect for women is included or countenanced. It is difficult, therefore, to understand why some advocate[28] for the Gnostic Gospels as preferable to the canonical Gospels.

The third movement Ratzinger identifies as having sought to eliminate the female dimension from salvation history is the aforementioned modern movement, *Solus Christus*.[29] He singles out for criticism its denial that humans, men and women, can respond and cooperate with grace. Such is, in fact, a major point of contention for Ratzinger in his assessment of many contemporary religious and theological movements and critiques. He is strongly critical of much modern biblical interpretation, particularly attempts to reconstruct Scripture. He does not reject, as some have suggested, modern theology or even feminist theology *as such*; rather, the issue is the method of interpretation that eschews engagement with Scripture as Scripture; in the instance above, for example, it is the ahistorical substitution of disputed texts in place of Scripture—a substitution that

---

26. Marvin Meyer, with Esther A. de Boer, *The Gospels of Mary: The Secret Tradition of Mary Magdalene, the Companion of Jesus* (San Francisco: HarperCollins, 2006), 62.
27. Ibid., 68.
28. Lesley Hazleton, *Mary: A Flesh-and-Blood Biography of the Virgin Mother* (New York: Bloomsbury, 2004), 177–80.
29. Ratzinger, "Sign of the Woman," 17; idem, *God and the World*, 301–302; idem, "On the Position of Mariology," 76.

ironically chooses texts that instantiate and reify the very prejudices and exclusions that they purport to rectify. Against this, Ratzinger, while not eschewing insights from historical criticism, seeks out positive, constructive answers in the received text of Scripture and in searching dialogue within the larger breadth and depth of the tradition of the Church, wherein fruitful vistas may be revealed, retrieved, and refined in new contexts and under new and changing conditions.

Having established the background to the development of his notion of a female line, we will now look at the methodology that underpins, or more specifically is the essential enabler, of the notion of a female line in the Bible.

The Biblical-Interpretation Approach Underpinning the Concept of the Female Line

Ratzinger's constructive visions of a female line in the Bible is (1) the outworking of a coordinated set of theological precommitments and (2) a practical application of his biblical-interpretation approach. In the present section, we will look at this within the context of the latter. Ratzinger's style of biblical interpretation consists of three basic principles: the unity of the Bible; the importance of typology; and the central role of the Church in mediating tradition in biblical interpretation and in the development of comprehension of revelation. He uses the historical-critical method in a very specific, ad hoc way, which informs his interpretation and excludes reconstruction of the text. The hermeneutical key for interpreting the Bible, for Ratzinger, is faith rather than history. This does not mean that he is more interested in the Jesus of faith in the Gospels than the Jesus of history; for him, the Jesus of faith *is* the Jesus of history. This makes his approach strikingly different from modern approaches in which the search for the historical Jesus through the reconstruction of the Gospel accounts predominate. Nonetheless, Ratzinger's method of biblical interpretation corresponds to that advocated by Vatican II. Indeed, the principles he outlines in "The Sign of Woman,"[30] where he first explicitly refers to a female line, reads like a restatement of the principles outlined in *Dei Verbum*, particularly in chapters 3 to 5. I will first explore each of Ratzinger's three principles individually and then his use and criticism of the historical-critical method. As part of this exploration, I will look at how his hermeneutical key, faith, contributes to his biblical interpretation.

Three Principles of Biblical Interpretation

The principle of biblical unity, as advocated by Ratzinger, accepts the Bible as *one* book. The books of the Bible, with their wide variety of literary genres, are nonetheless singular in their testimony and witness. Notwithstanding the fact that its authors did not write the Bible as one book, in Ratzinger's view Scripture is now one book with an inherent unity; consequently, theologians are to search for the "one voice" that speaks throughout the Bible. This means that the detail of each individual book of the Bible is to be interpreted through the whole of the Bible. In this way, individual details are not understood in isolation, but interpretation occurs through "Scripture interpreting Scripture," which thereby provides the context to release its meaning. Canonization, then, underpins the interpretative process: theological meaning is located in the horizon of the texts of the Bible as *the text of Scripture*, rather than as individual, isolated units. In short, his overall biblical-interpretation approach seeks the meaning of Scripture that arises from the Church's gathering of the individual texts into one book. In this way, the meaning that the author intended is important, but it is relativized and transformed by

---

30. Ratzinger, "Sign of the Woman," 9–40.

the subsequent action of the Church in its ongoing development of understanding God's self-revelation.

A second fundamental aspect of Ratzinger's biblical interpretation is his use of typological exegesis. As Ratzinger uses it, typology is an interpretative tool used to comprehend the fulfillment of the old covenant, its people and deeds, in the new covenant. Typology, or interpreting the New Testament through the Old Testament, is a method of interpretation found in the New Testament itself. Jesus used typological interpretation to explain who he was when he pointed to figures and images in the Old Testament to reveal who he was, for example, Jonah (Matt. 12:39), Solomon (Matt. 12:24), the Temple (John 2:19), and the bronze serpent (John 3:14). Peter, Paul, and the author of the letter to the Hebrews also used typology to interpret Scripture. In this, they were all drawing on a method already used by Judaism. As John N. D. Kelly has observed, typology was not an invention of Christian theologians, but the Old Testament itself understood the events of Israel's history as figures or types of what was to come.[31] We see a continuity of interpretation methodology from the old to the new covenant and the fathers in Ratzinger's biblical interpretation.[32]

Ratzinger's use of typology is grounded in his view of the theological significance of canonization—the Church's gathering the books of the Bible into one book—and the communal vision of reading Scripture in continuity with the Old and New Testament and the fathers. In fact, he believes that it was the loss of typological exegesis in modern theology that has led to a separation of the Old and New Testament in contemporary scholarship.[33] His view

---

31. J. N. D. Kelly, *Early Christian Doctrines*, 5th ed. (London: A&C Black, 1977), 71.
32. It could be argued, from Ratzinger's perspective, that it is not only the typological exegesis employed by the early church, but medieval exegesis in particular; in fact, this is very likely a carryover from his pre–Vatican II days, since his doctoral work was a study of Augustine's ecclesiology (first dissertation) and Bonaventure (*habilitationschrift*).

of typology and the impact of modern approaches to biblical interpretation is shared by the Protestant theologian G. W. H. Lampe, who observed in his 1957 essay, "The Reasonableness of Typology," that:

> The rise of modern critical study broke the chain of continuity which had hitherto existed between the modern reader and his medieval and early Christian predecessors. Until this development took place, the unity of the Bible was the fundamental premise upon which all were agreed. A common belief linked the authors of the New Testament books with their readers. This was the conviction which they shared; that the whole Bible spoke directly of Christ, in prophecy, type and allegory so far as the Old Testament is concerned, and the consequent belief that the historical context of a passage and the immediate intention which the original author had in writing it in the circumstance of his time were of relative minor importance. . . . The unity of the Bible meant in effect that a passage was valuable for its application to Christ or to Christians. . . . The various texts are all alike "scriptures," whose importance lies in their prophetic and typological significance rather than their historical context in the books from which they possessed in their literal sense for the writer who penned them. The unity of Scripture transcended the diversity of books and authors.[34]

Typological reading, then, for Ratzinger, is an exercise of reading Scripture *with* the Church; it is, as well, biblical interpretation as mediated by the Church's tradition. This connects fundamentally to a vision of the imbricate nature of Scripture, Church, and revelation—Scripture and the apostolic tradition are two forms of revelation that make up the deposit of the Church's faith. Scripture and apostolic tradition are not parallel, but complementary, forms of revelation. The Church builds upon and refines its comprehension

---

33. Ratzinger, Daughter Zion, 33.
34. Geoffrey W. H. Lampe, "The Reasonableness of Typology," in *Essays on Theology*, Studies in Biblical Theology 22, ed. Geoffrey W. H. Lampe and K. J. Woollcombe (London: SCM Press, 1957), 14–15; Lampe asserts that typology is essential for an understanding of the New Testament, and he gives the example of Stephen's speech in Acts 7, which, he contends, presupposes a typological correspondence between Christ and Moses (19).

through the guidance of the Spirit and the application of reason. In this way, the insights of each generation of the Church are integrated into the living understanding of the faith. In view of this, he rejects the search for the "original" within Christianity, as this suggests some pure form of Christianity uncorrupted by later developments. Instead, the development of the Church's comprehension is an integral aspect of historical Christianity. The problem he sees with some strands of current biblical interpretation is that "The purification of Christianity, the search for its original essence, is carried on today, in the era of historical consciousness, almost entirely by seeking its oldest forms and establishing them as normative. The original is confused with the primitive. By contrast the faith of the Church sees in these beginnings something living that conforms to its own constitution only insofar as it *develops*."[35]

The living nature of the faith means that the original is reflected upon so that the Church draws out its true meaning and implications. Ratzinger insists that each generation continues a deepening of the Church's understanding of God's Word:

> The Catholic Church knows in faith all what God has said to us in the history of revelation. Our understanding of it, of course—even the understanding of it that the Church enjoys—remains greatly inferior to the magnitude of what God has spoken. On that account there is a development of faith. Each generation, from the point of view of its own circumstances, is able to discover new dimensions of faith that even the Church did not know before.[36]

Allowing for the insights of each generation of theologians to be incorporated into the Church's understanding of God's word means that Ratzinger's approach is open to—indeed, expects—ever-deeper understanding of the meaning of God's word. Such deepening is

---

35. Ratzinger, *Daughter Zion*, 38.
36. Ratzinger, *God and the World*, 38.

guided by the Spirit acting in the Church. It means that the Christian faith, above all the belief in the incarnation and resurrection, is the criterion of the Church's understanding. These are the fundamentals of God's revelation, but they are not the totality of God's self-revelation, nor has that self-revelation been fully understood. This approach rules out a static faith anchored only in events that happened in the past and opens the door to a faith that grows as the capacity to understand it grows. Ratzinger's approach, however, is not a license to develop totally new theologies, but to build on what the Church has already comprehended. Hence, we have his thinking that the Church's understanding of Mary, as articulated in the Marian dogmas, is an entirely appropriate and logical development.

Ratzinger's Approach to History in Biblical Interpretation

Ratzinger's three principles of biblical interpretation do not mean that he rejects the historical-critical method. Rather, it means he utilizes it in a very specific, and ad hoc, way. I would argue that Ratzinger's approach identifies two different aspects of the historical-critical method: on the one hand is the attempt to reconstruct texts to discern the original, historical Jesus—this he rejects; on the other is a critical method of textual investigation as an ingredient to biblical meaning—this he accepts and utilizes. He uses history to understand and interpret history; that is, history is used as a mechanism to reveal the meaning of history. This is seen in his use of the name of the leader of the last messianic war, Bar Kokhba (Star of the Son) to explore the possible meaning for Christology and salvation of the brigand BarAbbas, the prisoner Pilate released during Jesus' trial.[37] The historical-critical method is a coordinated, if asymmetrical, or even subordinate, aspect of Ratzinger's hermeneutical approach; it is

---

37. Joseph Ratzinger, *Jesus of Nazareth: The Infancy Narratives*, trans. Philip J. Whitmore (New York: Image, 2012), 40–41.

a moment, really, of investigation that serves as part of the scaffolding to theological interpretation of Scripture. It is only one tool he uses among many, employed in support of other interpretative tools and never used as the *principle* tool of inquiry.

Ratzinger's attitude to the limitations of the historical-critical method is, in part, related to the surplus of meaning he finds in the biblical texts, which he thinks cannot be captured by the historical-critical method. For him, the data identified in the texts provide meaning when considered within the context of the whole Bible and the Church's tradition, which means that the Bible as a whole—or, as an integrated, coherent, singular text—is greater than the sum of its individual parts. As he states in *Jesus of Nazareth*:

> Historical-critical interpretation of a text seeks to discover the precise sense that the words were intended to convey at their time and place of origin. That is good and important. But—aside from the fact that such reconstructions can claim only a relative certainty—it is necessary to keep in mind that any human utterance of a certain weight contains more than the author may have been immediately aware of at the time. When a word transcends the moment in which it is spoken it carries within itself a "deeper value." This "deeper value" pertains most of all to words that have matured in the course of faith-history.[38]

In addition to the surplus of meaning in Scripture, there is the issue of the level of certainty provided by the historical-critical method and the attempt to reconstruct texts. On this, Ratzinger is dubious that history can deliver a level of certainty similar to the natural sciences; in his view, modern exegesis generates theories and hypothesis, not certainties.[39] The modern quests for the historical Jesus exemplify this problem. As James K. Beilby and Paul R. Eddy, in their introduction

---

38. Ibid., xix–xx.
39. Ratzinger, "Biblical Interpretation in Crisis: On the Question of the Foundations and Approach of Exegesis Today," lecture at St. Peter's Church, New York, January 27, 1988, http://www.catholicculture.org/culture/library/view.cfm?recnum=5989.

to *The Historical Jesus: Five Views*, state: "The culminating goal of any quester, of course, is to present an historically responsible reconstruction of Jesus of Nazareth, one that others find 'plausible'—hopefully even 'probable' (which is, of course, as good as it gets in the realm of historiography)."[40] A chief problem here is that plausibility and probability—as constitutive features—are subjectively and coordinately conditioned and contingent on one another. A reconstructed Jesus is only as plausible as it corresponds to what one accepts or admits as probable according to one's particular view of method and historical evidence. Moreover, the accumulation of historical data can never yield the reality of the subject—one cannot, in other words, be beckoned to faith in the Jesus reconstructed from historical bricolage. What can do this—faith—is what we turn to now.

Faith in Ratzinger's Use of History and Biblical Interpretation

Faith is the determinative hermeneutical key to Ratzinger's biblical interpretation, rather than history, and it is this that holds his three principles together. For him, the interpreter must have *sympathia* with the biblical text to truly comprehend it and that *sympathia* is the faith of the Church.[41] Faith as hermeneutic has important consequences: the starting point of his approach to the Bible is "trust" in the Gospel presentations of Jesus, that their depiction of Jesus represents the real historical Jesus.[42] But this is not a flat, reader-to-text relationship; rather, it is communal and ecclesial, ineluctably tied to the Church and the operation of the Holy Spirit in both the Church's development of its understanding of revelation and the

---

40. James K. Beilby and Paul R. Eddy, "The Quest for the Historical Jesus: An Introduction," in Beilby and Eddy, eds., *The Historical Jesus: Five Views* (London: SPCK, 2010), 52–53.
41. Ratzinger, "Biblical Interpretation in Crisis"; also, idem, *Jesus of Nazareth*, xxiii.
42. Ratzinger, *Jesus of Nazareth*, xxi.

manner in which the canon of the New Testament developed. As briefly discussed above, canonization is of paramount significance to meaning and the interpretative process. Marcion's attempt, probably as early as 150 C.E., to streamline some of the documents that became the New Testament, alongside eliminating the Old Testament, demonstrated that there was a body of text that was identified as in some way special for Christian faith; Marcion's actions instigated a formalized process by the Church of identifying the content of the scriptural canon. Karl H. Schelkle has argued that by 300 C.E. most of the writings of the New Testament had undisputed canonical status. As he puts it:

> The New Testament is the result of a collection with a long history and development. The final unity was not achieved by means of decrees issuing from the one superior authority of the Church, but in common and voluntary effort of the Churches of East and West, in Edessa, Constantinople, Alexandria, Rome, Carthage and Gaul. This shows how sure the Church was in her judgment of what was genuine and what was foreign to her spirit.[43]

The chief criterion for inclusion in the canon, according to Scheckle, was the congruence of the content of the writings with the apostolic tradition.[44] Ratzinger takes an analogous approach—or, rather, applies analogously the principles of canonization to hermeneutics and biblical interpretation. This elicits for him trust in the Gospels as accounts of Jesus precisely because he trusts the judgment of the apostolic and post-apostolic Church that collated these specific books into one book and passed these Gospels and other books down throughout history.[45]

---

43. Karl Hermann Schelkle, *An Introduction to the New Testament*, trans. Gregor Kirstein (Cork: Mercier Press, 1969), 229.
44. Ibid., 231.
45. Others take a different view. For example, John Galvin argues that the various interpretations of Jesus in the Gospels need to be assessed by reference to Jesus as such because "The extent and the theological significance of our historical access to Jesus are subject to dispute." John

Trust in the ecclesial witness and in the veracity of the Gospels themselves, as the Church's Scripture, underpins Ratzinger's approach to historical questions in biblical interpretation. That does not eliminate the need to investigate historical details but, rather, functions as a programmatic framework through which such investigation is undertaken. Equally, though, or perhaps more importantly, Ratzinger's hermeneutical approach is theologically conditioned, or determined, by its very subject—the person of Jesus Christ: it is the truth of Jesus Christ which he believes, and "trusts," is present in the account given of the reason for the early Church's faith in Jesus as the Christ, as contained in the four Gospels. Here, Ratzinger's approach brings history and faith, or, as we saw earlier, the historical and ontological, together. This approach is a mirror image of his arguments that reason and faith should not be separate to each other but should work together, that history and ontology are not contradictions but form a unity. In this case, faith and history should work together in the search for the truth of God's self-revelation in Jesus Christ: the historical nature of Jesus and his being are in union; they are not contradictions. But this also means that biblical interpretation goes beyond historical method, because to believe Jesus was truly God and that he communicated his divinity "exceeds the scope of the historical method."[46] History as an investigative method or endeavor cannot deliver this; only the subject can.

Ratzinger's approach to biblical interpretation is a response to changes that began in the 1950s, specifically the widespread approval of scientific and historical methods in critical scholarship. The theological hermeneutics that undergird his approach, though, are

P. Galvin, "Jesus Christ," in *Systematic Theology: Roman Catholic Perspectives*, vol. 1, ed. Francis Schüssler Fiorenza and John P. Galvin (Minneapolis: Fortress Press, 1991), 281.
46. Ratzinger, *Jesus of Nazareth*, xxiii.

not just a direct response to that decade, but connect to important dynamics of the era immediately preceding, particularly the Gospel-based portrayals of Jesus by Karl Adam, Romano Guardini, and others in the 1930s and '40s. These provided important modern anchors for Ratzinger, even as his theology developed and evolved in response to contemporaneous theological trends; defense of the fundamental tenets of Christian faith became his mission. He describes what happened as follows: "The gap between the 'historical Jesus' and the 'Christ of faith' grew wider and the two visibly fell apart. But what can faith in Jesus as the Christ possibly mean, in Jesus as the Son of the living God, if the *man* Jesus was so completely different from the picture that the Evangelists painted of him and that that Church, on the evidence of the Gospels, takes as the basis of her preaching?"[47]

Only if Jesus of Nazareth is the same figure as the Christ of faith is faith in Jesus of Nazareth as the Christ, for him, reasonable, and this can be equally applied to Mary. If they are identified as two separate figures—one historical and the other a doctrinal construct—the basis of faith is removed. The question of the historical nature of the Gospels is a question about the role or place of faith in God's actions in this world in intellectual thought. It is the nature of faith and God's actions, not history, that is in fact at the core of the search for the historical Jesus. The insistence that the Jesus of history and the Christ of faith are one figure, as are the historical Mary and the Gospel Mary, underpins his critique of attempts to reconstruct the historical Jesus distinct and separate from the Christ of faith depicted in the four Gospels. In 1988, in response to the prevalence of such attempts, Ratzinger offered a philosophical treatise on modern biblical interpretation, "Biblical Interpretation in Crisis."[48] In this paper, he restates and develops the criticism of the historical-critical

---

47. Ibid., xi.
48. Ratzinger, "Biblical Interpretation in Crisis."

method he put forward originally in *Eschatology*. Here we see a recurring theme being applied to biblical interpretation. His primary criticism of modern exegesis is that it fails to acknowledge its philosophical presuppositions, and so biblical interpretation, he argues, is in fact a philosophical debate. The philosophical issue of God's actions in this world is central to his critique of the search for the historical Jesus and his own biblical interpretation. The turning point toward what Ratzinger calls "the restriction to the positive, to the empirical, to the exact science," initiated by Kant, had consequences not just for modern theology, but for biblical interpretation. This leads to the central tenet of his criticism of the search for the historical Jesus, which is his claim that the majority of modern exegetes are "certain that it cannot be the way it is depicted in the Bible, and he looks for methods to prove the way it really had to be. To that extent there lies in modern exegesis a reduction of history into philosophy, a revision of history by means of philosophy."[49] Ratzinger's view is that the search for the historical Jesus is really a philosophical search, not history at all. Because he accepts that God can and does act in this world, he also accepts the biblical portraits of Jesus as the historical Jesus. God is the God of both spirit and matter. Matter falls within God's power and is subject to God, and it is in creative reason that God acts to reveal himself in his Word become flesh, Jesus Christ: the Jesus of history is coinherent with the Jesus of faith.[50]

The enterprise to reconstruct historical portraits of Jesus discloses more about the a priori philosophical and theological commitments and worldviews of the scholars than about Jesus himself. In fact, the exercise itself is quite circular and self-generating: the need to

---

49. Ibid.
50. Ratzinger, *Jesus of Nazareth*, 56–57; idem, *Principles of Catholic Theology: Building Stones for a Fundamental Theology*, trans. Sister Mary Frances McCarthy, S.N.D. (San Francisco: Ignatius, 1987), 29.

reconstruct the historical Jesus is the result of prior philosophical decisions to reject texts or data as historical, which elicits the need for a reconstituted picture more consonant with those same determining commitments. Enlightenment-era presentations of the historical Jesus, for instance, delivered accounts of Jesus shorn of miracles, eschatology, or material purported to derive from doctrinal tradition, such that the accounts corresponded cleanly and undisturbingly to Enlightenment beliefs. If the attempt to reconstruct the historical Jesus is itself generated by a rejection of the miraculous and supernatural—hence its elimination from the earthly life of Jesus—it is, then, in essence a *philosophical* assessment and worldview rather than historical. The reconstructions are not, and can ever be, history.[51] The validity of the assumption that is an essential point of departure for the entire enterprise to reconstruct the Gospels, that there is a disconnect between the Jesus of history and the Jesus of faith, depends on a prior assessment of God's activity in the world. The fathers, in contrast to Enlightenment accounts, employ a more "iconographic" reading of the Gospels: the divine *in* the human; the supernatural in the material. They transpose, in a sense, the profound theological insight of *homoousios*—Jesus as Son is one in being with the Father, that Jesus is both fully divine and fully human—in a hermeneutical register: the Jesus presented in the Gospels reveals, in his historical mode of life, the being of God who has come into human history and human flesh; the historical Jesus, as the Jesus of the Gospels, is the exegesis of the Father and is the revelation of God under the conditions of the materiality of human history and existence. The portraiture of the Gospels, then, for the Fathers, is an

---

51. I explore a number of issues with theology's engagement and use of history in my paper, "Current Problems with the Use of History in Modern Theology and Biblical Interpretation" (unpublished).

icon, a window, through which the union of the eternal Son with the Father is seen in the fleshy earthiness of the human life of Jesus.

The iconographic reading of Jesus as found in the Fathers offers a profound paradigm not only for understanding the coinherent unity of the historical and philosophical in biblical hermeneutics, but also for the complex task of articulating the identity of Jesus within the pattern that emerges. This is a particular challenge in modern and contemporary biblical interpretation. Indeed, there is not only a loss of clarity but also a concomitant danger of recapitulation of theological errors that the early Church rejected, most notably Arianism, in the search for a historical Jesus separate from the Jesus of faith. Those struggles, of course, involved not only the question of Christology but also, perhaps more fundamentally, the question of God. In this, answers to questions about the person of Jesus Christ coordinated with, and had direct implications upon, answers to questions about the God of Jesus Christ. In this way, the early christological disputes were ineluctably contests about the trinitarian identification of God. Catherine Mowry LaCugna ably demonstrates this in her book *God For Us*, wherein she discloses how the Nicene solution to the problem of Arianism proceeded on the basis of the theological insight that soteriologically the person of Christ *must* be identical—on both sides—with that which he mediates; and if Christ is one in being with God, that has significant consequence to *who* God is.[52] At the same time, while Nicaea posed a particular solution

---

52. LaCugna states that: "Theologians in the Greek East and Latin West found Arius' position intolerable because it jeopardized salvation through Christ: If Christ is not God, we are not saved through him. To answer Arius the Council of Nicaea (325) taught that Christ is *homoousios* with God. This immediately shifted attention away from the patent subordination of the economy to an intradivine realm, *theologia*, in which God and Christ, Father and Son, could be equal in substance. But this 'solution' created another problem. The unquestioned axiom that God cannot suffer was contradicted by the suffering of Christ; if he were truly God, God would suffer. The way around this was to say that Christ suffered in his humanity but not in this divinity, not as the Logos. The result was a small gap between *theologia*, in which God and the divining Christ were equal, and *oikonomia*, in which God and the human Christ

to the problem raised by Arianism in the fourth century, further clarification would be needed as to how the divine and human relate in Jesus. Such clarification was necessary because, as John Galvin maintains, with the defeat of Arianism the divine Jesus was emphasized and, after Nicaea, "eventually, the climate became emphatically anti-Arian, with heavy stress on the divinity of Christ in theology and general piety."[53] Over a century of debate would transpire before Chalcedon would assert that the two natures—divine and human—are united fully, unabbreviated, yet unalloyed in the singularity of his person.

It could be said, though, as Ratzinger does, that the early Church councils provided a negative blueprint for understanding the person of Christ. This is to say that the conciliar definitions, in particular Chalcedon, mark off the boundaries of what is expressible, while being more apophatic in terms of concretely defining the positive content—the negative adjectives of the Chalcedonian definition being exemplary here.[54] In light of this, it should be said that despite the absence of such in the early Church definitions, a competitive conception or formulation of the relationship between the divine and human in Jesus should not be envisioned. As Ratzinger insists, Jesus' divine nature takes nothing from his humanity; rather, the divine and the human *coinhere* mutually and noncompetitively in the single subject who is Jesus Christ—each fully and completely existent and expressed.

---

remained unequal." Catherine Mowry LaCugna, *God for Us: The Trinity and Christian Life* (San Francisco: HarperSanFrancisco, 1993), 8.

53. Galvin, "Jesus Christ," 1:264.

54. On this Ratzinger asks: "What does the formula mean positively, 'Christ has two natures in one person?' I must admit right away that a theological response has not yet completely matured. In the great struggles of the first six centuries, theology worked out what the person is not, but it did not clarify with the same definiteness what the work means positively." Joseph Ratzinger, "Retrieving the Tradition concerning the Notion of Person in Theology," trans. Michael Waldstein, *Communio* 17, no. 3 (Fall 1990): 450.

Much contemporary theology, in the purported absence of technical clarity and a perceived overemphasis in traditional dogma on the divinity of Christ, responds in the other direction, placing significant stress on the humanity of Jesus. But rather than understanding these exercises in heresiological terms—such as historical reconstruction as Arian retrieval—they may be more charitably thought as counterpoint exercises in clarifying technical responses to pivotal christological dilemmas. Answering the question, "What does it mean for Jesus to be one person in a human and divine nature?," may in fact open up an alternative perspective on the Jesus portrayed in the Gospels as a credible historical Jesus. Galvin argues that the Chalcedon statement "spoke of Christ as one 'in two natures' (not 'from two natures'), a clear rejection of monophysitism. The creed then confesses that the difference of the natures (divine and human) is not removed by their union but rather preserved, as the two natures are united in one person (*prosopon*) and one hypostasis."[55]

The space left open, then, by Chalcedon's failure to give concrete positive definition to the meaning of Jesus as two natures (divine and human) *in* one person might be thought as the generative context for the search for the historical or human Jesus. If this is correct, that the lack of a positive definition feeds into a continuing theory of a disconnect between the human and divine Jesus, then the urgency of developing such a positive definition is clearly demonstrated. Historical reconstructions, while providing a substantial possibility on one side of that register, fail significantly to round out what is needed; instead, the quest should be for the human Jesus of Nazareth who is the Christ, who is two natures in one person. Such is a call for a more coordinate, symbiotic relationship between historical criticism and theological or dogmatic hermeneutics.

---

55. Galvin, "Jesus Christ," 1:270.

For Ratzinger, it is theological interpretation of Scripture that provides a more substantive tool, one that could augment historical criticism in a way that could enable it to fulfill its potential. This would be what Ratzinger denotes as orthodox interpretation. There are precedents for such in Scripture: Paul's letters clearly demonstrate this need as does the fact that these letters themselves require interpretation, as the Second Epistle of Peter cautioned one early Christian community. So we must recognize that the issues related to biblical interpretation are as old as Christianity itself. Ratzinger, then, builds upon this scriptural and classical model, offering an approach to biblical interpretation approach and method that reflects what John Ashton maintains about the Gospel writers:

> The evangelists were interested neither in what we call the Jesus of history nor what Bultmann calls the Christ of faith, but in Jesus as Christ, the single object of our faith. The fundamental affirmations of the Christian belief were, as we have seen, "Jesus is the Christ" and "Jesus is Lord." And the evangelists' concern was precisely to hold together Jesus of Nazareth and the risen Christ in this single affirmation, an act of judgment in the sense of Maréchal and Lonergan, but above all an act of faith. They were neither historians nor theologians but combined the functions of both in declaring their own faith and eliciting the faith of their readers.[56]

Orthodox biblical interpretation takes as its determining object the person of Jesus Christ and, through assiduous investigation and reflection, provides the substantial concrete content that exists amidst the dialectical paradox of the Jesus of history who is the eternal Son—fully God *and* fully human. Yet, it should be noted, that Ratzinger does not here call for a flat return to the premodern theology of the fathers or the Middle Ages. Rather, he wants the debate to move forward so that the "the inner harmony between

---

56. John Ashton, *Why Were the Gospels Written? Theology Today* Series, no. 15 (Dublin: Mercier Press, 1973), 79.

historical analysis and hermeneutical synthesis" can be found. He states in his essay "Biblical Interpretation in Crisis":

> Certainly texts must first of all be traced back to their historical origins and interpreted in their proper historical context. But then, in a second exegetical operation, one must look at them also in light of the total movement of history and in the light of history's central event, Jesus Christ. Only the *combination of both* these methods will yield understanding of the Bible. . . . To recognise the inner self-transcendence of the historical word, and thus the inner correctness of subsequent rereadings in which event and meaning are gradually interwoven, is the task of interpretation properly so called, for which appropriate methods can and must be found. In this connection, the exegetical maxim of Thomas Aquinas is quite to the point: "The duty of every good interpreter is to contemplate not the words, but the sense of the words."[57]

What is essential for Ratzinger is that the meaning of God's self-revelation is central to biblical interpretation and that the textual origins of this self-revelation as identified by scholars are incorporated into the networked results of investigation, exegesis, and reflection.

Ratzinger recognizes that interpreting the Bible is a multiperspective discipline and that biblical interpretation and history are not one-dimensional but multidimensional. This opens the space for a broad approach from which the essence of Scripture's meaning can be distilled. Just like collating a view of a mountain consisting of views from the north, south, east, and west—which may at first sight appear to describe four separate mountains—a multiperspective-based view provides for a fuller, if seemingly contradictory, picture. Each interpretative principle used offers unique perspective and insights on the text considered. When combined with the perspectives offered by other interpretative principles, each principle also acts as a corrector to the potential excesses of the other principles used. By utilizing

---

57. Ratzinger, "Biblical Interpretation in Crisis."

traditional and modern methods in conjunction with each other, the best from each method can be secured while minimizing the individual method's weaknesses. Ratzinger's overall theological vision, herein, remains anchored in Scripture and revelation, in such a way that his approach agrees with LaCugna's exhortation that "what we believe about God must match what is revealed of God in Scripture."[58] And this vision, finally, crystallizes in conjunction with faith; it is, in fact, the liturgical and doxological that point to faith in harmony with history rather than faith in contrast to or in contradiction to history—the unity in Jesus of the historical and ontological.

Faith in History

Paul speaks of a knowledge of God that human wisdom cannot grasp hold of and subdue. It is this "wisdom" that must be incorporated into historical and theological interpretation. Faith is not something precritical that Enlightenment reason allows us finally to decode. Faith is something real and tangible that offers access to the truth. Faith is something that speaks so that reason can critique—but not something that reason negates or regulates to a second-class position. The encyclical *Lumen Fidei* ("The Light of Faith," 2013),[59] which we considered in chapter 1, provides important direction and makes significant contributions to the search for a comprehensive articulation of faith for modern theology. Indeed, it offers the starting point for the development of a concrete and tangible notion of faith that can be incorporated into history when utilized by theology.[60]

---

58. LaCugna, *God for Us*, 397.
59. Pope Francis I, *Lumen Fidei* (Dublin: Veritas, 2013), http://www.vatican.va/holy_father/francesco/encyclicals/documents/papa-francesco_20130629_enciclica-lumen-fidei_en.html.
60. I explore a number of issues with theology's engagement and use of history in my paper, "Current Problems with the Use of History in Modern Theology and Biblical Interpretation" (unpublished).

Lumen Fidei links faith to the Church's liturgy, which in turn opens a dimension through which John Courtney Murray's concern about the relationship between the Spirit, the Church, and historical development can be addressed.[61] In *Meeting Christ in His Mysteries,* Gregory Collins argues that the liturgy is a vision of the sacred mysteries of the Bible and the liturgical rites express the depths of those mysteries whose end is the mystical marriage of God and the self. He describes the liturgy as "like the church's consciousness, floating on the limitless depths of truth contained in revelation." He maintains that it is the Church's "primary source for all theological reflection, and dogmatic elaboration" and points to the fact that the dogmatic declaration of Jesus as Lord and God was preceded by the Christian community's liturgical worship of Jesus as Lord and God.[62] As he puts it:

> The liturgy itself is the primary catechesis and the place of theological interpretation. The same can be asserted of every liturgical feast and especially the paschal liturgy, the centre of the church's year. That is where Holy Scripture is at home. The theologian's task consists in cultivating the capacity given as a gift from God (but also demanding study and reflection) of recognising the connections between the mysteries, what the First Vatican Council called the *nexus mysteriorum,* the network or inter-connectedness of the mysteries.[63]

Adopting such an approach as a starting point for considering the historical nature of the influence of faith, theology and biblical

---

61. John Courtney Murray, "Foreword," in Cyril Vollert, *A Theology of Mary* (New York: Herder & Herder, 1965), 10–11. Courtney Murray is responding to Vollert's approach to the development of Marian dogma in the last two centuries, which he argues is "not tied down to the sole power of reason, but takes place under the influence of the Holy Spirit."
62. Gregory Collins, *Meeting Christ in His Mysteries: A Benedictine Vision of the Spiritual Life* (Dublin: Columba Press, 2010), 262–63.
63. Ibid., 69–70. The quote continues: "A theologian who cannot 'do' analogy or recognise connections between the multifaceted aspects of the mysteries is doomed to certain failure. As in life so in revelation and the theology which comments on it: truth discloses itself above all in the relationships we are able to discern between realities."

interpretation would takes its cue from Mary: to ask questions, to treasure and hold these things in the heart and ponder them. In that way, theology and biblical interpretation maintain a continuous movement toward integration and synergy, rather than atomization and reconstruction, in which each individual part is understood only as part of and in relation to the whole, and never as a stand-alone item. It will mean that faith, and what faith opens the believer to, is not something separate from, or in some way in contradiction to, interpretation; instead, faith will be an integral aspect of theological and historical interpretation. In so doing, theology and biblical interpretation, including its utilization of history, would engage with Scripture and tradition as a coherent whole that exhibits a harmony, notwithstanding the significant tensions which exist within that unity.

Reengaging with, and embracing, the embryonic nature of faith—faith as faith—would allow history, as used and understood in modern theology on the one hand, to be comprehensible; and, on the other hand, to be released to evolve into its full potential. Faith acts as a leaven to history. This leaven breaks through the cultural milieu influencing modern scholarship and opens up new horizons. So we may define history, what it can tell us, its methodology and tools, but for theology that is only part of the story. It is necessary that theology utilizes history in a manner that recognizes this fundamental difference of subject parameters. Theology needs to develop a specifically theological version of history in which the additional vivifying element of faith is fully and integrally present. To respond to the reality of God's activity in the world and the faith of the believing community, something more than reason is required for Christian faith and theology to coherently account for and explore its existence and historical development. The interpersonal nature of faith and relationality make definitive statements and declarations about them difficult. What we can definitely say is that when we use the modern scientific methods and autonomous reason to investigate faith and relationality, we are using tools without the capability to carry out that task. Faith and relationality require their own language and method, which would then be used in conjunction with reason's methods, as *Lumen Fidei* maintains. The task now facing theology, particularly those utilizing history or a historical approach, is to commence the long and difficult journey of articulating a theory of the interior world created by the grace of faith and how that affected, and continues to affect, the historical development of Christianity's self-understanding and the meaning and implications of God's self-gift.

A re-Enlightenment, in which the true meaning and reality of faith in response to God's activity to reach out to humanity, is required, such that it is not only what can be seen that scholars acknowledge but also, as *Lumen Fidei* insists, what can be heard. This would entail a rupture with the last couple of centuries certainly. But it might also heal the rupture that autonomous reason—the idea through which the Enlightenment eventually understood itself—created with both the previous millennia of the Judeo-Christian tradition as well as the Greek tradition of seeking to account for the vivifying element, complexity, and organization evident in the world and universe around us. The foregoing is an attempt to sketch out the key issues related to the use of history in theology as I see them, as well as an endeavor to contribute, albeit in a very limited way, to addressing these issues.[64] Much is left to consider and explore if we are to

---

64. Also see my articles "The Church in Dialogue with New Scientific Atheism," *The Way* 53, no. 1 (January 2014): 7–22; "Renewing Intellectual Discourse by Means of a New Philosophy of Knowledge for Non-Natural Sciences," *Religion & Education* (Volume 42, Issue 1, 2015), 2-16; and "The Role of the Judeo-Christian Tradition in the Development and Continuing Evolution of the Western Synthesis," *Telos* 168 (Fall 2014), 132-144. In these I attempt to explore the issues related to faith, reason, and knowledge in modern intellectual discourse.

come to grips with the difficulties scholars face when using history in theology and to develop our comprehension of the historical development of the Church's understanding of God's self-revelation.

3

The Female Line in the Old Testament

Ratzinger's reflections on the women of the Bible span much of his writings from the 1960s to the present and are scattered in various publications and documents. There is not one work, but many in various forms. His writings on the women of the Bible are not presented under the title "the female line in the Bible," though the notion of such a line certainly underpins them. I will attempt to synthesize Ratzinger's variegated writings in order to surface a coherent, unified theological understanding of the women of the Bible.[1] Five interlinking themes are evident in Ratzinger's writings

---

1. The key sources are Ratzinger's books *Daughter Zion: Meditations on the Church's Marian Belief*, trans. John M. McDermott, S.J. (San Francisco: Ignatius, 1983); *Mary: The Church at the Source*, trans. Adrian Walker (San Francisco: Ignatius, 2005), with Hans Urs von Balthasar; and *'In the Beginning . . .': A Catholic Understanding of Creation and the Fall*, trans. Boniface Ramsey (Grand Rapids: Eerdmans, 1995). The last book is a series of Lenten homilies given in 1981 and subsequently published in German in 1986 and first in English in 1990, by My Sunday Visitor). See also his articles "The Sign of the Woman," introduction to Pope John Paul II, *Mary: God's Yes to Man: John Paul's Encyclical* Redemptoris Mater, trans. Lothar Krauth (San Francisco: Ignatius, 1988), also in *Mary: The Church at the Source*, 37–60; "Thoughts on the Place of Marian Doctrine and Piety in Faith and Theology as a Whole" (originally published in the Pastoral of the German Bishops, April 30, 1979; it was republished three times over the next twenty-six years: under the title " On the Position of Mariology and Marian Spirituality

on the women of the Old Testament: (1) God as Creator and the human being as God's creation and as creature; (2) the dialectical phenomenon of the unblessed–blessed; (3) faith and grace; (4) the bridal people of God; and (5) God's covenant with Israel. Each of these themes is interlinked and all constitute the primary theme of relationship: relationship between God and the human being. In this, Ratzinger provides a theological interpretation of Scripture that opens a fresh vantage point within the depths of the biblical witness and the tradition of the Church.

The Creator and the Creature

Adam: The Human Being

Where much of modern theology gets entangled in fierce debate about cosmological origins and scientific processes, Ratzinger finds a rich theological story—one that establishes the primacy and fundamental constituency of relationship (between God and humanity, and human beings with each other), as well as portends the tragic dimension of created reality, in the creation stories of Genesis.[2]

---

within the Totality of Faith and Theology," trans. Graham Harrison, in Helmut Moll, ed., *The Church and Women: A Compendium* [San Francisco: Ignatius, 1988], 67–79; in *Communio* 30 [Spring 2003]: 147–63; and then again in 2005 in *Mary: The Church at the Source* 19-36; "'You are full of grace': Elements of Biblical Devotion to Mary'," trans. Josephine Koeppel, *Communio* 16, no. 1 (1989): 54–68; and "Man between Reproduction and Procreation," trans. Thomas A. Caldwell, S.J., *Communio* 16, no. 2 (1989): 197–211 (based on two addresses he gave in 1988). Other theological comments on the women of the Bible appear throughout his other work, and I will also draw on these. Other theologians' writings will be discussed in conjunction with Ratzinger's to draw out areas of similarity and uniqueness, as his writings on each of the women of the Bible are considered.

2. He deals with this topic extensively in his book *'In the Beginning . . .'* This series of Lenten homilies are a response to modern theologies that he believes have abandoned the doctrine of creation, criticizing two works in particular for their reductionist positions on creation: Johannes Feiner and Lukas Fischer, eds., *Neues Glaubenbuch. Degemeinsame christliche Glaube* (Basil-Zurich: Herder, 1973); and Bruno Chenu and François Coudreau, eds., *La foi des catholiques. Catéchèse fondamentale* (Paris: Le Centurion, 1984). In the first, Ratzinger argues that creation is hidden in the various chapters, and in relation to the chapter "The New Human Being," by André Dumas and Otto Hermann Pesch, Ratzinger is disturbed by their argument

In his judgment, the Genesis accounts present the human person as the created relational partner of God, which is the fundamental answer to the question of "Who is the human being?"[3] God is both the origin of the creature—forming humankind from dust—and the point of immediate relation to the human being God has created—breathing life into that human being.[4] The human being as such, then, is created *for* relation with God and created out of the relationality that constitutes the internal divine life.

But this is not just a story of divine origins—there is, for Ratzinger, a deeper christological and eschatological meaning to the creation story. In this, he typologically links the Genesis creation accounts with John's account of the new creation, the Word become flesh, which he regards as the conclusive and normative scriptural creation account:[5] "All things were made through him, and without him was not anything made that was made" (John 1:1, 3). Here, Ratzinger argues that Christianity, by reading the Old Testament anew from the perspective of Christ, most notably through the Pauline typological interpretation of Adam and Jesus seen in Romans 5, uniquely redefines the understanding of the human being. Understood as the second Adam, *Christ* answers the question: What is the human being? Christ himself is the full revelation and fulfillment of what it means to be human.[6]

---

that, "Concepts like selection and mutation are intellectually much more honest than that of creation," and that, "'Creation' as a cosmic plan is an idea that has seen its day" (433). In the second text, Ratzinger points to the fact that out of its 736 pages, only five full pages deal with creation, but do so in a totally unsatisfactorily existential manner that loses the reality of faith and God's activity (356) (cf. Ratzinger, *'In the Beginning . . . ,'* x–xii, 78–100). Ratzinger's response to such theological treatment of creation is based on the role the concept of *Creator Spiritus* plays in his overall theological framework. See Ratzinger, *The God of Jesus Christ: Meditations on the Triune God*, trans. Brian McNeil (San Francisco: Ignatius, 2008), originally published in German in 1976; idem, *'In the Beginning . . .'*; and idem, "Man between Reproduction and Procreation."

3. Ratzinger, *'In the Beginning . . . ,'* 42.
4. Ibid., 43–44.
5. Ibid., 14–15.

Here, a dual typology is at work in Ratzinger's exegesis: Adam *and* Christ. Adam, for Ratzinger, as in most traditional exegesis, is a representative figure, not simply a single (male) human being; he stands as the human being as such—as the created, earthly being. Equally, and perhaps primarily, Christ,—the second Adam—brings to fulfillment the full weight and potential of Adam. This is the Pauline move in Ratzinger discussed earlier, particularly the typological link between Adam and Christ in his understanding of humanity,[7] and thus his soteriology and anthropology.[8]

There is, for Ratzinger, only one humanity—vicariously represented by Adam and fulfilled in Christ. A single humanity also means a refusal of division amongst human beings themselves, difference and diversity within humanity notwithstanding. It is difference within always-greater unity, as all human beings *in their diverseness* are represented by the one human being *qua* human being. This certainly has its precedents in Scripture, particularly Paul's dialectical reading of Christ and Adam, and in the theological exegetical tradition of the Church, in early Christian thinkers like Athanasius and Cyril of Alexandria.

---

6. Ibid., 50.
7. Joseph Ratzinger, *Introduction to Christianity*, 2d ed., trans. J. R. Foster (San Francisco: Ignatius, 2003), 234–35. Here he states that "In the Bible this word ['Adam'] expresses the unity of the whole creature 'man', so that one can speak of the biblical idea of a 'corporate personality.'"
8. Ratzinger contends that "The picture which describes the origin of Adam is valid for each human in the same way. Each human is Adam, a new beginning; the origin of each human being is a creation" ("Man between Reproduction and Procreation," 206–207). This means for him that "There are not different categories and races in which human beings are valued differently. We are all *one* humanity, formed from God's *one* earth. It is precisely this thought that is at the very heart of the creation account and of the whole Bible. In the face of all human division and human arrogance, whereby one person sets himself or herself over and against another, humanity is declared to be *one* creation of God from his *one* earth. . . . there is only *one* humanity in the many human beings. The Bible says a decisive 'no' to all racism and to every human division." This theme of one humanity is also seen in his interpretation of the term "one flesh." Ratzinger would think that "psychic unity, all-embracing personal community" is a more accurate interpretation than the more common understanding as sexual intercourse (ibid., 205). He uses Delitzsch's description that is quoted in Claus Westermann, *Genesis 1/1–11* (Neukirchen-Vluyn: Neukirchener Verlag, 1974), 318.

Although Ratzinger's interpretation is, in effect, a retrieval of a theological reading deeply engrained in the tradition, the Church's traditional reading also contains other ways of reading that are less satisfactory. Parts of the tradition, for instance, have made much of the gender identification of the figure of Adam—his maleness—and the patterning of male–female relationships, supporting hierarchical gender relations on the basis of isolated passages in the creation and fall narratives.

Phyllis Trible, in her 1973 article "Eve and Adam,"[9] rereads the Genesis accounts in response to just these sort of patriarchal exegetical interpretations. Trible's concern to counter patriarchal exegesis undergirds her constructive reading of the Genesis creation accounts. Trible, similarly to Ratzinger, notes that the Hebrew word for Adam is ambiguous, in that it means the first man formed, as well as being the generic term for humankind; interestingly, she here asserts that, until the creation of the woman, Adam is androgynous. She underscores, in her account, the traditional commentators who infer an inferiority of woman due to Eve being created last and, in response, appropriates the biblical and literary device that the last may be first. In fact, she puts forward the idea that the literary device of a "ring composition" was used in the Yahwist Genesis account, which suggests an interpretation of equality between man and woman: "In Hebrew literature, the central concerns of a unit often appear at the beginning and the end as an *inclusio* device. Genesis 2 evinces this structure. The creation of man first and of woman last constitutes a ring composition whereby the two creatures are parallel. In no way does the order disparage woman. Content and context augment this reading."[10] Despite particular differences in emphasis, there is

---

9. Phyllis Trible, "Eve and Adam: Genesis 2–3 Reread," in Carol P. Christ and Judith Plaskow, eds., *Womanspirit Rising: A Feminist Reader in Religion* (San Francisco: Harper & Row, 1979), 74–81; originally published in *Andover Newton Quarterly* 13 (March 1973): 251–58.
10. Ibid., 75.

significant resonance in the deeper theological readings in Ratzinger and Trible.[11]

Eve: Life and Mother

Further concord between Ratzinger and Trible can be seen in their respective interpretations of Eve. Interestingly, Ratzinger also understands the creation of Eve as a new creation, a new beginning; it is, in fact, fundamental to his theological vision that Eve represents life.[12] He typologically links the creation of Eve from Adam's side with the Johannine notion of the new community of Christianity—the Church—pouring from the piercing of Christ's side on the cross, where the blood and water point to the Eucharist and baptism.[13] As the Church is formed from Christ's person—and a new living community created—so Eve, from Adam, and hence a new humankind (really, all humankind), is formed.[14] So, for Ratzinger,

---

11. Ratzinger's own approach is a striking break from the association of Adam with the male made by some of the church fathers, which have been rightly criticized for their misogyny, which Trible's rereading is trying to escape. Ratzinger's and Trible's understanding of the Hebrew word `adam reflects the Hebrew meaning of the word, as Pauline Viviano demonstrates in her commentary on the Yahwist creation account (Gen. 2:4b-23): "The first thing formed by Yahweh is 'the human.' This is not to be understood as an individual named Adam; rather, 'the Human' is the whole of humanity. That the author views this original creature as a representative of undifferentiated humanity and not as an individual is clear from the use of the definite article 'the' before 'humanity' in the Hebrew text." Pauline Viviano, *Genesis*, Collegeville Bible Commentary (Collegeville, MN: Liturgical, 1985), 15.
12. The Hebrew word *Eve* is a form of the Hebrew word for life. Ibid., 18.
13. Ratzinger, *Introduction to Christianity*, 240–42; See also idem, *God Is Near Us: The Eucharist, the Heart of Life*, trans. Henry Taylor (San Francisco: Ignatius, 2003), 43.
14. Ratzinger expresses the meaning of the fully open Christ as follows: "To be the man for others, the man who is open and thereby opens up a new beginning, means being the man in the sacrifice, sacrificed man. The future of man hangs on the Cross—the redemption of man is the Cross. And he can only come to himself by letting the walls of his existence be broken down by looking on him who has been pierced (Jn 19:37), and by following him who as the pierced and opened one has opened the path into the future. This means in the end that Christianity, which as belief in the creation acknowledges the primacy of the logos, the creative meaning as beginning and origin, also acknowledges it in a specific way as the end, the future, the coming one. Indeed, in this gaze at him who is coming lies the real historical dynamism of the Christian approach, which in the Old and New Testaments perfects faith into hope in the promise." Ratzinger, *Introduction to Christianity*, 241–42.

the creation of Eve is the formation of a new humanity, not just of women alone: Adam is "no longer a single individual but 'Adam' from whose side, Eve, a new mankind is formed."[15] The new humanity is a communal, rather than individual, reality. In their mutual creation, moreover, is a vicarious togetherness: the dependence of man and woman on each other and their unity as one humanity.[16] It could be argued that, for Ratzinger, Eve, and the female line that commences through her, represents communal life and that the new life to which he refers means that human beings can only exist within a community, which finds its typological fulfillment in the new community—the Church. The particular typological link for Eve, though, is with Mary: it is through Mary that Eve, as woman, reaches the pinnacle of fulfillment.[17] Although Ratzinger links Mary more to Christ than to Eve, he does contrast the two and argues that Eve expresses the ambiguity of biological becoming, where death is the condition of life such that to give birth to life opens oneself up to death,[18] whereas Mary gives birth to the death of death, to the one who is life, and therefore is the Mother of life and of the living.[19]

For Trible, Eve is a vicarious person as well. She also holds that the equality of man and woman is seen in the fact that the woman is taken from Adam's rib, which she asserts means solidarity and equality. It is here, she asserts, that the first specific term for the man as male appears, when Adam uses the word `ishshah` for woman, in response to `ish` for man. Trible sees the use of these specific words

---

15. Ibid., 241.
16. Ibid. He finds this idea reflected in the history of religions and in Plato's myth about how the human being came to be divided in two. The message is thought to be the same: human beings are divided into men and women, and each searches for the other to find their wholeness together. Ratzinger, *God and the World: Believing and Living in Our Time: A Conversation with Peter Seewald*, trans. Henry Taylor (San Francisco: Ignatius, 2000), 80.
17. Ratzinger, *Daughter Zion*, 65.
18. Ibid., 77–79.
19. Ratzinger, *God and the World*, 294.

as a pun. Thus, Trible asserts the meaning of the Yahwist creation account is that "The two are neither dichotomies nor duplicates. The birth of woman corresponds to the birth of man, but does not copy it."[20] Furthermore, she points out that `ishshah* (woman) is not a name, but a word that indicates gender. Gender, here, is a matter of differentiation—but, it is a differentiation that is concomitant with a greater unity. Difference grounds complementarity and relationality: woman is in relation to man but not subject to him. The relational nature of humanity and the nonhierarchical complementarity, as seen in Eve, is further reflected in Trible's exegesis of the Hebrew word `ezer* (helper),[21] which is used to designate Eve at her creation as "a helper fit for him [Adam]"; the term, interestingly, is not exclusive to Eve, but is used also of God—characterizing God as the helper of Israel. Thus, it is a term of relation that constitutes the person of Eve, that establishes the nature of the vicarious togetherness of the first parents, and one that is ultimately grounded in the character of God the Creator.

The Fall: Humanity's Alienation

A major area where Ratzinger and Trible part company is in their reading of the fall. Ratzinger interprets the fall as a narrative of the alienation of humanity from God, and of human beings from each other, while Trible focuses on the story as an etiological construction that underwrites hierarchical and subordinationist relations.[22] Where

---

20. Trible, "Eve and Adam," 77.
21. The Congregation for the Doctrine of the Faith's "Letter to the Bishops of the Catholic Church on the Collaboration between Men and Women in the Church and the World" (2004), also makes this point; http://www.vatican.va/roman_curia/congregations/cfaith/documents/rc_con_cfaith_doc_20040731_collaboration_en.html.
22. Trible seeks to understand the interaction between the man and the woman during and after the fall. Interestingly, with this different starting point, Trible comes to the same assessment as Ratzinger, in that human beings need to repent. She focuses on the fact the serpent speaks to the woman and not the man, and argues that the reason for this is unknown. However, to her mind, the silence of the text led to speculation, which she asserts enabled patriarchal

for Trible the story of the fall reveals important sociological and anthropological conditions but does not, at the same time, transcend much beyond those categories, the fall as a theological narrative plays an important role in Ratzinger's understanding of God, of humanity, and of salvation history. An essential implication of the fall narrative is the fracturing of the originary relationship between God and humanity in humanity's abandonment of the covenant—an attempt by humans to be free and to transcend the limitations of imposed by finitude. In this way, for Ratzinger, human beings become alienated from God—seeking to arbitrate their existence themselves, as autonomous beings rather than creatures of God—and from each other, introducing competition, violence, and consumption in relations with others. This is the original sin, and sin, in essence, is a renunciation of the truth, of our limits and our finitude, and of the fact that, as humans, we are creatures who have a Creator.[23]

As we can see in this, sin is not merely an abstract "thing" in the Genesis story. Rather, Ratzinger perceives Adam's deed in concrete terms: Adam and Eve, as the human beings representative of all

---

ideas to be read into that silence. In rejecting patriarchal exegesis of the fall, she asserts that the character portrayals are a striking contrast to prevailing culture: "The man is not dominant; he is not aggressive; he is not a decision maker. Even though the prohibition not to eat the tree appears before the female was specifically created, she knows that it applies to her. She has interpreted it, and now she struggles with the temptation to disobey.... If the woman be intelligent, sensitive, and ingenious, the man is passive, brutish, and inept" (Trible, "Eve and Adam," 79). After the act of disobedience, this contrast between the man and woman is no longer seen. The judgments to which they are subjected are not prescriptive but descriptive, a situation she describes as standing between creation and grace. The subjugation of the woman demonstrates that the man is corrupt as well as their shared sin. So, in rejecting the traditional exegesis of Genesis 2–3, and rereading it, Trible asserts that it in fact functions to liberate: "The Yahwist narrative tells us who we are (creatures of equality and mutuality); it tells us who we have become (creatures of oppression); and so it opens possibilities for change, for a return to our true liberation under God. In other words, the story calls female and male to repent" (ibid., 81). Rejection of patriarchy in anthropology is Trible's concern in her rereading of the fall, and this orientates her interpretation: the fall account describes the relationship between men and women but should not be determinative of it.

23. Ratzinger, *'In the Beginning . . . ,'* 67–71.

human beings, experience the rupture of relationality provoked by finitude and failure, while also simultaneously portending the possibility of the redemption that awaits.[24] Adam and Eve, in other words, reflect the collective nature of original sin and our redemption. Ratzinger himself maintains that the primary truth about human beings is that they are dependent, and that only love can redeem them because love transforms dependence into freedom. This is why he insists that original sin can only be understood when the Genesis story is read in the light of Christ.[25]

Ratzinger's interpretation, finally, underscores the dialectical *meaning* of the Genesis creation stories. In this, we see deeply interconnected answers to pivotal theological questions: What does it mean for there to be a Creator? What is the meaning of creation, and specifically the meaning of the human being? Why, if we are God's creation, can the human being appear as anything but a creation of God's? His approach to answering these questions is based on God's creative act as read in the light of Christ. At the heart of his understanding is the relationship between God and humanity, and between Adam and Eve, human existence as life in community. Moreover, throughout Ratzinger's interpretation of the women of the Bible, this relationality is central to understanding humanity and God. In connection to this, one further point needs to be made: where feminist writers seek to highlight the patriarchal nature of Israel or the biblical texts, Ratzinger takes for granted the abuse of power as well as the vulnerable situation of women in these societies as the historical and sociological realities of the fissiparous (that is, the tendency to splinter into separate parts or groups), and the haunted tragedy of alienated humanity. The women of the Old Testament, in fact, represent both typologically and really, in Ratzinger's view, the

---

24. Ibid., 71.
25. Ratzinger, *God and the World*, 87–88.

vulnerability of God's people in the world and their dependence on God. This approach is understandable in light of his presuppositions, though it should be noted that it can be—and has been—used to impose a patriarchal order and to justify the subordination of women. Ratzinger's insistence on reading Scripture as a whole and in the light of Christ, though, consciously attempts to mitigate such an abuse.

The Matriarchs: Faith and Grace

The dialectical approach evident in Ratzinger's reading of Genesis and the creation–fall cycle continues, and receives additional layers, in his interpretation of the Old Testament narratives of the matriarchs. It is here, in fact, that the dialectics of rupture–relationality and alienation–redemption become history. In these Old Testament narratives, that dialectical plays in a further "reversal of values," or transvaluation of contrasts: infertility/fertility and unblessed/blessed. Such transvaluation is seen, for instance, in the pairings of Sarah-Hagar, Rachel-Leah, Hannah-Penina.[26] The narratives of the matriarchs are, for him, the history of God's promises that come to fruition and are fulfilled in the reversal of impossibility—the barren are fruitful and the forlorn receive hope and promise. God's grace creates faith, hope, and anticipation—and, even more, brings them into being.[27]

Ratzinger's reading of these narratives, of course, connects theologically to ultimate fulfillment in the New Testament. The meaning of the conception and miraculous births in the Old Testament, in particular Sarah's conception of Isaac (Genesis 18), Hannah's conception of Samuel (1 Samuel 1–3), and the unnamed

---

26. Ratzinger, *Daughter Zion*, 18–19.
27. Ibid., 18n8. Ratzinger refers to his article "Fraternité," in Marcel Viller, et al., eds. *Dictionnaire de spiritualité ascétique et mystique: doctrine et histoire* (Paris: Beauchesne, 1992), 5:1141–67, which develops this theme.

mother of Samson (Judges 13:2ff.), are part of the phenomenon of the reversal of values.[28] Each of these miraculous births occurs at decisive turning points in the history of salvation and each is a manifestation of God's gracious mercy. This history leads to Mary's conception of Jesus as the fulfillment of this line of women—a fulfillment due to grace, not from man's power but from God's power alone.[29] The interconnection between the matriarch narratives and the New Testament—expectation and fulfillment as a divine act of grace—is particularly evident in the appropriation of Hannah's song as echoed in Mary's *Magnificat*.[30] In Hannah's hymn of praise to God when dedicating her son, and Mary's effluent doxology at the annunciation, they join and fulfill the line of women who voice Israel's praise of God's preference for the powerless and poor. As Irene Nowell puts it, "the `*anawin*, the humble people whose total reliance is on God."[31]

Gentile Women of Matthew's Gospel: Unexpected Lineage

Ratzinger employs this typological exegesis in a way that brings these themes to their fullest expression in an Advent sermon on Matthew's

---

28. Ratzinger, *Introduction to Christianity*, 277–78.
29. He states that "The meaning of the occurrence is always the same: the salvation of the world does not come from man and from his own power; man must let it be bestowed upon him, and he can only receive it as a pure gift." Ibid., 277.
30. Ratzinger, *Daughter Zion*, 18.
31. Irene Nowell, O.S.B., *Women in the Old Testament* (Collegeville, MN: Liturgical, 1997), 99. In a similar approach to Ratzinger's, Nowell perceives the themes of faith and grace in the story of Sarah. The human element of these stories is important for Nowell in a way not seen in Ratzinger's interpretation. The announcement stories, for her, demonstrate Sarah to be a strong but complex individual who is capable but also, due to fear, can be weak and deceitful. The importance of these stories is that they reveal that Sarah, along with Abraham, is chosen by God and is the mother of the promise. She views it as important that, after having driven out Hagar's son Ishmael, the next mention of Sarah, in spite of God's request for Abraham to sacrifice Isaac, is her death. Nonetheless, "She begins a long line of barren women who mother children of promise: Rebekah, Rachel, Hannah, mother of Samuel; Elizabeth, mother of John the Baptist. The line comes to its ultimate fullness in a woman who, although remaining a virgin, also becomes a mother. Through the power of God's spirit, Mary gives birth to the child who is hope for us all. Is anything impossible to God? Like Mary, Sarah is also a model of the church who mothers the people of God" (ibid., 13).

genealogy of Jesus, published in German in 1982.[32] In this homily, he reflects on the four Gentile women of Matthew's genealogy in the line of Mary.[33] It is in his exposition of this genealogy that Ratzinger refers explicitly to a "line" of theological genealogy—in particular, he identifies these four Gentile women as pre-figures of Christ in the history of salvation. In Matthew's genealogy, the line is not separated into male and female, but constitutes one line. The four Old Testament women in Matthew's genealogy are Rahab, the harlot who admitted the Jewish spies into Jericho;[34] Ruth, the Gentile who married a Jew, and who, when widowed, stayed with her mother-in-law in times of difficulties; Bathsheba, Uriah's wife, a Hittite who married David, accepted his God, and was mother of Solomon; and Tamar, whose right to have children was refused by Judah, but who compelled him to grant her wish and through whom the kingdom came to the tribe of Judah. For Ratzinger, these four women are a sign that Israel's genealogy is one of grace and forgiveness; it is not a genealogy of human greatness or achievement.[35] Four other women of Israel, Sarah, Rebecca, Leah and Rachel, he admits are traditionally seen as the great ancestresses. But it is the Gentile women Rahab, Ruth, Bathsheba, and Tamar, who appeared at decisive moments of Israel's history, who are the real ancestresses of Israel, because, through their faith, the story of God's promise is continued as God's

---

32. Originally published as: Joseph Ratzinger and Heinrich Schlier, *Lob der Weihnacht* (Freiburg, Basel, Vienna: Herder, 1982), 7–16.
33. For Ratzinger, Matthew's genealogy presents Jesus' ancestry, which at the same time describes his nature: Jesus is both a son of Abraham and "the true David, who fulfills the sign of hope which David had become for his people." Ratzinger, *Daughter Zion*, 40.
34. In Clement's First Epistle to the Corinthians, he refers to Rahab as follows: "Rahab the harlot owed her preservation to her faith and hospitality." Betty Radice, ed., *Early Christian Writings: The Apostolic Fathers*, trans. Maxwell Staniforth and Andrew Louth (London: Penguin, 1987), 27.
35. Joseph Ratzinger, *The Blessing of Christmas*, trans. Brian McNeil (San Francisco: Ignatius, 2007), 39–50.

faithfulness, God's relationality, and, especially, God's preference for the poor, the weak, the vulnerable, the outcast, and the exiled.

In agreement with Ratzinger, Peter-Ben Smit asserts that the five women (Rahab, Ruth, Bathsheba, Tamar, and Mary) of Matthew's genealogy are a key interpretive tool for the theological portraiture of Jesus. These characters as women, and particularly their class, sociopolitical, and ethnic location, add significant complexity and unique dimensions to the Gospel story. Smit points out, too, that the men with whom these women are most associated in the genealogy, Judah, David, and Jesus, are clearly messianic figures, and he argues that Mary's awkward pregnancy is prepared for through Tamar and Bathsheba. In relation to Rahab and Ruth and their association with David, Smit contends that they make Jesus' messianic genealogy an ethnically inclusive one, which is one of the overarching themes of Matthew's Gospel. As he states: "In various ways, therefore, the five *women* in Matthew's genealogy of Jesus interpret the ministry of Jesus from its very start (his birth)."[36] J. A. Loubser, in a similar interpretation of Matthew's genealogy, identifies its structure as important. He observes: "By naming them, their complete narratives and the polemics associated with them are called in to memory. Thus a metanarrative is established of female ancestors, preparing the audience for the (unexpected?) statement that Jesus, son of Mary is the Davidic Messiah."[37] In line with this, as well as the scholarship of Raymond Brown,[38] as well as Donfried, Fitzmyer, and Reumann, Ratzinger makes two additional theological assertions. He argues

---

36. Peter-Ben Smit, "Something about Mary? Remarks about the Five Women in the Matthean Genealogy," *New Testament Studies* 56 (2010): 191–207, at 207. I thank Dr. Brian Nolan of All Hallows College, Dublin, for drawing this article to my attention.
37. J. A. (Bobby) Loubser, "Invoking the Ancestors: Socio-Rhetorical Aspects of the Genealogies in the Gospels of Matthew and Luke," a lecture delivered at the International Meeting of the Society of Biblical Literature, Cambridge (UK), 2003, 6. Again I thank Dr. Brian Nolan for drawing this article to my attention.
38. Raymond E. Brown, et al., eds., *Mary in the New Testament* (London: Geoffrey Chapman, 1978), 81–83.

that these four women tend to be passed over in silence because they are embarrassments, blemishes on the history of Israel that disturb the purity of the genealogy of Christ. In this, he sees the message of Matthew's Gospel: the last shall be first. Again, a reversal of values and God's choice of the weak are stressed. However, there is a further and decisive meaning for Ratzinger: they point to the "Church of the peoples." They are thought to transform the genealogy of Abraham and David into the genealogy of the Church of Jews and Gentiles: "Indeed, one could say that in the genealogy, these four women push aside all the tremendously important 'history of men'; it is the women who are the real hinges on which the genealogy turns. Instead of a genealogy of supposedly male deeds, it becomes a genealogy of faith and grace. The real heart of this history, the continuing story of God's promise, is based on the faith of these women."[39] Ratzinger understands the faith of these four Gentile women as prefiguring and anticipating Mary's faith, her *Fiat*, through which the new beginning is made in Jesus Christ. By entering the sphere of Mary's yes, this beginning, relatedness, and union to Jesus, becomes a reality for everyone. As he puts it: "The Gospel [Matthew's] summons us to enter the door of the *Fiat*."[40]

The Judge Saviors: Unexpected Strength

In reading the Jewish and Gentile matriarchs as embedded histories of expectation and fulfillment of salvation, Ratzinger draws deeply from the theological exegesis of the great tradition of the early Church to provide a fresh angle on Scripture and constructive theology. In this, he also offers surprising improvisations on the interpretation tradition. A pivotal example of this can be seen in Ratzinger's reading of the female judges in the Old Testament. For Ratzinger, Esther and

---

39. Ratzinger, *Blessing of Christmas*, 46.
40. Ibid., 50.

Judith in the late Old Testament writings embody a new and entirely original typology, one that he reads in close conjunction with the ancient tradition of Deborah—the savior judge. Here, Ratzinger draws from the earliest interpretative wells of the Church, harkening back to Clement's First Epistle to the Corinthians, one of the earliest Christian writings outside of the New Testament, dated circa 96 C.E. Clement writes:

> Even females have frequently been enabled by God's grace to achieve feats of heroism. The blessed Judith, when her city was in a state of siege, begged permission from the elders to visit the enemy's camp; and then for love of her country and her beleaguered people, she took her life in her hands and went forth, and the Lord delivered Holofernes into the hands of a weak woman. Esther, too, in the Fullness of her faith, took a similar risk to save the children of Israel from the destruction that was threatening them. In fasting and humiliation she made her supplication to the all-seeing Lord of eternity; and when He saw the humbleness of her spirit, He delivered the people for whom she had put herself in jeopardy.[41]

Ratzinger, improvising on Clement, links these two women—Esther, a wife in the harem of a Persian king, and Judith, a widow—to the great mothers who are also in an oppressed state. Ratzinger maintains that "Both embody the defeated Israel: Israel who has become a widow and wastes away in sorrow, Israel who has been abducted and dishonoured among the nations, enslaved within their arbitrary desires. Yet both personify at the same time Israel's unconquered spiritual strength, which cannot boast as do the worldly powers and for that very reason knows how to scorn and overcome the mighty."[42] By embodying Israel's hope, the women as saviours stand beside, and in the same line as, the unblessed–blessed mothers as prophetesses and judges.[43] In the dialectic of strength and

---

41. Radice, ed., *Early Christian Writings*, 45.
42. Ratzinger, *Daughter Zion*, 20.

vulnerability, God's power and faithfulness are revealed and, in this way, these woman become "the mother[s] of life" and the people as a nation. Hence, Ratzinger says: "The great women of Israel represent what this people itself is. The history of these women becomes the theology of God's people and, at the same time, the theology of the covenant."[44]

A similar theme carries through in Ratzinger's interpretation of Israel's exile to Babylon. He states that through their experience of the exile, in Israel's defeat, the true face of God appeared: "It was in exile and in the seeming defeat of Israel that there occurred an opening to the awareness of the God who holds every people and all of history in his hands, who holds everything because he is the creator of everything and the source of all power."[45] In the midst of the vulnerability of the people—barrenness and exile—and in the reversal of roles and locations, hope, promise, expectation, and fulfillment come into being through God's grace. This is particularly narrated by the Old Testament *through* its pivotal female figures, and underscores the shape of faith, grace, and relationality that constitutes the fragility yet transcendence of human existence that is the subject of salvation history.[46]

---

43. Ratzinger here draws on Louis Bouyer's idea of the role of women in the Church, which he develops through the women of the Old Testament. See Bouyer, *Women in the Church*, trans. Marilyn Teichert (San Francisco: Ignatius, 1979), 14.
44. Ratzinger, *Daughter Zion*, 21.
45. Ratzinger, 'In the Beginning . . . ,' 11–12.
46. Megan McKenna, in her collection of reflections on women of the Bible, *Leave her Alone* (Maryknoll, NY: Orbis, 2000), places the book of Esther within the context of other ancient tales, specifically the story of Scheherazade in the collection *Arabian Nights*. McKenna asserts that it is a wisdom story, and that its purpose is to remind the Jews to remember that, even in slavery and exile, God is with them; consequently, they must be obedient to the covenant and trust in the community for survival. In contrast to Ratzinger, she raises the problematic elements of this story, specifically, what she refers to as the "killing orgy of the Jews" following their deliverance. Notwithstanding the problems with this aspect of Esther, McKenna understands the meaning of the story as follows: "This is the story's meaning: how God intervenes to protect, defend, and succour his people in the midst of danger and despair, working with the people who have repented and are being faithful now in exile. It is about God's power in history

The Covenant and The Song of Songs: Marital Relationship

The covenant and the women of the Old Testament are fundamentally linked in Ratzinger's theology. In *Daughter Zion*, he argues that the figure of the woman makes God's covenant with Israel comprehensible. This means, for Ratzinger, that the figure of woman is central to relationship with God in the Old Testament. The figure of woman enables the prophets to transform the covenant from the political and legal model of the ancient Eastern vassal indentures into a covenant of marital love between Yahweh and Israel. In this relationship with God, Israel, as woman, is virgin and mother.[47] Ratzinger observes that "For this reason the covenant, which forms the very basis of the existence of Israel as a nation and the existence of each individual Israelite, is expressed interpersonally in the fidelity of the marriage covenant and in no other way."[48] God is not joined by a goddess but, rather, by the chosen creature, Israel, daughter Zion, the woman, which implies that woman is essential to salvation history. For Ratzinger, it is only in the context of this covenant of marital love that the Song of Songs is comprehensible. For him, they are "profane love songs with a heavily erotic coloring," which, when accepted into the canon of sacred Scriptures, became an expression of God's dialogue with Israel.[49] In this way, Ratzinger follows the Judeo-Christian tradition. He asserts that the mystery of the love of God and Israel shines through the Song of Songs so that the election of Israel is a love story between God and his people. This love story is illustrated through the analogy of betrothal and marriage. This is the one occasion where he uses allegory in interpreting

---

and about how God's glory resides in his people who will be saved in spite of what history tries to do to them" (133).
47. Ratzinger, *Daughter Zion*, 21–23.
48. Ibid., 23.
49. Ibid., 24.

the Old Testament. The importance for him of the imagery of the love relationship between God and humanity is that this analogy is continued and built upon by Jesus in his description of himself as the bridegroom (Mark 2:19f.) and use of the other wedding banquet parables.[50] He understands this to mean that the Eucharist is now the presence of the bridegroom and that through the Eucharist we become one spirit, one person with Christ, which is a foretaste of the wedding feast of God. In this way, "everything moves through the passion toward the wedding of the Lamb."[51]

Ratzinger's understanding of the covenant is expounded in his book *Many Religions—One Covenant*,[52] which contains a number of lectures and articles presented between 1994 and 1997.[53] Here, Ratzinger argues that the covenant God established with Israel is not a reciprocal but an asymmetrical agreement. God established the covenant with Israel as a gift and a creative act of love: by giving man the law God gave him the path of life.[54] He notes that the asymmetric relationship of the covenant, in parallel to the image of bridal love

---

50. Joseph Ratzinger, *The Spirit of the Liturgy*, trans. John Saward (San Francisco: Ignatius, 2000), 141–42.
51. Ibid., 142.
52. The theology of the covenant is a theme that was of interest to Ratzinger since his student days. In response to recent scholarship, he outlined his own theological understanding of the covenant. He states that: "I first encountered the topic of the relationship between the two Testaments, and of their inner unity-in-diversity, in a course of lecturers delivered by Gottlieb Sohngen in the Munich Faculty of Theology in the winter semester of 1947–48. The questions have stayed with me ever since, but it was the new challenges of recent years that prompted me to take an active part in this dialogue, which theology is now pursuing with increasing interest." Joseph Ratzinger, "Preface," in *Many Religions—One Covenant: Israel, the Church, and the World*, trans. Graham Harrison (San Francisco: Ignatius, 1999), 19.
53. The articles published are: "Israel, The Church, and the World," at the Jewish-Christian meeting in Jerusalem in February 1994, in ibid., 21–45; "The New Covenant: On the Theology of the Covenant in the New Testament," presented at the Academy of Moral and Political Sciences, Paris, and first published in *Communio* 24 (1995): 193–208; "The New Manna," presented as a homily in Wolfesing near Munich in August 1997, in *Many Religions—One Covenant*, 79–88; and "The Dialogue of the Religions and the Relationship between Judaism and Christianity," presented at the Academy of Moral and Political Sciences, Paris, and first published in *Communio* 26 (1997): 419–29.
54. Ratzinger, *Many Religions—One Covenant*, 49–50.

(Ezekiel 16) of God's relationship to Israel, is in striking contrast to the God of Greek philosophy.[55] Greek philosophy, he points out, deduced that God as immutable could not enter a mutual relationship with mutable humankind without compromising divinity. Israel's God, in contrast, is a God of relationship who enters into a relationship with human beings through the covenant with Abraham and Moses.[56] For Ratzinger, the covenant defines relationship with God and demonstrates that God *can* and *does* enter into relationship with human beings, albeit asymmetrically, without any compromise to the nature of God—God relates in freedom and unabbreviated love. The trinitarian theology of the early church, particularly its doctrine of divine persons, underwrites Ratzinger's view here, providing what he identifies as a "God-in-relationship" to be what is narrated of God in the biblical stories.[57] The relational nature of God, as we saw in chapter 1, underpins, too, his concept of salvation history. But if he insists on the priority of God's initiative within this paradigm, the human response to God's initiative is thought to be equally important, even if it always remains a response to God's initiative.

---

55. Ibid., 51. In this regard he states: "The prophets' portrayal of God's passionate love goes beyond what is to hand in the purely legal forms of the Orient [marriage being understood in patriarchal terms]. On the one hand, given God's infinite 'Otherness', the concept of God must seem to be the most radical heightening of the asymmetry; and, on the other hand, the true nature of *this* God must seem to create a two-sidedness that is totally unexpected."
56. Ibid., 74–76.
57. Based on this he states: "When we say that man is the image of God, it means that he is a being designed for relationship; it means that, in and through all his relationships, he seeks that relation which is the ground of his existence. In this context, covenant would be the response to man's imaging of God; it would show us who we are and who God is. And for God, since he is entirely relationship, covenant would not be something external in history, apart from his being, but the manifestation of his self, the 'radiance of his countenance'" (ibid., 76–77).

Wisdom: Female Image of God?

In *Daughter Zion,* Ratzinger notes that Wisdom (*Sophia*), which emerges in the final books of the Old Testament, was probably adapted to Israel's belief system from Egyptian prototypes. Here, we see a glimpse of Ratzinger's use of the historical-critical method as a tool to deepen his understanding of the biblical texts. He interprets Wisdom to be God's first creature, who appears as the Mediatrix of creation and salvation history. In Wisdom, both the pure, primordial form of God's creative will and the pure *answer* is expressed. As Ratzinger puts it: "Creation answers, and the answer is as close to God as a playmate, as a lover."[58] Whereas the New Testament refers back to the Great Mothers, to the theology of daughter Zion and (probably) Eve so as to refer to Mary, Ratzinger points out, as he does in regard to the judge-saviors, that it is the Church's liturgy, not the New Testament itself, that correlates the Wisdom texts with Mary. The liturgy, here, is a crucial matrix for constructive and expansive theological interpretation of the Old and New Testaments and salvation history itself.

Ratzinger is critical at this point of the early to mid-twentieth-century liturgical movement, noting their objection to the liturgical correlation of the Wisdom texts to Mary; many within the liturgical movement claimed these texts to refer strictly to Christ, not Mary. Such was in keeping with the narrowly christological theology of the liturgical movement. Ratzinger does admit that he, for many years, subscribed to this viewpoint but changed his mind. He did so because, in his revised view, it misjudges the full meaning of the Wisdom texts. He claims that while the Wisdom idea is assimilated into Christology, not all of it is integrated, so that a "remainder flows to Mary." He asserts:

---

58. Ratzinger, *Daughter Zion,* 25.

> From the view point of the New Testament, wisdom refers, on one side, to the Son as the Word, in whom God creates, but on the other side to the creature, to the true Israel, who is personified in the humble maid whose whole existence is marked by the attitude of the *Fiat mihi secundum verbum tuum*. Sophia refers to the Logos, the Word who establishes wisdom, and also to the womanly answer which receives wisdom and brings it to fruition.[59]

Ratzinger argues, further, that the consequence of an elimination of Marian reference is the loss of an entire dimension of the biblical and Christian mystery. He maintains, against such an elimination, that the word *wisdom* itself is a feminine noun in both Hebrew and Greek, and this is not an empty grammatical phenomenon. To his mind, *Sophia* represents woman and what is feminine. Perhaps, a certain influence of Balthasar's understanding of Mary as the feminine element of the Church can be identified here. As well, Ratzinger's later Marian "conversion" contributes a layer to his claim that a part of the Wisdom texts refers to Mary.[60] The crux of the issue is, Who

---

59. Ibid., 27.
60. This issue is a difficult one within the Church's theological understanding of salvation history, as the Church has not worked through the issue to conclusion. In other words, there are differences of opinion. For example, Henri de Lubac maintains, in relation to Wisdom, that "Wisdom is not a hypostasis which, in its created aspect, is realized in the Virgin. As in the liturgy, it is a symbol" (De Lubac, *The Eternal Feminine*, trans. René Hague [London: Collins, 1971], 95). Given that De Lubac and Ratzinger are associated with the same theological grouping, their different approaches highlight the unanswered questions associated with Wisdom within Catholic theology and liturgy. In Irene Nowell's exploration of Wisdom, Wisdom is identified as woman in the three Wisdom books and as a stand-alone figure in the Old Testament. She does identify nuanced differences and a deepening of insight of who Wisdom is in each of the three Wisdom books (Nowell, *Women in the Old Testament*, 131–51). Nonetheless, "woman as the image of God" is how Nowell describes the depiction of Wisdom in Proverbs, Sirach, and Wisdom. As a consequence of viewing Wisdom as an image of God, if we speak of her we speak of God. Nowell describes Wisdom as follows: "She is a breath of God's power, the outpouring of God's glory. She is the shining of God's light. She is the perfect reflection of God's power and goodness. She can do all things. . . . She fills the prophets with God's word. She is the one who makes us friends of God. God loves those who live with Wisdom" (ibid., 150.) In Nowell's exposition, Wisdom is essentially left as a stand-alone figure in salvation history. The relational nature of Nowell's exposition consequently fails to find a space for further development and integration within salvation history or within the male or female lines of the Bible, even though she alludes to a line of women in her discussion of the matriarchs. Another approach is advocated by Jann Aldredge-Clanton, among others,

is Wisdom? and Who is Mary? In my view, the development of a more thorough and comprehensive response to this issue of Wisdom in the New Testament as a whole is an outstanding task for theology to address and attempt to resolve. But to do so, a comprehensive understanding of Wisdom in her appearance in Christ is required, parallel to that of Wisdom's appearance in Mary.

Ratzinger's notion of a female line, fulfilled in Mary and her typological representation of the Church, offers solid foundations for such theological development. On this basis, a starting point of this development could be that because Wisdom is not just part of Ratzinger's female line—that she is also part, and to a greater extent, of the male line—the male line and the female line do not just run in parallel, but intersect each other at the point penultimate to the incarnation. More accurately, they come together at Wisdom, and then from Wisdom diverge again into Christ and Mary and her symbolism in the Church. The female line runs in parallel to the male line, but the intersection through Wisdom is a striking and unexpected revelation arising from Ratzinger's notion of a female line. The meaning for salvation history of this movement offers a basis for a renewed and deeper comprehension of the movement from Wisdom to Mary and the Church, the body of Chris, and Jesus, God's new beginning in humanity.

---

who proposes the image of Christ-Sophia. In her view, this symbolism offers an inclusive faith community, which provides for a holistic divine image which affirms women. See Aldredge-Clanton, *In Search of the Christ-Sophia An Inclusive Christology for Liberating Christians* (Mystic, CT: Twenty-Third Publications, 1995), 172–73. We see important themes of feminist theology in her proposal for the theological development of Wisdom. This is something that is absent from Nowell's interpretation, which is focused on the meaning of Wisdom as a woman in the Wisdom literature. There is a wide spectrum of interpretation of Wisdom. Ratzinger's concept of a female line provides a valuable, perhaps indispensable, interpretative tool to address the open questions related to Wisdom, which offers an opportunity to clarify and further develop the meaning of Wisdom in salvation history.

Womb Imagery: Female Imagery Depicting God

One final theme in Ratzinger's writings that is important to note here is his interpretation of the use of womb imagery in the Old Testament, something that links into his Mariology and hence his concept of a female line. We see him draw from tradition in his discussion of the meaning of womb imagery for God's self-revelation: the Council of Toledo in the late seventh century refers to the "womb of the Father." The Hebrew word *rahamin*, which refers in the singular to the womb, the uterus, Ratzinger singles out as a powerful description of God's compassion for humanity in his *Communio* article "'You are full of grace': Elements of Biblical Devotion to Mary," and also in his book *Jesus of Nazareth*.[61] He bases his understanding on Scripture passages, such as Isaiah's use of the term when he draws on the love of a mother to describe God's love for humanity (Isa. 49:15; 66:13). He asserts that this understanding of the term *rahamin* arises from the manner in which the Semitic language concretized its thought. Bodily organs were used to describe God through human dispositions and attitudes. He states that: "As 'heart' stands for feeling, loins and kidneys for desire and for pain, so the womb becomes the term for being-with another."[62] In this interpretation he utilizes the historical-critical method to draw out further meaning in an attempt to comprehend Scripture's depiction of God's relationship with humanity. Even here it is not just the knowledge of how the word was understood at the time of writing that is important for Ratzinger, but what it reveals about the God of Scripture in light of Christ.

---

61. Joseph Ratzinger, *Jesus of Nazareth*, trans. Adrian J. Walker (London: Bloomsbury, 2007), 139; and idem, "'You are full of grace'," 67–68.
62. Ratzinger, "'You are full of grace'," 67.

His use of womb imagery synchronizes, albeit in a reserved manner, with the constructive use of female language and imagery for God in feminist theology. For both, such imagery is at heart a matter of God's self-revelation. Womb imagery, for instance, provocatively captures the mystery and intimacy of origin, relationality, and bond. The Old Testament appropriates such natal imagery to depict God's creation and mothering into being of a people. The ancient and medieval tradition applied such images—some quite startling—to the eternal trinitarian relations of the Godhead, as analogies, employed with apophatic acumen, to portray the theological concepts of begetting and generation, and to get at the creative fecundity of the triune onto-relations. Such imagery parallels the revelatory significance, as Ratzinger notes, of the New Testament depiction of Jesus' addressing God as "Father," in which that act of dialogical naming simultaneously reveals their constitutive identities *as* Son and Father. As we have discussed earlier, the relational nature of Jesus' address to God as "Father," particularly in prayer, is integral to Ratzinger's understanding of Jesus and of Christianity as a whole. He states that "The essential events of Jesus' activity proceeded from the core of his personality and that this core was his dialogue with the Father."[63] Likewise, the term "Son" is the key to Christianity's interpretation and is what makes everything else accessible and intelligible.[64] This name-act narrated in the Gospels is, in essence, the playing out in history—in the historical life of Jesus—that which the Nicene Fathers articulated as *homoousios*, the consubstantiality of the Son with the Father; it is this hidden mystery of being that is unveiled in the dialogical manifestation of "Sonship."[65]

---

63. Joseph Ratzinger, *Behold the Pierced One*, trans. Graham Harrison (San Francisco: Ignatius, 1986), 18.
64. Ibid., 16–18.
65. Ratzinger, *God of Jesus Christ*, 89.

These terms, then, are not merely accidental names, but are revelatory of the relationship between the Son and the Father and thereby are normative for the triune God in the sense of being universal and unchanging.[66] It is important to note, though, that for Ratzinger, as well as Hans Küng, these names—Father, Son—do not and should not be taken to emphasize God *as* masculine or male. Küng argues that:

> Using the name Father in addressing God does not denote any sexual differentiation in God: God cannot be claimed solely for the male sex. God is not at the same time male: in the Hebrew Bible God also has feminine, maternal traits. Accordingly, the address 'Father', when used of God, is a patriarchal symbol (an analogy) of the trans-human, trans-sexual reality of God, who is the origin of all that is feminine and motherly; it cannot in any way be used as the religious basis for a paternalistic society.[67]

For Küng, as for Ratzinger, the use of the term "Father" is not to be taken as a literal depiction of God: God is neither male nor female and, as God is the Creator of all things, God is then the *origination* of male *and* female, of *paternity* and *maternity*. It is here that analogy both captures fundamental, constitutive realities about God, and, at the same time, the place where language and image fail—the apophatic barrier that breaks all language finally.

But the apophatic caution should not lead us to negate imagery too quickly. On the one hand, womb imagery, as found in the great tradition of the ancient and medieval theologians and exegetes, provides some critical purchase to contemplation of the intimate mysteries of God's internal and external relations, while, concomitantly, destabilizing our conceptual and linguistic constructions. On the other hand, there is a christological fine-tuning

---

66. Joseph Ratzinger with Vittorio Messori, *The Ratzinger Report*, trans. Salvator Attanasio and Graham Harrison (San Francisco: Ignatius, 1985), 97.
67. Hans Küng, *Women in Christianity*, trans. John Bowden (London: Continuum, 2001), 3–4.

of such imagery and referents; the Gospels present, for instance, Christ appropriating to himself maternal and motherly language, as well as to the Father (e.g., Matt. 23:37; Luke 13:34), as denoting the divine love and compassion for God's creatures. For Ratzinger, moreover, the Marian dimension in Mary, the Mother of Jesus, is a demonstration of God's motherliness.[68] Taken together, it is not only revealing, or constitutive of, God's love and care, but also an eschatological set of images—portraitures of the relational matrix that opens out and elevates humankind in deification, in eschatological union with the triune God.

Of course, such imagery is bounded—it cannot apply without reserve. More positively, it provides a space of critique not only of but with traditional concepts and language. In this, that the primary referent, as christologically conditioned, is *God*, human objects of reference are critiqued and redefined: God as "Father" becomes the divine critique of human fatherhood; in the same way, "mother" is redefined by this very reality of God's maternity—*ad intra* and *ad*

---

68. Ratzinger improvises on this imagery further by linking this typologically with the image of the dwelling of God in the womb of Israel, in the Ark of the Covenant, which for him becomes a reality in the Virgin Mother of God. In this way, drawing on René Laurentin's work (*Struktur und Theologie der lukanischen Kind-heitsgeschichte* [Stuttgart, 1967], 75–82; and *Court traité de theologie mariale* [Paris, 1953], 25) in relation to Luke's Mariology, he posits that "Thereby the symbol of the ark attains a uniquely powerful reality: God in the flesh of a human being which is now his dwelling in the midst of creation" (Ratzinger, "'You are full of grace'," 57–58). Continuing this line of argument, which includes the typological link between Israel, the bridal people of God, and Mary, Ratzinger connects the image of the womb with the image of the Pietà and considers it to be a living translation of the word *womb*. For Ratzinger, in the Pietà, Mary's grief over her son reveals God's maternal pain and com-passion. He believes that because suffering is a fundamental part of life, the image of the sorrowful mother has gained great importance for Christianity. He goes as far as saying that only in the sorrowful mother is the image of the cross concluded, so that the pain of the sorrowful mother reveals the transformation of death into the redemptive being-with of love (ibid., 54–68). Ratzinger's subsequent link of the womb with the Pietà is an explication of both the womb imagery and of the Pietà, rather than necessarily a typological link as such. It does, however, illuminate the true meaning of God's compassion for humanity. What he is trying to do is to concretize in Mary God's compassion in the New Testament, as the womb does in the Old. The danger, though, is that this could be misunderstood as in some way divinizing Mary, so that she is no longer a human being but divine. This is, in fact, something that his Mariology rules out.

extra.⁶⁹ The relationality of God, in this way, just is that reality into which humanity is created and drawn—God *is* the womb in which we come to really be: "The womb is the most concrete expression for the intimate interrelatedness of two lives and of loving concern for the dependent, helpless creature whose whole being, body and soul, nestles in the mother's womb."⁷⁰ He uses the term "being-with another" to describe the meaning of the womb, and this links the image to other important aspects of his theological ideas and positions. As we saw earlier, for Ratzinger, God's nature is to be entirely "being-for" (Father), "being-from" (Son), and "being-with" (Holy Spirit), and the human being is God's image only when he or she follows this pattern.⁷¹ This reality is concretized for him in the bodily term *rahamin*,⁷² "womb." This concretization of thought in human imagery is again strikingly seen in his theological interpretation of Mary as the personal concretization of the Church, a topic we turn to now.

---

69. Ratzinger, *God of Jesus Christ*, 30–31, 33.
70. Ratzinger, *Jesus of Nazareth*, 139. He also maintains that the Bible identifies the mother's womb with the depth of the earth, particularly Ps. 119:73, "Thy hands have made me and fashioned me," and Ps. 139:13, 15, "thou didst knit me together in my mother's womb," as well as Job 10:8-10, "Remember that thou hast made me of clay." In these references, which identify the mother's womb with the depth of the earth, he links the images with the origin of Adam, each human being: "Your hands have fashioned me, like clay you have formed me" (Ratzinger, *Man between Reproduction and Procreation*, 206–7).
71. Joseph Ratzinger, "Truth and Freedom," trans. Adrian Walker, *Communio* 23, no. 1 (1996): 16–35.
72. Ibid. Ratzinger demonstrates the reality of this situation in his reflection on truth and freedom. In the scenario of pregnancy, the being of one person, the fetus, is interwoven so much with its mother that it can only survive through physical unity with her, but this unity does not dissolve the separate existence of the being of the fetus. He observes: "To be oneself in this way is to be radically from and through another. Conversely, this being-with compels the being of the other—that is, the mother—to become a being-for, which contradicts her own desire to be an independent self and is thus experienced as the antithesis of her own freedom" (ibid, 27.) This scenario describes the essence of human existence in general and in particular to human beings' relationship with God. It also demonstrates how his understanding of God and man and his understanding of freedom converge. Only by accepting the limits of freedom does man remain truly human. Demands for total liberation and freedom in the end lead to the emancipation from being a human being, from the essence of being human. We remain truly human when we live *for, from,* and *with* others.

4

The Female Line in the New Testament

The female line in the New Testament consists of Mary and her symbolism of the Church. Mary's response to God, her yes, and the incarnation, God become flesh, are the fundamental elements of Ratzinger's Mariology and the pinnacle of his "female line in the Bible." I will first look at Mariology in general and then at the Marian dogmas. Ratzinger's approach can be understood as an attempt to identify the correct place of Marian piety in Catholic theology and faith. This is demonstrated by two of his key texts in relation to his female line and Mariology in general. The first, *Daughter Zion*,[1] seeks to "help towards a new understanding and appropriation of what should not be lost in the Church's Marian belief." It is not written as a comprehensive treatise; rather, it seeks to identify the layers of meaning upon which a larger work can be built.[2] Whether the three lectures of 1975 upon which this book

---

1. Joseph Ratzinger, *Daughter Zion: Meditations on the Church's Marian Belief*, trans. John M. McDermott, S.J. (San Francisco: Ignatius, 1983). This book is based on three lectures he gave in 1975 and published in German in 1977.
2. Ibid., 7–8.

is based were influenced by *Marialis Cultus* (1974), in which Paul VI provided guidance for theologically appropriate Marian devotion, is not clear. In the lectures Ratzinger sought to provide clarity on the theological basis of Mary in Christian faith and theology. As a result, his approach is complementary to *Marialis Cultus* with its emphasis on clarifying appropriate Marian devotion in relation to divine worship, particularly in the liturgy. The second text, "On the Position of Mariology and Marian Spirituality within the Totality of Faith and Theology," was originally published in the Pastoral of the German Bishops, on April 30, 1979. In this article, the aim of which is self-evident from the title, Ratzinger seeks to situate Mary correctly within Catholic faith and theology.

An important element of Ratzinger's writings is his criticism of the view that Mariology is an infiltration of pagan religions and ideas into Christianity, as well as a refutation of the criticism that Mariology endangers and threatens Christology. Ratzinger in particular rejects Hans Küng's criticism of Catholic Marian piety. In *Daughter Zion*, he refers to Küng's "exceptionally coarse resumption of the old, liberal hypothesis" in reference to the title of Mother of God.[3] He sees the call for enabling diverse forms of piety, including what he refers to as the attitude of "leave the Romans their madonnas," as a response to a rationalizing trend. In response, he asserts that Marian piety cannot be based on customs, and seeks to outline the theological basis for Marian piety. For Ratzinger, far from endangering Christology, Mariology is required if Christology is to be understood correctly.[4] It is not just in defense of Christology that Mariology plays a significant role; instead, his view is that the very development of Christology requires the Marian element to be present. He states in this regard:

---

3. Ibid., 10n1.
4. Ibid., 31–37.

Only when it touches Mary and becomes Mariology is Christology itself as radical as the faith of the Church requires. The appearance of a truly Marian awareness serves as the touchstone indicating whether or not the Christological substance is fully present. . . . In Mariology, Christology was defended. Far from belittling Christology, it signifies the comprehensive triumph of a confession of faith in Christ which has achieved authenticity.[5]

It is upon this theological foundation of Mary's role in explicating the Christian faith that Ratzinger's understanding of Mary is based and developed.

Mariology in Ratzinger's Theological Thinking

Ratzinger builds his Mariology on Luke's and John's Gospels, specifically Luke's infancy narrative, and John's description of Mary as woman. He calls these two evangelists the "Marian authors of the New Testament."[6] His view is that Mary is essential to a correct understanding of Christian faith and that this role in clarifying salvation history is particularly important in this era.[7] In response to the post–Vatican II theological discussions on Mary he identifies six important points relating to Mary that complete the Catholic faith. First, Marian dogma and tradition has to be rooted in authentic Christology, and is in direct service to faith in Christ, not primarily devotion to Mary. Second, Mariology, specifically the Marian dogmas, is based on the correct integration of Scripture and tradition. Third, Mary links together the Old and New Testaments, Israel and Christianity. Fourth, Mary brings to Christian faith the reasons of the heart, feeling, providing a coordinated balance with reason. Fifth,

---

5. Ibid., 35–36; see also idem, *God and the World: Believing and Living in Our Time: A Conversation with Peter Seewald*, trans. Henry Taylor (San Francisco: Ignatius, 2000), 354.
6. Ratzinger, *Daughter Zion*, 31.
7. Joseph Ratzinger with Vittorio Messori, *The Ratzinger Report*, trans. Salvator Attanasio and Graham Harrison (San Francisco: Ignatius, 1985), 105.

Mary, as figure and archetype of the Church, prevents faith from being reduced to an abstraction, an instrument for a program of social and political action. Sixth, Mary, through her courage and obedience, is an example that every Christian should follow. He suggests that Mary "continues to project a light upon that which the Creator intended for all in every age," for she proclaims the Magnificat and the overturning of the worldly orders of power and status by the marginal, the outcast, and the exiled.

Church-Centered Mariology

In addition to his biblical theological interpretation, explored in chapter 3, the interpretation of Mary through the Church and vice versa, specifically Mary's personification of the Church, plays an essential role in Ratzinger's theology. As noted earlier, prior to Vatican II, he admits that he was heavily influenced by the liturgical movement, but he was later convinced of the indivisibility of Mary and the Church through Hugo Rahner's book *Our Lady of the Church*, as well as the work of other theologians of the period.[8] The later importance to his theological position of the indivisibility of Mary and the Church is made clear through his statement: "I think that in fact this rediscovery of the inter-changeability between Mary and the Church, the personification of the Church in Mary and the universal dimension acquired by Mary in the Church, is one of the most important theological rediscoveries of the twentieth century."[9] Hugo Rahner anticipates *Lumen Gentium* in understanding Mary as

---

8. Namely, Alois Muller, Karl Delahaye, René Laurentin, and Otto Semmelroth. See Joseph Ratzinger, "On the Position of Mariology and Marian Spirituality within the Totality of Faith and Theology," trans. Graham Harrison, in Helmut Moll, ed., *The Church and Women: A Compendium* (San Francisco: Ignatius, 1988), 67–79, at 69–70.
9. Ratzinger, *God and the World*, 353.

the *typos* of the Church while Ratzinger, later, builds on *Lumen Gentium*'s reassertion of this ancient aspect of Catholic theology.[10]

Rahner published *Our Lady and the Church* (1951) to demonstrate that, within the church fathers' writings, Mary is understood to be the symbol of the Church. In his view, the early Church saw in Mary's earthly life the highest mystery of theology. As a consequence, the fathers viewed Mary and the Church as a single figure, which means that everything said about Mary in the Gospels also applies to the Church. Rahner states that "In Patristic thought Mary is the *typos* of the Church: symbol, central idea, and as it were all that is meant by the Church in her nature and vocation."[11] For him, this denotes that Mary is the "type of what is to come."[12] Rahner finds a clear and very early example of the indivisibility and interchangeability of Mary and the Church in patristic writings in Hippolytus, the disciple of Irenaeus, himself a disciple of Polycarp, who was a disciple of the apostle John. In reference to the words of Moses, "Through God's blessing his land shall remain his own, and be blessed with the dew of heaven" (cf. Deut. 33:13), Hippolytus states that "This was said of Mary, who was the blessed land, and the Word was made flesh, coming down as the dew. But it can also be said of the Church, for she is blest by the Lord as a holy land and a paradise of bliss, and the dew of the Lord, the Redeemer Himself. For this holy land has inherited all the Lord's blessings from the holy House, from the virginal birth, as these latter ages have shown."[13] Another example Rahner quotes is from St. Ephrem, the Syrian father (306–373 C.E.): "Mother Earth it was that bore all flesh, and was accursed. But for

---

10. *Lumen Gentium*, nos. 52–69, in Austin Flannery, ed., *Vatican Council II: The Basic Sixteen Documents: Constitutions, Decrees, Declarations* (Dublin: Dominican Publications, 1996).
11. Hugo Rahner, *Our Lady and the Church*, trans. Sebastian Bullough (Bethesda, MD: Zaccheus Press, 2004), 7–8.
12. Ibid., 9.
13. Ibid., 10–11; Rahner takes this quote from *The Blessings of Moses* 15 (*Texte und Untersuchungen* 26, I [1904]: 66).

the sake of the flesh that is the Church incorruptible, this fleshy earth was blessed from the beginning, for Mary was the Mother Earth that brought the Church to birth."[14]

Rahner's rediscovery demonstrates quite effectively, through his exposition of patristic thought, that it is misguided to seek the fundamental principle of Mariology in Mary herself. By necessity, the fundamental principle must be external to Mary, for Mary is a human being, and Christianity is God's self-revelation. The fundamental principle of a theology of Mary is Christ, for there is no Mariology without Christ; it is God the Father, Son, and Holy Spirit who transforms Mary from an ordinary girl in Israel's history into Theotokos, the Mother of God. Christ as the fundamental principle of a theology of Mary allows for a synthesis and integration of all aspects of Mary into Christianity while preventing any inappropriate development of Mariology without Christ.[15] It allows for the integration of five out of the six attributes, which Cyril Vollert explores, as a possible primary principle: The Divine Maternity; The Mission of the Co-redemption; Twofold Principle: Mother and Associate; Mother of the Whole Christ or Universal Mother; Mary, Prototype of the Church; Fullness of Grace.[16] This integration of the five attributes would itself then clarify the appropriateness of the sixth, Mary's co-redemption. In such an integration, each option would be refined and built upon in light of each other in a manner that offers something more than each on its own. Church-centered Mariology offers the space to carry out that synthesis and the

---

14. Rahner, *Our Lady and the Church*, xi; Rahner takes this quote from *Evangelii concorantis Expositio* (ed. Moesinger, 49).
15. For as Karl Rahner maintained, the fundamental idea of Mariology is that Mary is the perfect Christian because she is the most perfect instance of Christianity, in that she received God in his Incarnate Word with her whole nature, body, and soul, not simply as some abstract thought: "All that faith says about the realization of redemption, about salvation and grace and the fullness of grace, is realised in Mary." Rahner, *Mary, Mother of the Lord*, trans. M. J. O'Hara (Edinburgh & London: Nelson, 1963), 37–38.
16. Cyril Vollert, *A Theology of Mary* (New York: Herder & Herder, 1965), 58–98.

integration of all attributes of Mary into a coherent whole while remaining anchored in her fundamental principle, Christ.

The rediscovery of the interchangeability between Mary and the Church plays a major role in Ratzinger's theological framework, although he does have a slightly nuanced difference in emphasis from Rahner, in that he states that within the fathers' writings there is a "preliminary adumbration of the whole of Mariology, albeit without naming the name of the Mother of the Lord: *Virgo Ecclesia*, the *Mater Ecclesia*, the *Ecclesia Immaculata*, the *Ecclesia Assumpta*—everything that will one day be Mariology is present here as Ecclesiology."[17] Ratzinger, while acknowledging that the fathers' references to the Church in personal terms refer to Mary, thinks the fathers implicitly developed Mariology in relation to the Church, and later explicitly developed it in relation to Mary in reference to the Church. Ecclesiology comes first, and through its development and refinement Mariology is to be understood. This has important consequences for the development of the recent Marian dogmas. The teachings existed from the time of the fathers, clothed in ecclesiology, awaiting their full implications to become evident when an explicit Mariology developed. One final point should be made here, the implications of this interchangeability of Mary and the Church on Ratzinger's own ecclesiology, with its emphasis on the Church as God's self-gift and communion, have yet to be fully drawn out.

Bernard of Clairvaux: Commencing a New Emphasis in the Thought on Mary

An important and significant change of emphasis on how the Church perceived Mary begins with St. Bernard of Clairvaux's writings in the twelfth century. This change had an impact on the Church's

---

17. Ratzinger, "On the Position of Mariology," 74.

awareness of the indivisible link between the Church and Mary that Rahner and Ratzinger identify in the fathers' writings. According to Ratzinger, Bernard of Clairvaux began the process of fusing the teachings of patristic ecclesiology with the teachings on Mary found in Christology, and it is from here that a Mariology distinct from ecclesiology began to emerge.[18] Ratzinger as well as Rahner agree with Thomas Merton that this was an appropriate development of the Church's tradition in that Bernard's Mariology draws out in an explicit manner what had previously been implicit in the Church's faith and theology. Merton states that

> Saint Bernard stands at a critical point in the development of theological teaching on the Mother of God. Before him it can be said that there was, strictly speaking, no such thing as a completely developed "Mariology." The principles were there. The seeds had long lain hidden in the fertile soil of tradition. They had pierced the surface of the ground in the early Fathers and in such great ecumenical councils as that of Ephesus. But in Bernard they first reached maturity and become ready for the harvest. His Marian doctrine is a luminous synthesis of all that tradition had indicated before his time, and the loving explication of deep truths which had hitherto lain hidden implicitly in the mystery of the Incarnation itself. I have already said that Bernard's writings on Mary are the most beautiful pages he ever composed. However, they are more than poetry, more than beautiful style; they are great theology. To say Bernard has developed a strict Mariology is to say that he has drawn from Scripture not only food for affective piety, but also principles of a new theological synthesis.[19]

---

18. Ibid.
19. Merton continues that "The marrow of his teachings is concentrated in the Homilies on the *Missus Est* (the Gospel text of the Annunciation) and seven great sermons for feasts of Our Lady. . . . Better than anyone else, Saint Bernard saw that the love of Jesus and Mary as so inseparable as to be the same. We cannot love Him without the same time loving her, and our only reason for loving her is that we may love Him better. The logical consequence of this is Saint Bernard's belief that everything that comes to us through our One Divine Mediator comes to us also, and by that very fact, through Mary. '*Totum nos habere voluit per Mariam.*'" Thomas Merton, *The Last of the Fathers* (London: Catholic Book Club, 1954), 86–87, 88–89. I thank Dr. Teresa Whitington of the Central Catholic Library in Dublin for drawing my attention to Merton's work on St. Bernard and in particular his comments on Bernard's Mariology.

It is clear that Bernard knew his homilies were an innovation of the fathers' approach, but one he considered remained within that tradition. Bernard's approach in praise of Mary can be seen in this short passage: "Blessed Mary! She lacks neither humility nor virginity. And what unique virginity. Motherhood did not stain but honoured it. What extraordinary humility. Fruitful virginity did not tarnish but exalted it and matchless fruitfulness went hand in hand with both virginity and humility."[20] In acknowledging that these homilies take a new and different approach to Mary, Bernard states that so long as what he says is not in contradiction of the fathers, they should not displease anyone.[21] This is an example of what Ratzinger would refer to as the development of the Church's faith through successive generations, which is an essential principle of his biblical interpretation approach. Bernard, like Ratzinger, was capable of innovation within the tradition of the Church. From the Gospels, through the Christology and ecclesiology of the fathers, and Bernard's joyful praise of Mary, the Church's understanding of Mary deepened and opened up an unexpected perspective. It might be argued, however, that this process also opens the faith up to the danger of obscuring the basis for understanding the, which in turn leads to forgetfulness and a loss of the actual foundations of the individual tenets of the faith.

This, indeed, is what happened to the understanding of Mary as the symbol of the Church. Hugo Rahner asserts that Bernard's development of a Mariology focused on the person of Mary meant

---

20. Bernard of Clairvaux, Homily I:9, *Homilies in Praise of the Blessed Virgin Mary*, trans. Marie-Bernard Said, O.S.B. (Kalamazoo, MI: Cistercian Publications, 1993), 12. It is important to note that these homilies praised Mary not in isolation from, but together with, Jesus Christ.
21. Ibid., 3, 58. In his introduction to these homilies, Chrysogonus Waddell points out that Bernard's Marian reflections were unoriginal and conservative, and that he did not contribute to the Marian teachings that were being developed in the twelfth century such as the immaculate conception (Bernard opposed this teaching), Mary's bodily assumption, and her spiritual maternity. Waddell, "Introduction," in ibid., xvi–xvii.

that the cult of Our Lady, which developed from the early Middle Ages, was distinct from and unrelated to the Church.[22] This led to the eclipse of Mary as the symbol of the Church, which in turn led to an unbalanced understanding of Mary and the Church, arguably affecting the development of theology in subsequent centuries. Indeed, the debate on Mariology's place in theology and faith since the promulgation of the two latest Marian dogmas demonstrates this very point. This evolution of Mariology demonstrates why Ratzinger places such importance on the Church's tradition in theology and biblical interpretation. It also demonstrates the challenge the Church faces in remembering all the various aspects of that tradition to ensure that the basis of the Christian faith can be understood in each age.

Mary and the Church as a Single, Personal Figure

Notwithstanding this later development and subsequent forgetfulness, Ratzinger has demonstrated that, from the beginning, Mary and the Church were understood as a single figure. In spite of their interdependence, however, the development of Mariology and ecclesiology occurred at separate times. He points to the angel Gabriel's greeting to Mary, "Rejoice, O you who are full of grace. The Lord is with you" (Luke 1:28), as the fundamental interpretation of Mary; indeed, he maintains that the Archangel Gabriel's address of Mary is the nucleus of Mariology. The address is found four times in the Greek version of the Old Testament: Zeph. 3:14; Joel 2:21; Zech. 9:9; and Lam. 4:21. Each time it is an announcement of messianic joy. Zephaniah's version, addressed to Israel, daughter of Zion, tells her that God would come as a savior and dwell in her. In Ratzinger's view, Mary personifies what was prophesied, in that

---

22. Rahner, *Our Lady and the Church*, 116.

Mary is the daughter of Zion in person.[23] Ratzinger, building on René Laurentin's work, interprets Mary as the daughter of Zion:

> Mary is identified with the daughter of Zion, with the bridal people of God. Everything said in the Bible about the Ecclesia is true of Mary, and vice versa: what the Church is and shall be, she discovers concretely by looking at Mary. Mary is her Mirror, the pure measure of the Church's being, because she stands completely within the boundaries of Christ and God, and is "indwelt" by him. And why else should the Ecclesia exist except to become God's dwelling on earth?[24]

Ratzinger's argument is that, in the early Church, what was said of Mary was said of the Church, that she was the symbol of what is to come. Given Rahner's demonstration that, within the fathers' writings, the Marian dogmas appear in relation to Mary and the Church, this means that they are a continuation of the Gospels' understanding; this is not a latter-day, inappropriate innovation that overly creative theologians have disconnected from tradition. Rahner and Ratzinger's position is that Mary and the Church are theologically indivisible and interchangeable. In other words, neither Mary nor the Church can truly be understood without the other, and each is understood through the other. This relationship also links Mary with Israel and is a fundamental tenet of his understanding of the concept of "the female line in the Bible." Ratzinger argues for the reasonableness of the identification of Mary with Israel thus: "It is no less part of the framework of biblical theology than the systematic interpretation of the Adam-Christ type is part of the doctrine of

---

23. Joseph Ratzinger, "'You are full of grace': Elements of Biblical Devotion to Mary'," *Communio* 16, no. 1 (1989): 56–58. In reference to Mary as the true daughter of Zion, Ratzinger asserts that through it Mary's true nature is revealed: "In the address of the angel, the underlying motif in the Lucan portrait of Mary surfaces: she is in person the true Zion, toward whom hopes have yearned throughout all the devastations of history. She is the true Israel in whom Old and New Covenant, Israel and Church, are indivisibly one. She is the 'people of God' bearing fruit through God's gracious power" (Ratzinger, *Daughter Zion*, 43). Also see idem, *Introduction to Christianity*, 2d ed., trans. J. R. Foster (San Francisco: Ignatius, 2003), 271–73.
24. Ratzinger, "'You are full of grace'," 58.

original sin. Through the Lucan equation of the true daughter Zion with the listening-believing Virgin it is fully present, in essentials, in the New Testament."[25] Just as Ratzinger identifies original sin as a theological fact,[26] it can be argued, by extension, that the personal identification of Mary and the Church with Israel is also a theological "fact." For Ratzinger, Mary is the Church in person because the Church embodies what she anticipates: through Mary, the Church is concretized.[27] In his view, Mary as type of the Church reveals the personal form of the Church, because "in theology, the person is not traced back to some state of affairs: on the contrary the state of affairs is traced back to the person."[28]

The importance of the personal in Ratzinger's theology reflects the influence of personalism derived from Balthasar's theology, but it is an influence that Ratzinger develops in a distinct manner. Where Balthasar would refers to the link between Mary and the Church, he does so in relation to Mary as the *feminine* aspect of the Church. The contrasting ideas of masculinity and femininity in Balthasar do not appear in Ratzinger's thinking. For example, in relation to Mary and the Church, von Balthasar states that:

> The Church is primarily feminine because her primary, all-encompassing truth is her ontological gratitude, which both receives the gift and passes it on. And the masculine office, which has to represent the true giver, the Lord of the Church (albeit with the Church's feminine receptivity), is instituted in her only to prevent her forgetting this primary reality, to ensure that she will always remain a receiver and never become self-assertive possessor and user.[29]

---

25. Ratzinger, *Daughter Zion*, 68.
26. Ibid., 66.
27. Ratzinger, *God and the World*, 353.
28. Ratzinger, "On the Position of Mariology," 73.
29. Hans Urs von Balthasar, "The Marian Mold of the Church," in Joseph Ratzinger and Hans Urs von Balthasar, *Mary: The Church at the Source*, trans. Adrian Walker (San Francisco: Ignatius, 2005), 140.

Ratzinger, in contrast, does not assign essentialist characteristics to Mary, or to the Church as typologized by Mary; for him, Mary is, rather, a free, active, personal agent—and it is the personal and relational that receives his fundamental theological attention. The relational nature in his view of Mary is important for how his Mariology developed and is grounded in the relational nature of his overall theological thinking.[30] Ratzinger emphasizes the personal and human aspects, which have important consequences, particularly in that such emphasis avoids abstract ideas and embraces the concrete human person. It may also reflect Ratzinger's attempt to continue the Old Testament's use of language to concretize its thought, as was seen in his discussion of the Hebrew word *rahamin*, "womb," when articulating God's relationship to humanity.

The absence of a notion of the eternal feminine, or an emphasis on femininity as receptivity, or feminine characteristics in contrast to specifically masculine characteristics, from Ratzinger's Mariology distinguishes his work not only from Balthasar but others with whom he was theologically closely associated, such as Henri de Lubac, among others. De Lubac, in his study of Teillard de Chardin's poem *The Eternal Feminine,* notes that the poem directly links the principle of the eternal feminine with the Virgin Mary. De Lubac posits that Mary, for de Chardin, universalizes this principle.[31] In contrast, Ratzinger refers to Mary as the personification or personal concretization of the Church, as exemplified in patristic ecclesiology, particularly reference to the Church in personal terms and the

---

30. Hans Urs von Balthasar, "Epilogue," in Louis Bouyer, *Women and the Church*, trans. Marilyn Teichert (San Francisco: Ignatius, 1979), 113; idem, "Mary and the Church's Doctrine and Devotion," in Ratzinger and Balthasar, *Mary: The Church at the Source*, 110–11, 140; idem, "How Weighty Is the Argument from 'Unjustified Tradition' to Justify the Male Priesthood," trans. Lothar Krauth, in Moll, ed., *The Church and Women*, 159.
31. Henri De Lubac, *The Eternal Feminine*, trans. René Hague (London: Collins, 1971), 117–19. Also see Jaroslav Pelikan, "The Mater Gloriosa and the Eternal Feminine," in *Mary through the Centuries: Her Place in the History of Culture* (New Haven: Yale University Press, 1996), 165–75.

indivisibility of Mary and the Church.[32] Rather than the universalization of an abstract concept, like the eternal feminine, for Ratzinger the Church is a person. This marks a significant difference in Ratzinger's understanding of Mary and her place in Catholic faith and theology and is based on the central role that the concept of person, and hence relationship, plays within Ratzinger's theology and anthropology.

The idea of the feminine in distinction and in contrast to the masculine is found in Louis Bouyer's *Women and the Church*, which Balthasar fully endorses, as well as in Balthasar's own writings.[33] Bouyer associates the male with God the Father, an idea that sits uncomfortably with the Judeo-Christian concept of God as transcending sexuality.[34] Balthasar comments in relation to Bouyer's work that "the role of the man consequently acquires a particularly open bi-polarity where women's role exhibits closure."[35] Bouyer and

---

32. As already noted, he articulates his approach as follows: "In theology, it is not the person who is reducible to the thing, but the thing to the person" (Ratzinger, "On the Position of Mariology," 73).

33. Balthasar, "Epilogue," in Bouyer, *Women and the Church*, 113. Also see idem, "Mary and the Church's Doctrine and Devotion"; and idem, "How Weighty Is the Argument."

34. Bouyer, *Women and the Church*, 49. Bouyer states that "Man, the male, insofar as he is such, is defined by the following paradox: he essentially represents that which goes beyond him, which he is incapable of being in and of himself, in which he cannot even take part except by his participation through grace in the sonship of the only eternal Son, who himself represents the father from whom he proceeds and from whom all things proceed: God in the inexhaustible vitality of his absolute transcendence. But, once again, on the natural plane, man is able to be a father only in a very partial and ephemeral way, while on the supernatural plane he can represent divine fatherhood only through his dependence on the unique image of the Father which is the only begotten Son. Woman, on the contrary, simply represents the creature in its highest vocation, by which it is conjoined with God himself in his creation and even in his fatherhood." In Bouyer's use of the abstract terms *male/masculine*, and *female/feminine* in salvation history, he uses these in too literal a sense. He fails to anchor these reflections within the witness and people of the Bible.

35. Balthasar, "Epilogue," in Bouyer, *Women and the Church*, 114–15. The quote continues: "As a representative of the Creator God, the man is more than himself, and yet, at the same time, as a mere transmitter who can as such *only* represent, he is also less than himself. Once this, in my opinion, irrefutable assessment is applied to the relationship between the bride-Church (as a conceiving, birth-giving, and nurturing reality) and the ecclesial ministerial office, it seems that no objections against it would hold up." These comments highlight his concern in this discussion to validate the male only priesthood.

Balthasar's emphasis on a contrast of masculine and feminine characteristics, and Balthasar's view of femininity as receptivity mean their ideas, like de Lubac's, essentialize gender characteristics and roles, as well as universalize abstract notions in disconnection from the history of the women of Scripture. Bouyer and Balthasar attempt to demonstrate from this construct the validity of an exclusively male priesthood. In contrast, Ratzinger seeks to interpret the meaning for salvation history of the women of the Bible—not under essentialized traits and assignments, but as human beings who have vital, active, generative significance for the history and story in which they participate. It is not about an *idea* of what woman, the feminine, or the female is. Instead, it is about the lives and actions of these women and what they tell us about God's relationship with humanity and salvation history.

The combination of the link between the idea of the eternal feminine and the ideas of femininity as receptivity, along with the contrasting of strictly feminine characteristics with masculine characteristics in the Mariology of some mainstream and conservative theologians of the last fifty years,[36] allowed non-Judeo-Christian ideas to infiltrate inappropriately into mainstream Catholic theology and anthropology. But the "Letter to the Bishops of the Catholic Church On the Collaboration between Men and Women in the Church and the World" (2004) rejects what it describes as "a passivity inspired by an outdated conception of femininity"[37] in relation to Mary and the Church. It is difficult not to read this statement as

---

36. In addition to de Lubac, Balthasar, and Bouyer, also see Jutta Burggraf, "Women's Dignity and Function in Church and Society," trans. Lothar Krauth, in Moll, ed., *The Church and Women*, 110; and Barbara Albrecht, "Is There an Objective Type 'Woman'?," trans. Maria Shrady, in ibid., 36.

37. The Congregation for the Doctrine of the Faith, "Letter to the Bishops of the Catholic Church On the Collaboration between Men and Women in the Church and the World" (2004), no. 16, http://www.vatican.va/roman_curia/congregations/cfaith/documents/rc_con_cfaith_doc_20040731_collaboration_en.html.

anything but a rejection of those aforementioned ideas, particularly given its insistence that feminine values are "above all human values."[38] The Letter's anthropology is based on the Genesis accounts of creation and fall, leaving no room for the ideas of the eternal feminine or Aristotelian femininity as receptivity. The specific influence of Ratzinger, Walter Kasper, and Karl Lehmann can be identified with this rejection.[39] It is a correction of an important and powerful idea in the anthropology of leading twentieth-century Catholic theologians who were their close theological associates, which rightly troubles feminist theologians. The Letter's rejection of these ideas has freed Christian anthropology from a toxic and disruptive idea that is in fact antithetical to it. As a consequence, it has provided space for the further development of an authentically Christian anthropology that rejects radical contrasts and, rather, understands the human being to hold within it femininity and masculinity while simultaneously acknowledging the complementarity of the female and male of humanity.

A Problematic Aspect of Ratzinger's Mariology

Nonetheless, there is a problematic aspect to Ratzinger's understanding of Mary, namely, his view of her as in some way special or of specific significance to women. One aspect of this is

---

38. Ibid., no. 14.
39. I argued in the literary review in my PhD thesis and my subsequent paper, "A Critique of the Theological Direction the Congregation for the Doctrine of the Faith's Letter on Collaboration between Men and Women, 2004, provides to Christian Anthropology," presented at the European Society for Catholic Theology's Emerging Scholars conference, August 28, 2013, that the articles in Moll's *The Church and Women* are organically linked to this Letter, even if significant development and refinement are also evident in the Letter as compared to the articles that appear in that volume. On this point, the rejection of the eternal feminine and the associated contrasting of femininity and masculinity is evident in Walter Kasper, "The Position of Woman as a Problem of Theological Anthropology," trans. John Saward, in Moll, ed., *The Church and Women*, 59; and Karl Lehmann, "The Place of Women as a Problem in Theological Anthropology," trans. Robert E. Wood, in ibid., 18–19.

that Ratzinger's argument that the Marian dimension is required to anchor the emotions into faith.[40] The notion that Mary is in some way special for women, however, also appears in the writings of those critical of feminist theology such as Jutta Bergraff and Barbara Albrecht, as well as within feminist theology, for example, Tina Beattie, Lesley Hazelton, and Mary Daly. The fundamental problem with this notion is that it presupposes that Jesus, as a man, has some special significance for men. Viewing Mary as special for women—or its corollary, that Christ is special for men—is highly problematic theologically, for it misses the theological meaning and importance of both Jesus and Mary for salvation history. It could be argued, in fact, that the theological problem is that it transposes a kind of Nestorianism onto the issue of gender: assigning special significance to Mary and Jesus along gendered lines is analogous to the Nestorian heresy of separating the natures of Christ. The true Christian message is lost unless both Jesus and Mary, with the events and meaning of their lives, are presented together: God's grace seeking a response. One without the other loses the value of both, or more precisely, Christ the Son without Mary the Mother, or vice versa, is simply not the fullness of Christianity: only in unity can Christology or Mariology exist. Without Mary there is no incarnation; without Christ there is no Theotokos or *ecclesia*.

Marian Dogmas: Touchstone of Marian Controversy

Ratzinger's Mariology and biblical interpretation are fundamental to his understanding of the Marian dogmas. In *Daughter Zion* he asserts that the dogmas "*cannot* be deduced from individual texts of the New Testament; instead they express the broad perspective embracing the unity of both Testaments. They become visible only to a mode of

---

40. Ratzinger, *God and the World*, 299.

perception that accepts this unity, i.e., within a perspective which comprehends and makes its own the 'typological' interpretation, the corresponding echoes of God's single history in the diversity of various external histories."[41] The multitooled approach to theology and biblical interpretation Ratzinger employs is vital to an appreciation of the Marian dogmas. Where these are not extensively used, the Marian dogmas can, as will be seen in Küng's thinking, appear alien to true Christianity. This indicates the importance of biblical interpretation to theological inquiry and how it is determinative of theological findings. It is not just an issue of interpreting the Bible but of theology as a whole. For Küng, the veneration of Mary developed during what he refers to as the "Hellenization Byzantine" paradigm, and he links this development with the long tradition of mother goddesses in Asia Minor. In Küng's view, it is the historical background that enables and accounts for the dogmatic statements about Mary. Even though his four guiding principles related to Mary identify her importance as a witness to Jesus Christ, he does not accept this role within the Marian dogmas.[42] Instead, he asserts that the existing goddess tradition enabled the development and acceptance of the veneration of Mary through the cults such as the "perpetual virgin," the "mother of God," and "queen of heaven," prayers invoking protection, liturgical commemoration of Mary, along with the hymns to her, the naming of churches after her, the institution of the Marian feasts, and the creation of the first images of Mary. He asserts that it was only in the East, particularly in

---

41. Ratzinger, *Daughter Zion*, 32.
42. In an attempt to counter the problems he identifies in Mariology, Küng outlines four guidelines for Marian thought: first, the two descriptions of Mary that appear in the Gospels, the historical and the symbolic figures, need to be recognized. Second, as a human being and a mother she is a witness to Jesus' true humanity. Third, Mary's faith is not exceptional or special, but goes through a development and points the way for Christian faith. Fourth, Mary points to the cause of her Son, and Jesus' cause is God's cause. Hans Küng, *Women in Christianity*, trans. John Bowden (London: Continuum, 2001), 57–59.

Ephesus, where the citizens worshiped the "Great Mother," that Mary could be declared Theotokos, the Mother of God, and Mariology be established. He maintains that a theological price was paid for this declaration. Citing the fact that the Council of Chalcedon's need to correct the Monophysite misunderstanding to which the Council of Ephesus gave rise, he states that this led "to a reification of the understanding of the divine Sonship and the incarnation." He also asserts that it is responsible for mistrust of Christianity among the Jews and misunderstanding from the Muslims.[43]

Küng seeks to integrate the theological with the historical; however, his historical conclusions are open to question and criticism. Küng contrasts the East's development of Mariology with its absence in the West, and he points to the lack of any mention of hymns, prayers, and feasts of Mary from Augustine's writings as an example of the late development of devotion to Mary in the West. He also states that it is only from the fifth century that Mary is referred to in a Latin hymn, that only in the sixth century did Rome incorporate the title "Mother of God" into the text of the Mass, and that the feasts of Annunciation, Visitation, Birth, and Purification were introduced in the seventh century. His thinking is in striking contrast to Hugo Rahner's demonstration in *Our Lady and the Church* of the fathers' theological development of ecclesiology and the numerous statements Augustine made in relation to Mary and Mother Church.[44] J. N. D. Kelly, in fact, maintains in *Early*

---

43. Ibid., 52–53.
44. An example of Augustine's writings linking Mary and the Church, drawn from Hugo Rahner's study of patristic writings on the indivisibility between Mary and the Church, quotes from one of his Christmas sermons, as follows: "Today the Virgin Birth is celebrated by the virgin Church. For her it was that the Apostle said: 'I have espoused you to one husband, that I may present you as a chaste virgin to Christ' (2 Corinthians 11:2). Why as a chaste virgin, unless because of her purity in faith, hope and charity? The virginity, which Christ desires in the heart of the Church, He assured first in the body of Mary. But the Church could only be a virgin if she has a spouse, to whom she could give herself entire; and He is the virgin's son" (Rahner, *Our Lady and the Church*, 31). He takes this quote from sermon 178, 4 (*Patrologia Latina* 38, 1005).

Christian Doctrines (1977) that Mary was theologically important well before Augustine. He notes that Hilary and Zeno of Verona defended Mary's virginity, and that Zeno took up the antithesis between Eve and Mary, equating Mary with the Church. Kelly, however, asserts that Jerome, Ambrose, and Augustine contributed most to Mariology in the West.[45] Ratzinger's Mariology, anchored in biblical and theological foundations, retrieves this trajectory noted by Rahner and Kelly within the Western tradition—an Augustinian Mariology. Ratzinger's approach is enveloped in a process of historical investigation of the development of thought in the tradition of the Church, so the historical development of these dogmas is an integral aspect of his considerations. The theological meaning, however, always remains in the ascent in his considerations.

Ratzinger makes a distinction between the dogmas of Mary's motherhood of God and her virginity as historical facts, and the more recent dogmas of the immaculate conception and the assumption, which are, he argues, theological facts based on typology. The difference between these two types of dogmas is that the former are ecclesial confession and the latter veneration. Central to Ratzinger's understanding of the Marian dogmas is that they are based on his

---

45. J. N. D. Kelly, *Early Christian Doctrines*, 5th ed. (London: A&C Black, 1977), 496. For example, Ambrose (337–397 C.E.) stated that "Christ's Mother is a virgin and likewise is His bride the Church" and it was, according to Rahner, his student Augustine who worked out the idea of the Church's virginity in relation to the mystery of Mary. Rahner quotes Augustine in a Christmas Day sermon comparing the virginity of Mary and the virgin Church: "The virginity, which Christ desires in the heart of the Church, He assured first in the body of Mary. But the Church could only be a virgin if she has a spouse, to whom she could give herself entire; and He is the virgin's son" (Rahner, *Our Lady and the Church*, 31). Rahner takes this quote from sermon 178, 4 (*Patrologia Latina* 38, 1005). Similarly, the motherhood of Mary and the Church are understood by Augustine in relation to the other: "Mary's Son, spouse of the Church! He has made His Church like to His mother, He has given her to us as a mother, He has kept her for Himself as a virgin. The Church, like Mary, is a virgin ever spotless and a mother ever fruitful. What He bestowed on Mary in the flesh, He has bestowed on the Church in the spirit: Mary gave birth to the One, and the Church gives birth to the many, who through the One become one" (Rahner, *Our Lady and the Church*, 35). He takes this quote from sermon 195, 2 (*Patrologia Latina* 38, 1013).

theological reading of Scripture, both the Old and New Testaments, and they are declarations about God's actions with respect to humanity, and are, as indicated above, primarily christological. In this, the biological, or corporal, nature of these dogmas is integral to their meaning.[46] We will now consider each dogma in turn.

The Historical Dogmas: Virgin and Mother—Mary's Virginity in Her Maternity

Mary's Virginity

The theological meaning that Ratzinger assigns to the virginal conception is God's new involvement in history so that Jesus is the true Adam who comes from God. This is new creation within the old creation, which reflects the theological link he makes between the Genesis creation cycles and the New Testament narratives. For Ratzinger, the virginal conception leading to the birth of Jesus is both in continuity with the Old Testament births of the matriarchs and a break from them—it is the fulfillment of this line of unexpected births, a fulfillment that comes from outside. To highlight this point, he contrasts Jesus' conception and vocation to those of John the Baptist and Jeremiah, whose births are unexpected but occur from within the natural process. In this way, Jesus is more than a prophet of the Old Testament line:[47] he is the Son and his being is the fruit of the Spirit.[48] At the same time, even where Ratzinger sees a radical break

---

46. Ratzinger, *Daughter Zion*, 33–61; see also idem, "On the Position of Mariology," 74–77; and idem, *God and the World*, 303.
47. In relation to Christ, Ratzinger, building upon Balthasar's work, states: "If the Son is truly incarnate this event really reaches into the 'flesh' and, inversely, because man is one and entire, the 'flesh' reaches into the personal centre of the Logos. Despite the indestructible distinction of natures between God and man, Incarnation means a concrete unity of life. In Jesus' being as man this unity so realises itself that his whole human life enters into the filial exchange of the Son with the Father, thinking and existing from the Father and to the Father" (Ratzinger, *Daughter Zion*, 49–50).
48. Ibid., 42, 47–49.

in Jesus' conception, that is understood as part of a theology of grace and salvation: salvation comes to the world in history as a gift from God. Just as with the matriarchs of the Old Testament, it is not man's power that brings about salvation but God's power alone.[49]

Questions about Jesus' background are, for Ratzinger, about his "deeper origin and hence true meaning."[50] He sees this inquiry not only in Luke and Matthew but also in John, which provide the biblical basis of Mary's virginity. He accepts these accounts as interpreted historical accounts. In relation to the account of Jesus' birth in Luke and Matthew, he argues that the traditions and sources on which these are based cannot be reconstructed, and to attempt to do so through hypotheses is futile. His view is that the evangelists interwove the symbolic structure of these accounts with the historical strands of Old Testament promise. The new beginning of Jesus' birth exists in parallel to the continuity of God's action in history.[51] In Luke's account he highlights that there appears to be a Hebrew text from which it is drawn, given the semitism contained within it that do not appear in the remainder of that Gospel. The infancy narratives themselves are interpreted history, a storied account of God's new in-breaking, generated from Israel's Scripture, history, and experience, and given a new dynamism through theological interpolation: "There is a reciprocal relationship between the interpreting word of God and the interpreting history: the word

---

49. Ratzinger, *Introduction to Christianity*, 277–78.
50. Joseph Ratzinger, *Jesus of Nazareth: The Infancy Narratives*, trans. Philip J. Whitmore (New York: Image, 2012), 2.
51. Ibid., 8–9. In the genealogies, Matthew presents Jesus as a son of Abraham and the true David who fulfills the sign of hope, while Luke starts with Adam, which indicates that Jesus fulfills Israel's hope and answers the question about human nature. With regard to these genealogies Ratzinger states: "Both are convinced that Jesus can be the maturing fruit of history only because in him a new power has entered in to the withered tree of history—because he is not only 'from below'. He is certainly the fruit of this tree, but the tree can only bear fruit because it is rendered fertile from without. Jesus' origin is from below, yet simultaneously from above—and this is no contradiction. He is entirely man precisely because he does not have his origin only in this earth" (Ratzinger, *Daughter Zion*, 41).

of God teaches that 'salvation history,' universal in scope, is present within the events. For their part, the events themselves unlock the word of God and manifest the true reality hidden with the individual texts."[52] Old Testament history and expectation—exposited by Israel's prophets—becomes in the New Testament, especially here in the infancy narratives, universal promise and fulfillment. On one level, the prophetic message of Isaiah that a virgin will conceive and bear a son (Isa. 7:14; Matt. 1:22) is for Mary and her son Jesus; on another level, though, the prophesy has no context to which it applies, and Ratzinger maintains that this prophesy is addressed to humanity as a whole—human history is fulfilled at just this point.[53]

Dispute about the historical accuracy of the virginal conception and birth was alive from the earliest Christian times. For example, the *Gospel of Philip* states:

> Some said Mary became pregnant by the Holy Spirit. They are wrong and do not know what they are saying. When did a woman ever get pregnant by a woman? Mary is the virgin whom none of the powers defiled. This is greatly repugnant to the Hebrews, who are the apostles and apostolic persons. This virgin whom none of the powers defiled [wishes that] the powers would defile themselves. The master [would] not have said, 'My [father who is] in heaven,' if [he] did not also have another father. He would simply have said, '[My Father].'[54]

Nonetheless, the virginal conception, as a physical reality rather than a symbolic narrative, has been part of the Church's teachings from a very early stage. In response to rejection of the virginal conception in the post-apostolic period, Ignatius, third bishop of Antioch after Peter, asserts in his Epistle to the Ephesians: "Under the Divine dispensation, Jesus Christ our God was conceived by Mary of the

---

52. Ratzinger, *Infancy Narratives*, 17.
53. Ibid., 49–50.
54. Marvin Meyer, with Esther A. de Boer, *The Gospels of Mary: The Secret Tradition of Mary Magdalene, the Companion of Jesus* (San Francisco: HarperOne, 2006), 43.

seed of David and of the Spirit of God; He was born, and He submitted to baptism, so that by his Passion He might sanctify water. Mary's virginity was hidden from the prince of this world; so was her child-bearing, and so was the death of the Lord. All these three trumpet-tongued secrets were brought to pass in the deep silence of God."[55] Ignatius's letter tells us a number of important things. First, in an important early hub of Christianity with deep Jewish roots,[56] the virginal conception was vigorously defended and asserted. Second, it was associated with other core Christian mysteries. Third, it demonstrates that the virginal conception of Jesus was a controversial tenet of Christian faith from the early second century, if not before.

In continuity with this quite early tradition, Ratzinger underscores the deep interconnection between the virginal conception of Jesus and a wider network of theological ideas. Retrieving the dogmatic and confessional theology of the early church, Ratzinger understands the virginal conception as an ultimate theological confession and articulation of the power and mystery of God acting in the world and human history—that history and the laws of nature are not closed to God. The virginal conception as a dogmatic illumination of God's disruptive grace *in* history, as Ratzinger understands it, is demonstrated powerfully by Raymond Brown, who notes the theological counterpointing between the virginal conception and the resurrection: "[The virginal conception and the resurrection of Jesus] imply unique divine interventions from outside the flow of history. They are events that belong to the eschatological period, to that moment when the limits of history yield to God's freedom from space and time."[57] For Ratzinger, and Brown here, the virginal conception

---

55. Betty Radice, ed., *Early Christian Writings: The Apostolic Fathers*, trans. Maxwell Staniforth and Andrew Louth (London: Penguin, 1987), 66.
56. Raymond E. Brown, *The Virginal Conception and Bodily Resurrection of Jesus* (New York: Paulist, 1973), 50.

is dogmatic resistance to antimaterial Gnosticism—ancient and modern. Ratzinger's acceptance of the virginal conception, as God's freedom to act within the material conditions of history and matter, is in contrast to what he sees as the modern return to the ancient heresy of Gnosticism: a philosophy of emancipation hostile to creation, a philosophy that separates the biological and the spiritual, and holds body and birth in disdain, seeking meaning in transcendence of the material nature of existence. He rejects the notion that the virgin birth has only spiritual meaning rather than being a biological fact, because this would reject the body, which is the antithesis of faith and "denies the very spiritual reality which is the principal concern of the faith in the God become flesh."[58]

Ratzinger also rejects the charge that the virgin birth is a relatively late tradition. In his book *Infancy Narratives* (2012), based on the work of Joachim Gnilka, he maintains that these narratives are part of family tradition, which ultimately comes from Mary, and argues that such tradition only became public after Mary's death. This tradition, when it became public, informed the early Church of the meaning of Jesus, deepening the christological understanding of the event of the virginal conception and birth.[59] In *Daughter Zion* (1977) he maintains that even if the literary form of the tradition is late, it existed in another, presumably oral form, and its reception into the public tradition does not mean it is separate from the larger tradition. He also points to the two mutually independent narrative traditions of the virgin birth in Matthew and Luke to support a possible circulation within the tradition of the nascent Church. Moreover, these should not be taken as historical religious parallels or syncretistic adoptions of virgin-birth traditions from other religions by the early Church.

---

57. Ibid., 1.
58. Ratzinger, *Daughter Zion*, 53.
59. Ratzinger, *Infancy Narratives*, 16, 53.

He concedes that there may be "motifs" elsewhere similar to the Christian assertion, but, where these arise, he sees them as expressions of psychological archetypes longing for fulfillment.[60] Here Ratzinger has support again from Brown, who rejects religious parallels as sources for the Christian doctrine and asserts that the religious myths of a divine being impregnating a woman refer to something quite different from the conception described in the Gospel infancy narratives.[61]

Mary's Motherhood of God

In relation to Mary's motherhood of God, the biological *and* theological aspects are central to Ratzinger's understanding. It is not an either/or: the birth of Jesus from Mary is *both* biological and theological. This paradigm is similar to his insistence that faith and reason work together, not separately. In his theology, the drawing together and synthesizing of things that appear to be separate is a recurring theme that is seen once again in his Mariology. Mary, as Mother of God, is at the center—the matrix—of salvation history; she is the place where Christ is given flesh, where history opens as the material location of the union of God and creature in divine love. Mary is mother of God because she is the Church in person. He states:

---

60. Ratzinger, *Daughter Zion*, 54–57. Also see idem, *Infancy Narratives*, 54–56.
61. Brown, *The Virginal Conception*, 61–62. Ratzinger's arguments do not encompass the whole gamut of arguments against the rejection of the virgin conception. Brown raises one important issue Ratzinger does not, in that he contends that those rejecting the virgin conception need to explain the persistent rumors in the Gospels of Jesus' illegitimacy and irregular birth. On the other hand, Brown believes that what he describes as the "'high' explicit Christology" of the virgin conception needs to be reconciled with the "lower implicit Christology" of the ministry of Jesus. This is something that Ratzinger does not address, which could be due to his radically different approach to biblical interpretation, as seen earlier. The method of biblical interpretation is highly determinative of the approaches that Ratzinger and Brown each take to the virgin conception. Ratzinger's starting point is that he trusts the Gospel accounts, while Brown's starting point is that he searches for historical evidence to confirm the virgin conception. As a result, Ratzinger is able to accept the virgin conception while Brown, although accepting it in faith, believes the historical-critical method is unable to determine its historical nature.

"the moment she utters her Yes [at the Annunciation], Mary is Israel in person, she is the Church in person and as person. Doubtless, she is this personal concretisation of the Church by physically becoming the Mother of the Lord through her *Fiat*. But this biological fact is theological reality in that it realises the most profound spiritual content of the Covenant which God wishes to make with Israel."[62]

Mariology is never Mariology on its own, but always part of the whole Christian faith. He maintains that Mary's Motherhood of God is the most concrete expression of the faith's interconnectedness.[63] Mary is a symbol of faith and the Church in her historical and physical actualization of the reality of God's flesh that itself gives birth to the renewed existence of humanity and the new community that exists in its gathering within that mediated reality.[64] In this way, Mary's virginity in her maternity is much more than a debate about Mary for Ratzinger; it is central to the entire Christian faith. It is about Christ and it is about God's creature, the human being and their relationship. The answers to the questions posed by Mary's virginity and her motherhood of God determine, for Ratzinger, the content of Christian faith.

There is a point of theological dispute in Ratzinger's discourse on Mary's motherhood and virginity that should be noted. In *Daughter Zion* Ratzinger maintains that the birth of the Son had to be a virgin birth:

---

62. Ratzinger, "On the Position of Mariology," 75.
63. Ibid.
64. In this regard Ratzinger states that: "In the framework of the New Testament's faith the testimony to Jesus' birth from the Virgin Mary is not an idyllic nook of devotion, a tiny, private chapel of the two evangelists, an optional extra. The question of God is at stake. Is God a depth of being somewhere which, as it were, nourishes the deep roots of all things in some unimaginable way, or is he the one who acts with power, who knows and loves his creation, is present to it and effectively works in it from first to last, even today? The alternatives are simple: does God act or not? Can he act at all? If not, is he really 'God'? What does the word 'God' mean anyway? Faith in God, who has *remained* the creator in the new creation—*Creator Spiritus*—is at the centre of the New Testament and is its primary motive force" (Ratzinger, *Daughter Zion*, 60–61).

> The Virgin Birth is the necessary origin of him who is the Son and who as Son first endows the messianic hope with a permanent significance extending far beyond Israel. In this "new birth" (the Roman liturgy says *nova nativitas*), which simultaneously included the abandonment of earthly fertility, of self-disposal, and of the autonomous planning of one's own life, Mary as Mother is truly "the bearer of God"; she is more than the organ of a fortuitous corporeal event. To bear the "Son" includes the surrender of oneself into barrenness. Now it becomes clear why barrenness is the condition of fruitfulness—the mystery of the Old Testament mothers becomes transparent in Mary. It receives its meaning in Christian virginity beginning with Mary.[65]

This assertion that the virgin birth was the necessary origin of the Son, however, is in fact a major correction to his remarks in relation to the Sonship of Jesus in *Introduction to Christianity* (1968). In the earlier work, while assenting to the virginal conception, he asserts that it is not theologically necessary for Jesus' divine Sonship:[66]

> According to the faith of the Church, the Divine Sonship of Jesus does not rest on the fact that Jesus had no human father; the doctrine of Jesus' divinity would not be affected if Jesus had been the product of a normal human marriage. For the Divine Sonship of which faith speaks is not a biological but an ontological fact, an event not in time but in God's eternity; God is always Father, Son and Spirit; the conception of Jesus means, not that a new God-the-Son comes into being, but that God as Son in the man Jesus draws the creature man to himself, so that he himself 'is' man.[67]

Why this change? In *Daughter Zion* Ratzinger clarifies his argument and accepts Balthasar's criticism[68] of its earlier iteration. Ratzinger

---

65. Ibid., 51–52.
66. Brown draws on Ratzinger's statement in *Introduction to Christianity* to support his argument that the divine Sonship rests on the baptism and transfiguration of the Synoptic accounts and the Christology of Paul and John. Brown sees Ratzinger's argument as important, as to his mind Ratzinger is "relatively conservative" (Brown, *The Virginal Conception*, 41–42).
67. Ratzinger, *Introduction to Christianity*, 274–75.
68. Balthasar, "Conceived by the Holy Spirit, Born of the Virgin Mary," in Ratzinger and Balthasar, *Mary: The Church at the Source*, 148–54. Balthasar asks whether the one with the unique relation to the Father can have an earthy father as well. Balthasar maintains that if Jesus had an earthly

refers to "the limits of my frequently cited observation" and admits that he did not make his point clearly enough, saying that he only wanted to highlight the distinction between the biological and the ontological levels of thought as well as to clarify that the ontological statements of Nicaea and Chalcedon are not, as such, identical with the statements about the virgin birth.[69] This explanation for the statement in 1968, in contrast to his later statement in 1977, is linked to his "Marian conversion" and the overall movement of his thought to the truth of the tradition of the Church, particularly given his insistence in *Principles of Fundamental Theology*, as was seen earlier, that there is no contradiction between the nature of history and ontology. Nonetheless, Ratzinger did not remove or update the offending passage from subsequent editions of *Introduction to Christianity* to provide the clarity he states it lacked. This would indicate that he believes there are theological issues that remain to be fully explored and resolved.

The Theological Dogmas:
The Immaculate Conception and the Bodily Assumption

The Immaculate Conception

Ratzinger maintains that Mary's relationship with God, in which she reserves no part of herself and that she is full of grace, means God dwells in her: Mary is daughter Zion in person. Following the fathers' lead, Ratzinger relates the dogma of the immaculate conception to

---

father, he could not have said "no one knows the Father but the Son" nor mediate for humanity. In the Old Testament births of Isaac, Samson, Samuel, as well as John the Baptist, he posits that the human-father role was decisive even if God nonetheless "quickened the dead seed and barren womb." In the conception of Jesus, Balthasar argues that the (un)fruitfulness of the man or woman is replaced by the act of renunciation, an act through which Joseph crosses the threshold of the new covenant. The birth of Jesus is not a continuity of the Old Testament births but something new that is God's initiative alone, and the human father played no role bar that of foster father.

69. Ratzinger, *Daughter Zion*, 51n11.

original sin. As seen in chapter 3, Ratzinger posits that original sin means that each human being is alienated from God and this damages the network of relationships within humanity and among human beings. However, Mary, as the Mother of God, was "full of grace," and the Church came to understand that Mary belongs to Christ more than to Adam. This was so because, as he puts it, original sin is the contradiction between the will of the Creator and man's empirical being, and this contradiction is lacking in Mary. As he puts it: "God's judgment about her is pure 'Yes,' just as she herself stands before him as a pure 'Yes.' This correspondence of God's 'Yes' with Mary's being as 'Yes' is the freedom from original sin."[70] This raises the question of Mary's freedom to respond to God. Ratzinger's answer is that Mariology, in fact, demonstrates that the doctrine of grace does not impede the autonomy of humanity but is the "definitive Yes to creation." Mary is full of grace but that grace still requires Mary's free yes, her positive assent to God. The Old Testament theology of woman, seen typologically in the great women of Israel and personified by Mary, expresses the free reality of creation and the fruitfulness of grace: it is in Mary's believing response that she demonstrates the freedom of humanity, a freedom that is fulfilled in love.[71] In this regard Ratzinger observes that "The doctrine of the *Immaculata* testifies accordingly that God's grace was powerful enough to awaken a response, that grace and freedom, grace and being oneself, renunciation and fulfillment are only apparent contradictions; in reality one conditions the other and grants it its very existence."[72] Mary, as a creature, here corresponds to God in such a way that she is "a creature [who] has become response."[73] Drawing on Bernhard Langemeyer, Ratzinger sees Mary as the holy

70. Ibid., 70.
71. Ibid., 27–29.
72. Ibid., 71.
73. Ibid., 65.

remnant who will be saved, but a response from that remnant is necessary. Grace, yes—but a grace in freedom and for freedom.

Discussing the immaculate conception, Ratzinger defends and explicates the Church's tradition of Marian teachings. In his acceptance of the immaculate conception he acknowledges the long historical background to the dogma in which, during the Middle Ages, the Dominicans and Franciscans engaged in significant debate and wherein the Franciscans, arguing that Mary could not have been burdened by original sin, prevailed. The Franciscan victory, as Hans Küng notes, marked a transition in emphasis of Mary's glorification over her humanity; Küng, like Ratzinger, Hugo Rahner, and Thomas Merton, identifies this as a shift from Bernard of Clairvaux's writings. He views this shift negatively in that it subordinated Mary's earthly role to her cosmic role and idealized and exulted the "heavenly" Mary. As a result, a sinless Mary was retroactively constructed, which led to her humanity playing a very minor role in her veneration. Küng asserts the popular Marian piety of the Middle Ages predominated in the development of Marian teaching during that time. Much of this popular piety revolved around Mary as the embodiment of mercy and intercessor with her Son, as Küng observes: "This Madonna expresses in a unique way what millions of people often felt about Mary: she is the helper particularly of ordinary people, the oppressed, the anxious and the marginalised. A piece of Mariology 'from below' becomes visible here, which contrasts with the dogmatic super-theories of 'Mary' among theologians, monks and hierarchs."[74] Küng argues that Pius IX "burdened the Church" with just an etherealized dogma of the immaculate conception, severed from the bodily and material earthiness of her historical

---

74. Küng argues that this "explains the popularity of the biblical 'Ave Maria' from the twelfth century on; together with the 'Our Father' it became the most widespread form of prayer" (Küng, *Women in Christianity*, 55).

witness.[75] Ratzinger, sympathetic to Küng's historical argument, attempts to reclaim that biblical Mariology "from below" in conjunction with a retrieval of the ecclesial exegesis of the fathers: the view of Mary and the Church as typologically united. Rather than an etherealized cosmic matriarch, Mary is, for Ratzinger, as Ambrose stated in the fourth century: "the type of the Church, since each is a virgin unspotted (*Virgo immaculata*)."[76]

The Bodily Assumption

Ratzinger employs a similar move—synthesizing a biblical, "from below" view with an ecclesial theological interpretation—in relation to the bodily assumption of Mary, which Ratzinger recognizes as an especially difficult dogma. This difficulty is not theological, but a challenge to understand what the terms *heaven* and *body*[77] mean, and how they relate to humanity's future. The essential point for Ratzinger is that "Mary is wholly with God, entirely with Christ, completely a 'Christian',"[78] and that being in full communion with God means a different and new bodily existence. Grace, God's grace, transforms the human being. Ratzinger distinguishes the assumption, which is theological, from the resurrection of Jesus, which is

---

75. Ibid., 56.
76. Rahner maintained that the fathers' understanding of the immaculate conception was that, in response to the fall, the Church, as Eve and Mary, although victorious in the end, is continually at war in history (Rahner, *Our Lady and the Church*, 19). Rahner takes this quote from Ambrose's commentary on Luke II, 7 (*Corpus Scriptorum ecclesiasticorum latinorum* 32, 4, 45). In reference to Justus of Urgel (d. 527), Venerable Bede (d. 735), Haymo of Halberstadt (d. 853), and Bruno of Asti (d. 1123), he states: "The Church is immaculate, because she is cleansed by the waters of baptism, because she is already on the way to the unobstructed vision of God, because she is washed with the blood of Christ, because (in spite of sin and darkness among her children on earth) she stands already glorious without spot or wrinkle before God" (ibid.). Rahner refers to writings from Justus of Urgel (*Patrologia Latina* 67, 980); Bede (*Patrologia Latina* 91, 1155); Haymo of Halberstadt (*Patrologia Latina* 117, 327); Bruno of Asti (*Patrologia Latina* 164, 1263).
77. In relation to the issue of the form of the body see Joseph Ratzinger, *Eschatology: Death and Eternal Life*, 2d ed., trans. Michael Waldstein and Aidan Nichols (Washington, D.C.: Catholic University of America Press, 1988), 146–50.
78. Ratzinger, *God and the World*, 305.

theological *and* historical, and argues that it is the veneration of Mary that gives the dogma its content and orientation. Or, in other words, Mary is not to be worshiped as God but, rather, venerated, as she is and remains a human being. This veneration was "prophesied" in Luke, which identifies the veneration of Mary as a commission for the Church: "Behold, henceforth all generations shall call me blessed" (Luke 1:48).[79]

An important part of Ratzinger's understanding is that Eve expresses the ambiguity of life: in birth, death is presupposed. However, if Mary gives birth to God—the death of death—from this birth there only comes life.[80] Ratzinger thinks that human mortality arises from humanity's attempt at "autarchy." But where there is pure self-dispossession, where an attempt at self-sufficiency does not exist, there is grace and no death even when we die, a situation that applies to Mary "in a definitive, unconditional way, because she stands for the Church itself, for its definitive state of salvation, which is no longer a promise awaiting fulfillment but a fact."[81] And because it applies to Mary, it applies to the Church: linking the Lukan commission of 1:48 with Ephesians 2:6,[82] which he refers to as something like an ascension of the baptized, Ratzinger states that the assumption is only the highest form of canonization. And in Mary's assumption—that is, the ascent of her body in a new, graced existence—so is the Church's bodily future and ascent typified or, rather, realized: "[S]he who is wholly baptized, as the personal reality of the true Church, is at the same time not merely the Church's promised certitude of salvation but its bodily certitude also. The

---

79. Ratzinger, *Daughter Zion*, 72–75.
80. Ratzinger, *God and the World*, 294.
81. Ratzinger, *Daughter Zion*, 77–79.
82. "And God raised us up with Christ and seated us with him in the heavenly realms in Christ Jesus."

Church is already saved in her: the new Israel is no more to the rejected. It has already ascended into heaven."[83]

Again, we see here how Marian dogma and Mariology point beyond themselves. For Ratzinger, Mary is not just Mary the individual, but the concretization of the Church as person, and the Marian dogmas are the articulation of that reality. The effect of the assumption on theology in general, according to Ratzinger, is that it justifies the expansion of Marian spirituality beyond Advent, which is its liturgical locus, into the whole of Christian faith. With the bodily assumption of Mary into heaven, "Advent expands into the eschaton."[84] Thereby, the medieval expansion of Marian spirituality into all the saving mysteries remains faithful to biblical faith and therefore is an appropriate development of the liturgy. Ratzinger's argument chimes with Hugo Rahner's assertion that the dogma "is no more than a confirmation of the doctrine of the Church previously given in the encyclical on the Mystical Body of Christ."[85] Rahner demonstrates that this dogma is anchored in the fathers' writings, illustrated in their correlation of Mary's assumption to "the woman arrayed with the sun, with the moon at her feet" (Rev. 12:14, 17). Rahner maintains that when the Church celebrates the assumption, she is celebrating her own final glory.[86]

---

83. Ratzinger, *Daughter Zion*, 80–81.
84. Ratzinger, "On the Position of Mariology," 78–79.
85. Rahner, *Our Lady and the Church*, xi.
86. Ibid., 128. He also quotes Alcuin, a theologian in Charlemagne's court in the 780s and 790s, as stating: "The woman clothed with the sun is the Blessed Virgin Mary, who was overshadowed by the power of the Most High. But in her we can also understand the race of men that is the Church, who is not called 'woman' to suggest weakness, but on the contrary because of her strength in daily bringing to birth new peoples to build up the Body of Christ. The Church, then, is 'clothed with the sun'" (ibid., 115). Rahner takes this quote from Alcuin's commentary on the Apocalypse V, 12 (*Patrologia Latina* 100, 1152); the quote continues as follows: "according to Scripture: 'As many of you as have been baptised in Christ have put on Christ' (Galatians 3:27), for Christ is 'the sun of justice' (Malachi 4:2) and 'the brightness of eternal light' (Wisdom 7:26)."

Perhaps due to the controversial nature of Mary in ecumenical discussion, Marian dogma is often viewed with hostility, as retrograde and a barrier to unity—this was Ratzinger's view until his post–Vatican II Marian conversion. Consequently, Marian dogmas are criticized and rejected while other statements of the magisterium with similar content are accepted or quietly forgotten, such as Pius XII's "Mystical Body of Christ."[87] Rahner's positive assessment, alongside the criticisms by Küng and Mary Daly of the Marian dogmas, demonstrate the urgent need for a thorough theological articulation of the basis of Catholic Mariology and Marian dogma to counter its rejection in modern times, a rejection that arises in part from the loss of the foundations of Mariology. Fritz Arnold, in *Like Mary: Towards Christian Maturity in the Twenty-First Century*, argues that the dogma of the assumption reflects the seriousness with which God takes partnership with humankind,[88] and that the theological dogmas of Mary, which explicate Christology, point to humanity. Arnold contends that "We should understand the official declarations about Mary more as promises of what we are called to. What has happened to her is promised to all of us. The Spirit of God wants to bind himself to us deeply within. Those who let go to God totally and accept the offer of a binding partnership with Him, are entirely raised up by God, and virtually divine attributes become theirs."[89]

This approach provides an alternative lens to view both the dogmas of the immaculate conception and bodily assumption that may make them more accessible and perhaps more comprehensible than heretofore, thus enabling a renewed engagement with Mary by theology. Mary is a historical human being whose glorification reflects the fullness of grace that she received from God in her role

---

87. Rahner, *Our Lady and the Church*, xi.
88. Fritz Arnold, *Like Mary: Towards Christian Maturity in the Twenty-First Century*, trans. Denis Green (Dublin: Columba Press, 2001), 34.
89. Ibid., 35–36.

as Theotokos, the bearer of God. It is this fullness of grace, through which the Word became flesh, that leads to and necessitates the glorification. That glorification and veneration is of the human Mary who was transformed by the grace given by God the Father, Son, and Holy Spirit. It is the human Mary who is glorified, for it is this Mary through whom the incarnation takes place, in whom the Word became flesh. She was touched by God in a manner experienced by no other human being. Rowan Williams argues specifically in relation to the immaculate conception that grace is always there before us, in the life of Mary, Israel, and everyone; that the only real beginning is in God's call—the story begins with God's call, God's beckoning to us. Grace is always before us. God granted Mary the grace she needed to be the Mother of God.[90] So, as with the search for the historical Jesus, the answer to the concern for the historical, humanized Mary is to bring together in a harmony the earthly Mary with the Mary of the eschaton: she is truly one figure.

For Ratzinger, Mary enables a correct understanding of Christ and Christianity, but Mary is not a stand-alone figure within the faith nor is she to be worshiped as God or a demi-god. Rather, by being integral with Christian faith, by standing with the Church and the bridal people of God, she releases the true meaning and potential and promise of Christianity. The Marian dogmas arise from the matrix of christological and ecclesial confession. God the Father, Son, and Holy Spirit are the source of this grace and in that way they are trinitarian dogmas: the theological reality of Mary as a human being in relationship with the triune God is the basis for all future development of Mariology and Marian dogma. In that way, God redeems humanity through the incarnation of the Son, through the

---

90. Rowan Williams, "Holiness and the Sovereignty of Grace: Mary's Discipleship," at the Ecumenical Society of the Blessed Virgin Mary Congress, Magdalene College, Cambridge, September 23, 2014.

Holy Spirit, and through Mary's response to the annunciation—these are, as a network of confessions and witness, integral to redemption.

Mary as Person: Ratzinger's Female Line in the New Testament

Mary as Person—Christ as Person

The incarnation of the Son through Mary's yes, her *Fiat*—her response to God's call—is the fundamental building block of Ratzinger's understanding of Mariology and it is the high point and completion of his female line. The incarnation, for Ratzinger, is not just an isolated yes, but a yes deeply embedded in the Old Testament faith that Mary concretely embodies. The indwelling of God in Israel in the Old Testament and the marital image of the covenant is concretely realized in a new way in Mary's yes, in her faith and body. Ratzinger's New Testament female line, in and through Mary, is christological, hence trinitarian and ecclesiological. From the christological point of view, the incarnation is the coming into history and human flesh of the eternal Son—fully God, the Son becomes fully human through Mary. And, from the ecclesial point of view, there is Mary as type, the personal concretization, of the Church. Here, the indispensable role of Mary in Christology and ecclesiology is evident, for Mary is essential for both in their historical coming-to-be; but it also points to the trinitarian mission that undergirds the story of Mary, as reflected in the term *Theotokos*—she is the mother of the Father's Son through the Holy Spirit.

Moreover, Mary's role in the historical unfolding of the trinitarian economy of salvation reveals yet another aspect that is critically important to Ratzinger, and connects his Mariology even more deeply to his Christology and doctrine of God—relationality. Time and time again Ratzinger finds in Mary a person who fulfills the criteria for personhood that her Son reveals. As discussed in chapter 1, the phenomenon of "pure relationality" defines Ratzinger's notion of person, and is constitutive to his doctrine of God *and* anthropology.[91] To recap, Ratzinger maintains that

> I believe a profound illumination of God as well as man occurs here, the decisive illumination of what person must mean in terms of Scripture: *not* a substance that closes itself in itself, but the phenomenon of complete relativity, which is, of course, realised in its entirety only in the one who is God, but which indicates the direction of all personal being. The point is thus reached here at which ... there is a transition from the doctrine of God into Christology and into anthropology.[92]

In his article "'You are full of grace': Elements of Biblical Devotion to Mary," presented in 1988 for the Marian year, Ratzinger presents a summary of his thinking on Mary as person.[93] Here, Mary is exemplary of the human person as free relation—with God, with others, with herself, and the history of her community (Israel)—but, even more, she is the generative matrix of divine–human relations given concrete historical and fleshly reality. She is, in other words, the free relational agent who bears and brings into the world—who exhibits in herself, too—divine partnership with humanity. In this way, she exemplifies the epiphenomenon of Christian existence: "the fundamental phenomenon into which we are placed by the Bible is the God who speaks and the human person who is addressed, the phenomenon of the partnership of the human person who is called

---

91. Joseph Ratzinger, "Retrieving the Tradition concerning the Notion of Person in Theology," trans. Michael Waldstein, *Communio* 17, no. 3 (1990): 439–54, at 443–47.
92. Ibid., 445.
93. Ratzinger, "'You are full of grace'." Ratzinger's collection of articles on Mary are contained in Ratzinger and Balthasar, *Mary: The Church at the Source*; also see *Daughter Zion*. Ratzinger's article on the theological notion of person (see n. 91) was published in English in 1990 in *Communio* (it was originally published in German in 1973). While the article "You are full of grace" was published in 1989. The timeline of the publication of these two articles to me is significant, and I would argue that his article on the theological notion of person was published in the same journal soon after his article on Mary, "'You are full of grace'," in part at least, to draw out the depth of meaning of his idea of Mary as person and to clarify aspects of his article on person.

by God to love in the word." Mary as person, in her relationship, communion, and dialogue with God, means humanity's response in freedom to God's initiative and activity in history. And, Mary, as Theotokos, means that Mary also belongs to the name of God, as the human partner who brings into the world the One who is the relationality of God made flesh, and thus made to relate and mediate those relations vicariously on both sides. Mary thus is the human face of God's maternal side and is the mother of the faith.[94] As it is through relationship with God that God becomes known to humanity, the person of Mary then expresses this reality, and she lives what she signifies, living in relation to God without reserve: "she is permeable to God, 'habitable.' She lives so that she is a place for God."[95]

One may see, further, the synchronicity between Ratzinger's Christology and Mariology. There is, in effect, a reciprocity and mutual conditioning: as Mary gives historical flesh to the human Jesus, so the person of Christ gives shape and color to Ratzinger's understanding of Mary as person. As well, the person of Mary connects simultaneously to ecclesiology, in that she demonstrates how the Church, as a person, is to live and exist: total openness to God, wholly receptive, living from her relationship with God.

---

94. Ratzinger, "'You are full of grace'," 63–65.
95. Ibid., 58. Drawing again from Gabriel's salutation to Mary, Ratzinger demonstrates what it means for Mary to live in relation to God without reserve, and does so in two ways. First, he highlights that the Greek word for grace is derived from the same root-word as for joy and enjoy: grace is joy, and that grace is a relationship between the I of the human being and God. He rejects the idea that grace is an attribute belonging to an individual, which correlates to the rejection that person is an attribute of the substance of God. As God is person, so grace is a relationship. Being full of grace means, for Ratzinger, that "Mary is a person who is totally open, who has made herself wholly receptive, and has placed herself, keenly and without limits, without fear of her own destiny, in the hands of God. It also means she lives entirely out of and within her relationship with God" (ibid., 60).

Person as Dialogical Communion with the Triune God

Mary's relation to God—as a dialogical communion marked by openness and receptivity—is illumined for Ratzinger through the biblical narrative of Mary's meditative prayer. The Greek word for "ponder" comes from the word *dialog*, which indicates that when Mary pondered the words of Gabriel's address she entered into a dialogue with the Word, wherein, to understand its meaning, she both addresses the Word and allows herself to be addressed. In this he sees Mary entering into the Spirit-led meditative remembrance central to John's Gospel. For Ratzinger, the events are translated into words, which Mary penetrates by taking them into her heart. By putting and holding them together, Mary discerns the meaning of the whole and allows the meaning to unfold rather than grasping at it and looking for immediate, explicit comprehension. He refers to this elsewhere as seed in fertile soil.[96] Person as fertile soil is openness to God, dialogue and communion with God and, hence, with others. I maintain these are the attributes of a human person. Ratzinger links Mary's divine maternity with her openness for God's Word. Listening, meditating, and conceiving God's Word allow her to receive the Holy Spirit within herself so totally that the Word becomes flesh in her.[97] Importantly, Mary's divine maternity includes the cross of being at God's disposal and is fulfilled not only when bearing Jesus in her womb, but also in doing the will of God.[98] In Ratzinger's reading, the incarnation occurs through her relationality with God, which enables dialogue with God, where Mary both listens to God and receives the Holy Spirit within her. It is the relationship that allows for dialogue and communion.

---

96. Joseph Ratzinger, "My Word Shall Not Return to Me Empty!," in Ratzinger and Balthasar, *Mary: The Church at the Source*, 17.
97. Ratzinger, "'You are full of grace'," 63.
98. Ibid., 67.

What becomes clear here is that the second, or new, creation, like the first creation of Adam, occurs through dialogue in relation and communion with God. In this first creation, God speaks Adam into existence; in the second creation, or new creation, though, God does not speak without a human partner. Rather, God speaks to Mary, who in turn engages and responds by engaging in dialogue in openness. This dialogue with the human being who is daughter Zion in person is in striking contrast to the sole activity of God at creation, where it is God's dialogue and initiative that creates. Here, with Mary, it remains God's initiative and activity, but that initiative awaits a response from Israel; this response, not simply God's activity, is fundamental to Ratzinger's thought on Mary and Christianity. This dialogue, mediated by God's messenger, culminates in the Logos, the Word of God, taking flesh: Adam, the human being, is renewed through Zion and the daughter of Zion's relationship in communion and dialogue with God. This demonstrates the network of relations that is Israel, which brought forth the body that was prepared for the Word become flesh. Mary's response is the apex of the network of relations that commenced with Abraham's faith response; it is not an isolated yes but a yes embedded in the fertile soil that is Israel. Creation is God's work but, for the new creation, the final Adam and the birth of the Church, God's initiative awaits a response to the relation and dialogue God initiated. Through this dialogue between the divine and the created human, God enters into relationship with humanity in a totally new way while the human being remains fully and completely a human being. This is the reversal of Eve's dialogue, so central to the fathers' understanding of Mary, and here, too, dialogue is central to the events. This again underscores the communal element to Eve and the female line: Eve *dia*logues. Eve heard the serpents suggestive question, "Did God really say you were not to eat from any of the trees in the garden?," and, having engaged with this question, responded to the serpent, which culminated in her disregarding God's command not to eat of or touch the tree in the middle of the garden (Gen. 3:2-6). Eve followed her own plans and desires, eating of the tree and offering some of the fruit to Adam, the human being. So it is not just dialogue and relation that person necessitates but relation, communion, and dialogue with God, in which we open toward others and the Other in truth, love, and freedom. The Fall occurs in the dialogue of humanity and not in relation to an isolated Adam. The sin is the sin of Adam but it is in that way the sin of humanity; the sin infects the whole network of the community of humanity. Mary's Yes to God creates a new network for humanity through communion with God, the Father, Son and Holy Spirit, which overcomes the original sin.

Mary concretizes Ratzinger's notion of person in that, through her fulfillment of the female line in the Bible, the Christian understanding of the human being develops in parallel to the Christian understanding of the triune God. Humanity reaches its fulfillment and highest possibility in God's becoming human through Mary as the realization of what it means to be human. This is another way of saying what Gregory Nazianzus stated so famously: God became human that we might become God (divinized). In and through Mary, human salvation is given a genealogy that both culminates and is fulfilled in her and ushers from her as the origin of a new manner of existence. The fruit of Mary's person, in Ratzinger's understanding, opens to the human being the possibility of being like God, being in total relation.

Mary as Person: Trinitarian Implications for Society

Following from this, a practical application of the concept of "the female line in the Bible" comes into view. The New Testament, through Christ, reveals the fulfillment of salvation history, beginning with Mary's act of total relationality to God without reserve. The Trinity is revealed through Mary's act, and this reality indicates that human interaction with and response to the Trinity plays a significant role within salvation history. The Trinity does not exist because of humanity, but for humanity it is revealed through Mary's response to God, just as God was revealed in Old Testament times through human encounter, relationship, with God. Michael Downey, in *Altogether Gift: A Trinitarian Spirituality*, refers to the doctrine of the Trinity as providing the grammar through which we seek to comprehend the mystery of God.[99] He maintains this grammar is a gift that provides us with the correct way to speak about the mystery of God, and thus further reflection on the Trinity must remain within the rules of grammar the doctrine provides.[100] Within Downey's discussion of the Trinity, the incarnation is a vital aspect, yet Mary plays only a minor, if not sidelined, role. Yet, such exclusion is not exclusive to Downey, but is a fairly common feature of much recent trinitarian theology, which often lacks attention to Mary even where the incarnation is of decided importance. This can be seen, for instance, even in modern discourses on the Trinity such as those of Karl Rahner and Catherine LaCugna, both of which sought to give new life and new direction to consideration of the Trinity. While Rahner does explore Mary in relation to the Father, Son, and Spirit, as we saw earlier, in his reflections on Mary in *Mary, Mother of the Lord*, she is not included in his discourse on the Trinity. This is particularly striking given the importance he places, in his discourse on the Trinity, on the fact that only the Son is man, only the Logos becomes flesh, which of course points to, and necessitates, Mary. He underlines that neither the Father nor the Spirit have this mission,

---

99. Michael Downey, *Altogether Gift: A Trinitarian Spirituality* (Dublin: Dominican Publications, 2000); this book originated as a joint project with Catherine Mowry LaCugna; however, following her untimely death in 1997, Downey pursued and completed the project himself.
100. Ibid., 40–59.

which distinguishes the second person of the Trinity from the first and third. Rahner maintains that "Here we are not merely *speaking* 'about' this person in the world. Here something occurs 'outside' the intra-divine life in the world itself, something which is not a mere effect of the efficient causality of the triune God acting as one in the world, but something which belongs to the Logos alone, which is the history of one divine person, in contrast to other divine persons."[101]

Despite Rahner's lack of attention to Mary in his discourse on the Trinity, the uniqueness of the Logos's role points to the uniqueness of Mary's role as a human being for humanity in relation with God. This unique role belongs to her alone. She is Theotokos, Mother of God. It is Mary alone who provides the human flesh of Jesus Christ—fully human and fully divine. Mary has a unique role that she alone fulfills in the history of humanity. Mary provides the grammar to articulate and further develop the Church's comprehension of God's trinitarian relationship with humanity.

Declan Marmion and Rik van Nieuwenhove have observed that, within recent trinitarian theology, the relational and dynamic aspect of God is emphasized, and that this image of God, as being-in-relationship, is viewed as the correct paradigm for the Church and for the social and political spheres to emulate. In this regard they state:

> Given the political and social dimensions of much current theological reflection, it is not surprising that God is perceived not only as the source of our salvation, but also as the foundation and paradigm of society and liberation. If the Trinity is a symbol of interdependence and communion, this has consequences for humankind made in God's triune image and likeness. Despite current revival of Trinitarian theology, however, the impression remains that the revolution in our image of God, in our conception of the Church, society, and indeed in all our

---

101. Karl Rahner, *The Trinity*, trans. Joseph Donceel (New York: Herder & Herder, 1997 [1967]), 23; also see 31n27.

relationships, implied in the doctrine of the Trinity, has yet to be fully implemented.[102]

The full implementation of trinitarian relationships in society and within all relationships requires first and foremost an acceptance of the God of Jesus Christ, which would limit such implications to believing Christians in society. But even at that, the pattern of the triune God, truth, love, and freedom, means that the *implementation* or *deployment* of such a pattern onto others or society would negate the freedom that is inherent in the Trinity. Certainly, the pattern of relationality of the Trinity is *the* pattern of relationality and thus it cannot be imposed in a sense of an implementation project, wherein a certain process of relationality is imposed from the outside and "rolled out," as if a mechanism to improve efficiency and achieve perfection. The *should* that arises for humanity from God's revelation cannot be turned into the *is* of a specific perfect process or type of relational behavior. Freedom allows choice, another way. As saint John Paul II said, freedom is not about doing what we want but about doing what we ought. Freedom in love is creative, which allows creativity in response to our relationality with and origin in God; it does not call for uniformity in response. Indeed, that creativity, freedom in love, enables and allows for ever-new response to the perennial evolution and change in challenges and dynamics that confront human beings as individuals, communities, and humanity as a whole throughout our lives and throughout time. One size does not fit all, and it is creative love and freedom in truth with which each human being, each community, and humanity itself are called to engage to respond to others and the Other every day, every year, at all times.[103]

---

102. Declan Marmion and Rik van Nieuwenhove, *An Introduction to the Trinity* (Cambridge: Cambridge University Press, 2011), 28.
103. Mary Frances McKenna, "Moral Values and Social Consensus in Democratic Secular Society: Challenges and Responsibilities," *The Heythrop Journal*, 56 no. 4 (July 2015): 663–76.

Critical to this is the reality that Judeo-Christianity recognizes the fall. Due to the fall, as we saw earlier, we are alienated from God and from ourselves; humanity as the image of God has been distorted. The triune God is perfect love and perfect freedom. Seeking to fix society's failings by applying this image in conjunction with the pattern of relations of the Trinity without recognizing humanity's alienation from God can only fail. The letter "On the Collaboration between Man and Woman" (2004) states on this matter that although God's original plan is "upset and darkened by sin, it can never be abrogated," and that to heal this situation "The logic of sin needs to be broken and a way forward needs to be found that is capable of banishing it from the hearts of sinful humanity. A clear orientation in this sense is provided in the third chapter of Genesis by God's promise of a Saviour, involving the 'woman' and her 'offspring' (cf. *Gn* 3:15). It is a promise which will be preceded by a long preparation in history before it is realized."[104]

Here we see a path opened to continue to reflect on the implications of God's trinitarian self-revelation for the Church, the world, and for humanity's relationship among itself and with God. Applying this approach to theological reflection on trinitarian society would take account of the reality of humanity as being the image of God but also of the fact that we, in our current state, are alienated from God and ourselves. Mary provides the approach and the grammar for how the implications of the Gospel message can, and should, be applied in the Church, society, and humanity itself. Mary's response in freedom that sprang from the communion of Israel, in uniting her will with God's will, is the starting point for that reflection.

---

104. "Letter on the Collaboration between Men and Women," no. 8, also see nos. 5–9.

The question for us to consider now is: How would the understanding of the Trinity, particularly in relation to humanity's interaction with it, develop and deepen in light of Ratzinger's concept of "the female line in the Bible"? Or, in other words, how do the interlinking realities of the Trinity, the incarnation, and Mary and her symbolism of the Church relate to one another, and what do those relations mean for salvation history? Downey asserts that "person" names what is distinct in the triune God and "nature" names what is common to the three.[105] The paradigm can be used to understand humanity's relationship with God. Person is what God and humanity can have in common, while humanity's nature is what is distinct from God. Mary as type and symbol of the Church, as the Church in person, in her total relativity without reserve with God, provides the human response to the reality of the Trinity, which opens the space for the Church, the body of Christ. I would argue that theology should now develop the meaning of the term *mother* in Christianity, based on both Scripture and tradition, in the manner it did Father, Son, and Holy Spirit. I believe that this will open up a new horizon on God and humanity. Mary and the Church as mother are the source of such development. There is no danger of Mary and the Church as mother encroaching on God or of transforming God into one being in four persons. Rather, the relation between the persons of God—Father, Son, and Spirit—with the persons of Mary and the Church is the point of departure for such development. Mary is type, symbol, and mother of the Church because she responded to God by uniting her will to God's will without reserve, by being person, not by grasping for equality with God but by emptying herself (Phil. 2:5-11). It was through this process that God became flesh and dwelt among us. Through her response to God she enters relationship with

---

105. Downey, *Altogether Gift*, 53.

God in such a way that the Son became incarnate within her flesh and she gave birth to him, our new humanity. We have here the preliminary lines of the meaning of mother in relation to Father, Son, and Holy Spirit: Mary, Theotokos, is the prototype of divinized humanity. Mary, as person, is *Hodegetria*—she who shows the way. Mother, then, is bringing Christ into this world through relationality, communion, and dialogue with the Father through the Holy Spirit.

In Ratzinger's understanding of person, both Paul's body of Christ and John's relativity play significant roles. By combining two of Ratzinger's theological ideas discussed earlier—the human line (male and female) in the Bible culminating in person and the idea of the "we" of God into which Christ gathers us—a mechanism to develop the trinitarian aspect of Christian faith and anthropology becomes available. In this way, the idea of trinitarian society can be provided with theological foundations. As we discussed earlier, Ratzinger asserts that Christ adds the idea of "we" to the idea of "I" and "thou."[106] God is not an "I" but a "we," the "we" of the Father, Son, and Holy Spirit. This is the trinitarian "we." The "we" of the Trinity prepares the way for the human "we."[107] The human "we" Christ creates is the Church, his body, symbolized by his mother Mary, who is type of the Church. "The female line in the Bible," which finds its completion in Mary, both enables the integrating space of Christ to emerge in the world and also is the symbol of that continuing human "we" that is gathered by Christ and is directed to the Father. Ratzinger's concept of person is provided content by Mary; it is concretized by her. In this way, she also provides the

---

106. Ratzinger, "Retrieving the Tradition," 452–53. Ratzinger states in this regard that "Christ, whom Scripture calls the final Adam, that is, the definitive human being, appears in the testimonies of faith as the all-encompassing space in which the 'we' of human beings gathers on the way to the Father. . . . he is the integrating space in which the 'we' of human beings gathers itself toward the 'you' of God."

107. Ibid., 453.

content of the human "we." Mary both enables this "we" through her response to God and also is this "we" through her personal concretization of and indivisibility with the Church.

Paul's reference to Christ as second Adam, in Ratzinger's view, refers to the fact that Christ is to gather humanity, the whole creature Adam, in himself.[108] How this operates can be glimpsed through Ratzinger's use of Scripture to interpret the incarnation. The incarnation comes about through the unity of wills between the Son and the Father, which means that the incarnation required acceptance. He sees in Heb. 10:5-7 an interpretation of Ps. 40:5-8, which he maintains understands the process of incarnation as an actual dialogue within the divinity, and that the incarnation was achieved through Mary's yes to the triune will of God. "'A body you have prepared for me', says the Son to the Father (Heb 10:5) and in response he sees Mary saying, 'Sacrifice and offerings you have prepared for me. . . . Behold, I have come to do your will'" (Heb. 10:5-7; Ps. 40: 6-8). Ratzinger interprets this to mean: "The body was prepared for the Son, through Mary's putting herself entirely at the disposal of the Father's will and thus making her body available as the tabernacle of the Holy Spirit."[109] For Ratzinger, in the harmony of Mary's yes with Jesus' yes, the wills of Jesus and Mary coincide, which enables the incarnation and humanity's redemption.[110] This movement is pointed toward the Church but also toward the human being's relationship with the triune God, to a Christian anthropology that takes Christ as its starting point and moves toward the

---

108. For Ratzinger this means that "The reality that Paul calls . . . the 'body of Christ' is an intrinsic postulate of this existence, which cannot remain an exception but must 'draw to itself' the whole of mankind (cf. John 12:32)" (Ratzinger, *Introduction to Christianity*, 236).
109. Joseph Ratzinger, *God Is Near Us: The Eucharist, the Heart of Life*, trans. Henry Taylor (San Francisco: Ignatius, 2003), 14.
110. Joseph Ratzinger, *A New Song for the Lord: Faith in Christ and Liturgy Today*, trans. Martha M. Matasich (New York: Crossroad, 1995), 60.

corresponding relationship with the Father and Spirit; and, hence, to a Christian anthropology that is christological and thus trinitarian.

Mary's personal concreteness of the Church and the renewal of the covenant, God's relationship with Israel, through Mary's yes to God are the continuation and high point of God's covenant relationship with Israel. This means that Mary, and through her "the female line in the Bible," are central to understanding salvation history and God's continuing relationship with humanity. As a result, Mary's response to God is of the essence of humanity's relationship with God. In view of this, both Mary and "the female line in the Bible" should be explored in much greater depth to develop the Church's understanding of the encounter of humanity with the triune God. In this they will touch on all aspects of theological thinking and open new layers of meaning and comprehension of God's relationship with humanity, as well as who and what the human being is. At the core of this exploration must be the response Mary offered on behalf of humanity to God and what such human *response* to God means for both God and the human being. The harvest of such exploration may result in the development and deepening of the Church's understanding of humanity's relationship with the triune God, indeed, the comprehension of the triune God. From here a theology of trinitarian society may also evolve.

I would propose, based on our discussion so far, that trinitarian society exists where Christians live within the wider community as a communion of persons who live for (the Father), from (the Son), and with (the Holy Spirit). Importantly, trinitarian society has no structures, no organization, and no policies. The communion of persons operates within the wider society by being for, from, and with the other and God, and encounters and engages the world as such. Trinitarian society's life and energy is sourced from the Church; it is not humanity's construction but God's. It is a communion of persons in relation to God and turned toward other persons, which is openness toward others, and never individualism pursuing an independent agenda. Mary as person provides the model of person in trinitarian society: persons live out of their lives in relation to God, making space for God in the world; persons respond in dialogue and allow that dialogue and the events that surround it to evolve and mature so that its true meaning can grow and bear its fruit—they are fertile soil for God's Word. The communion arises from those who respond to God as person, living in relation and dialogue, such that one "I" cannot make that response for any other "I." Trinitarian society knows no boundaries of nation or state, and membership depends simply on human beings' response to God as person. By living and existing for, from, and with, Christians infuse society with trinitarian Truth and love—like the scent of a flower. Trinitarian society is like and acts as St. Teresa of Avila (1515–1582) told us:

> Christ has no body but yours,
> No hands, no feet on earth but yours,
> Yours are the eyes with which he looks
> Compassion on this world,
> Yours are the feet with which he walks to do good,
> Yours are the hands, with which he blesses all the world.
> Yours are the hands, yours are the feet,
> Yours are the eyes, you are his body.
> Christ has no body now but yours,
> No hands, no feet on earth but yours,
> Yours are the eyes with which he looks
> compassion on this world.
> Christ has no body now on earth but yours.

5

The Female Line in the Bible

Innovation within the Tradition of the Church

Ratzinger's concept of "the female line in the Bible" demonstrates that the women of the Bible have a central role in salvation history. Ratzinger's concept specifically highlights the fact that the women of the Bible represent Israel, the Church, and communal life. It also demonstrates how the human being can achieve and fulfill his or her highest possibility and potential in relation to God. "The female line in the Bible," as a theological hermeneutic, is both christologically grounded and shaped, and is a creative, faithful appropriation of the Church's traditional teachings on Mary. In fact, by putting together the constituent blocks of the Church's teachings in an innovative and unique way and constructing a theological "grammar," Ratzinger opens up the possibility of new modes of understanding and comprehending salvation history. This constructive vision reveals that salvation history is not simply a one-sided, exclusive act of God. Rather, it is a history where the response of human beings, men and women, of faith to God's call and promise, however asymmetrical, is essential and indispensable because such is a call to and provision of the fulfillment of the fundamental role of the human being in the communion of faith and union with God. Relationship with and response to God is the deeper meaning of salvation history that the female line underscores. Perhaps it is really only a reminder of this reality; even so, it is an important and timely reminder. Ultimately, the female line demonstrates that relationship with God—and through that primary relationship, relations with each human being—is the foundation of this history of salvation and redemption.

The female-line hermeneutic also teaches that faith is not exclusive to the isolated individual, but really belongs to the communal community—for faith is communal in nature. Just as each human being does not exist as an individual alone but only in community, as the Genesis creation accounts demonstrate, so faith comes to each human *through* the communal community of faith and creates the network of relations that sustains renewed existence. From the vantage point of the Church's Scripture, the faith of this community can be traced from its earliest instantiation in the creation-and-fall narrative cycle, its growth across the successive generations of Israel's history starting with Abraham's call through to Mary's response to God at the annunciation and its apex in the incarnation, God taking flesh. What this means is that the network of relationships arising from the one human line in the Bible, incorporating the male and female lines, builds throughout the history of Israel's relationship with God, and it is from this network that Mary's relationship and response to God emerges. Mary's yes is part of Israel's yes: Mary is daughter Zion, Ark of the Covenant. The entry of Jesus, the Son, into this world is the fruit of Mary's faith, which is the fruit of Israel's faith. Through Israel's faith, Mary's faith is born, and from this birth the incarnation occurs, which completes "the human line in the Bible."

This history is now carried on through the Church's continuing yes, which is itself witness to God's yes to all.

Mary is integral to Christology and ecclesiology, and is so through her relationship with the triune God. The incarnation is a trinitarian act of the Father, Son, and Holy Spirit. The Son's unique role as Word become flesh is actualized in history through Mary's faithful response to be Mother of God, Theotokos, an act in which the Son, by his own faithful, obedient response through the Holy Spirit, carries out the external mission of the Father toward creation. As the Gospels narrate it, the Father sends the angel Gabriel to Nazareth to proclaim to Mary: "The Holy Spirit will come upon you, and the power of the Most High will overshadow you; therefore the child to be born will be holy; he will be called Son of God" (Luke 1:35-36). Mary as Theotokos, then, is a term that can only be unpacked as a trinitarian term—really, a trinitarian reality. Mary is Theotokos because the Son is the second person of the Trinity, a reality we know through God's self-revelation as Father, Son, and Spirit. Mary, as Mother of God, in her relationship with God points to the fullness of God, three persons in one being.[1] The Mother with her Son points to the Father and the Holy Spirit. The relationship initiated by the triune God with Zion, fulfilled in the daughter of Zion, culminates in the incarnation. Mary as person is the dwelling place of God. The pattern of incarnation occurred biologically only once but it is the pattern of encounter with the God of Jesus Christ that allowed Paul, and every Christian, to say, "It is no longer I who lives but Christ who lives in me" (Gal. 2:20). It is from here that the full meaning of the term mother in relation to God the Father, Son and Spirit should be explored and developed: Mother in relation without reserve with

---

1. For further consideration on how the trinitarian and christological aspects of Mary, Theotokos and type of the Church, can be developed, see my article "New Directions in Mariology within Fundamental Theology. Mary, Mother of God, Theotokos, Type of the Church, Illuminator of the Fullness of Christian Faith and Theology" Theology March 2016; 119 (2).

Father and Son in the Holy Spirit will yield the true meaning of the term mother for the God of Jesus Christ.

In this way, Ratzinger gives a fresh hearing to the women of the Bible and underscores their ineluctable importance to salvation history: even more, Ratzinger's theological interpretation draws the universal dynamic of salvation history as a human affair in which both the male and female lines are intrinsic and indispensable to God's involvement with, and salvation of, humanity. Ratzinger's approach to biblical interpretation releases to its fullest the meaning of Scripture and enhances the Church's understanding of revelation and faith. It also demonstrates how each generation can contribute to the development of the Church's understanding of Christian faith and highlights the value of synthesizing traditional and modern methods of biblical interpretation to address theological issues anew.

Alongside Ratzinger's acceptance of feminist theology's criticism of how women have been treated in the history of the Church, he shows how the riches of the Church's tradition might be retrieved in such a way as to synchronize with the pressing concerns that contemporary feminist theology raises. He finds such a solution particularly in a more complete, synthesized view of salvation as the complementarity—and union—of the female and the male lines, converging in the new patterns of renewed relationality in the Church—a new pattern brought into being in the person of Jesus Christ. Through this, Ratzinger demonstrates that women hold an essential place in Scripture and Christianity. In this way, he calls into stark question the patriarchal nature of Scripture interpretation and patterns of exegesis, as highlighted by feminist theology. The problem, it could be argued, is not with Scripture, but theologians, and how they have interpreted Scripture in a way that has missed the essential female role within salvation history and the theologically pivotal nature of this female line in dogmatic interpretation. What this tells us is that the work of theologians is very much a work in progress and each generation can, and should, contribute to tradition through refining, pruning, and innovating in continuity with the river of tradition. The Church's comprehension of Christian faith and theology is still an evolving one, in which certain elements await coherent articulation while others need to be critiqued so that tradition is pruned of casuistical and accidental traditions.[2]

Two key issues are at the forefront of the discourse on women and Christianity: first, the theological meaning and place of the women in the Bible; and, second, the debate about the experience and treatment of women within the Church. Unless these issues are clearly differentiated and explicitly identified, they will cause significant confusion. The emphasis on patriarchy and subordination of women within Scripture can lead theology to miss some highly unhierarchical situations and aspects of the Bible. Where this happens, theology fails to perceive the Bible's highly attuned lens for the dynamics of the abuse of hierarchy. For example, in the book of Numbers, the daughters of Zelophehad claimed before Moses the rights to their father's inheritance. Normally, in such situations where there were no sons the daughters did not inherit their father's

---

2. The issues of patriarchy and of the subordination of women are now widely accepted as significant themes in modern theology. There is a danger that theologians who maintain these issues as integral to Scripture and tradition are, to varying extents, *reacting to* rather than *developing from* the biblical text and the tradition of the Church. So long as the *reacting to* is a pruning, refining, and building up of the exegesis in the tradition of the Church, there is no danger of losing the richness of the women of Scripture in the process. As part of that, the recognition that the biblical texts exist alongside, but separately from, the exegesis is paramount to enabling us to retain what needs to be retained and burning what needs to be burned. Here lies the challenge of exegesis today in relation to the women of the Bible: the ability to prune away the inappropriate contemporary thinking of each generation so that the tree of tradition may continue to bear fruit. The appalling statements, or more precisely anti- or un-Christian statements, made about women by some theologians from the beginning of the Church, such as the assertion of the natural subordination of woman to man, an idea that runs throughout the history of exegesis and theology right up to the present, needs to be pruned from the casuistical and accidental traditions to reveal tradition. When looked at through the lens of Ratzinger's concept of the female line, in conjunction with his concept of person, it is clear that no such statement denigrating women or the female can stand in Christian theology.

property. Moses went before God, who responded, "The daughters of Zelophehad are right; you shall give them possession of an inheritance among their father's brethren and cause the inheritance of their father to pass to them. And you shall say to the people of Israel, 'If a man dies, and has no son, then you shall cause his inheritance to pass to his daughter. And if he has no daughter, then you shall give his inheritance to his brothers'" (Num. 27:7-9). In the book of Esther (1:16-21), the fate of Queen Vashti was sealed not by her husband's hurt pride; in fact, he managed to get over that fairly quickly. Rather, the courtiers wanted Queen Vashti to be made an example of so that their own wives would not repeat her insubordinate behavior! Esther 1:9-22 reads:

> Then Memu'can said in presence of the king and the princes, "Not only to the king has Queen Vashti done wrong, but also to all the princes and all the peoples who are in all the provinces of King Ahasu-e'rus. For this deed of the queen will be made known to all women, causing them to look with contempt upon their husbands, since they will say, "King Ahasu-e'rus commanded Queen Vashti to be brought before him, and she did not come." This very day the ladies of Persia and Media who have heard of the queen's behavior will be telling it to all the king's princes, and there will be contempt and wrath in plenty. If it please the king, let a royal order go forth from him, and let it be written among the laws of the Persians and the Medes so that it may not be altered, that Vashti is to come no more before King Ahasu-e'rus; and let the king give her royal position to another who is better than she. So when the decree made by the king is proclaimed throughout all his kingdom, vast as it is, all women will give honor to their husbands, high and low." This advice pleased the king and the princes, and the king did as Memu'can proposed.

Another such powerful example is Huldah. The high priest Kilkiah consulted Huldah on behalf of King Josiah upon the rediscovery of the Book of Laws, which had been passed down from Moses (2 Kgs. 22:3—23:3; 2 Chron. 34:14-33). These passages demonstrate that attempts to affirm the female in Christianity by rejecting or reconstructing Scripture means losing not just the role that these, and many more women, play within Christian faith and Scripture, but the respect and esteem with which they were held as well. Moreover, the dynamics that have been identified with patriarchy are those associated with the abuse of hierarchical position and power regardless of gender, race, or age. Recalibrating the discussion toward the human aspect, rather than associating these dynamics to specific categories, will enable a fresh, albeit painful, exploration of the potential negative dynamics of relations among human beings. This, of course, is not to say that women, for many reason, are not at a significant ongoing disadvantage in relationships with other human beings. But it is a call to ensure that a fuller, more complete perspective of relations among human beings is considered in its totality rather than through only one aspect.

The value of Ratzinger's concept is that it offers a new perspective on salvation history, which opens a pathway to reenergizing theology and hence opens new horizons for Christianity. From Ratzinger's concept, the following can be extrapolated. First, the women of the female line represent the communal aspect of humanity and its relationship with God. In Eve's creation, communal life commences; Eve is mother of all the living. However, from the fall on, Eve, life, is subjected to constant pain in childbearing; to give birth, she will be in pain.[3] Second, the typological link between Eve's pain in childbearing and God's indwelling in Israel, culminating in the birth of Christ through Mary, cannot be ignored and should be developed further in conjunction with the birth of the child to the woman in Revelation. Part of this typological interpretation

---

3. Gen. 3:16: "To the Woman he [God] said: 'I will multiply your pains in childbearing, you shall give birth to your children in pain. Your yearnings shall be for your husband, yet he will lord it over you.'"

would include Eve's conception and the birth of Cain, which occurs immediately after humanity's expulsion from the Garden of Eden (Gen. 4:1). Third, by typologically interpreting Eve, and Eve's pain in childbirth through the concept of the female line, birth through pain is a fundamental part of "the female line in the Bible," and so of Israel's path. Faith through the pain of birth, viewed both in a theological and biological way, allows God into the world: faith is a path of pain but that path is also the path of true life. Each of the births is accompanied by the brutal action of worldly power: after the birth of Cain and Abel, Cain murders Abel out of jealousy for the Lord's favor; Herod seeks to murder Jesus; and the dragon seeks to eat the child of the woman in Revelation. The prince of this world, the dragon, humanity's dark side, reacts against the birth of God and faith in this world. In my view, the reality of pain in childbearing that runs through the female line from Eve, through to Mary and the woman of Revelation 12, is an integral aspect of salvation history and faith. This reality needs to be incorporated fully within tradition.

Finally, how does Ratzinger's concept of a female line, along with his perspective on salvation history and `adam, the human being, apply to humanity's situation today? First, Ratzinger demonstrates that Christian faith, at heart, is a relationship with God available to us through the communion of faith. It is God reaching out to each human being and the created, invited response by the human being. In this way, Ratzinger's concept provides each Christian with a model of faith pointed toward the Creator through the Church. It thereby prevents Christian faith from becoming focused erroneously on the individual's experience alone. Second, Ratzinger's concept demonstrates that the widely held view that Mary is in some way special exclusively for women is a fundamental misunderstanding and misrepresentation of Christian faith and revelation. Only together, as a whole, do the Mother and the Son reveal the meaning of salvation history for humanity, and by doing so point to the Father and Holy Spirit. God acts through human beings' positive response to his initiative, and such responses arise from being in relation with God through the communion of faith: Mary and the Church in relation with God the Father, Son and Holy Spirit.

Ratzinger's concept of "the female line in the Bible," as we have seen, offers the opportunity to develop our understanding of key aspects of Christian faith and theology. One such issue is the link between the liturgical celebration of the feasts of the Annunciation and the Incarnation. Ratzinger acknowledges that "the true stature of this event [the annunciation] has only gradually been recognised in the course of history."[4] This reality is reflected in the fact that the Feast of the Annunciation plays a relatively minor role in the Church's liturgical calendar. The Feast of the Annunciation generally falls within Lent, and very occasionally within Holy Week, which means that the Church fails to fully register the monumental nature of the event, Mary's yes, her response to God in total relatedness. It means that the faithful's religious expression neglects to include the indivisible link between the annunciation and the incarnation. The incarnation occurs in freedom, not passivity; God seeks a response, but that response always remains a response in freedom. The revelation of the Trinity within history at the annunciation, Mary's yes to God, and the Word's subsequent taking flesh are fundamental tenets of the Christian faith and theology. But to be truly comprehended, they must be viewed together in total relationality toward each other and not as disconnected parts.

By separating the liturgical celebration of the feasts of the Annunciation and the Incarnation, something substantial and fundamental to Christianity is lost. The Word's incarnation occurred

---

4. Joseph Ratzinger, *God and the World: Believing and Living in Our Time: A Conversation with Peter Seewald*, trans. Henry Taylor (San Francisco: Ignatius, 2000), 293.

due to Mary's response to God's call, her yes to God. The Church's liturgical calendar misses this fundamental tenet of Christianity. God did not descend into history through God's action alone, but God found a response in Israel that culminated in Mary's response. The value of the concept of "the female line in the Bible" is demonstrated by the fact that it shines a light on the fulcrum and indivisible nature of the annunciation and incarnation for the fulfillment of salvation history. It points to both the problem and the solution. The problem here is that, in the Church's liturgical calendar, the celebration of the Feast of the Annunciation is not a major event and is not celebrated with its necessary corollary, the Feast of the Incarnation. To address this problem, the annunciation and incarnation should be celebrated together. Furthermore, due to their indispensable importance of the annunciation in salvation history, this combined celebration should be part of the preparation for the Passion. The Passion would then be placed in its proper context. As a consequence, consideration should be given to celebrating the feasts of the Annunciation and Incarnation as a major event of the Lenten season.

The specific combination of Ratzinger's notion of a female line in the Bible and his notion of person in God and humanity provides an unexpected and unique vision, anchored in Scripture and the Church's tradition, of Christian faith and salvation history. This vision provides solid ground to respond to the challenges and critiques of Christianity and its history in this and all eras. Specifically, it offers a vision of Christian anthropology that orientates us to the Father through the Son in the Holy Spirit while recognizing our alienation from God and each other. In doing so, it offers the path out of that alienation. Anchored in the network of relationships that God initiated with Abraham and brought to fulfillment in Jesus Christ through Mary's Yes, a network of relationships that is a communal, dialogical relationship with God, each individual in total rationality with the triune God, can overcome that alienation by being person. In that, we follow in the way of Mary, who as person responded to God with yes, through which the Logos became flesh and dwelt among us.[5] The continuing network of yeses that arises directly from Abraham and Mary's yeses, means that the human line in the Bible continues within history as the body of Christ. More than that, the human line demonstrates the place of the human being, `adam, within the communal of humanity, Eve. And it is through Jesus and Mary that we discover how the fall, in which the sin of the human being negatively affects humanity, is overcome.

---

5. See Mary Ford Grabowsky's *The Way of Mary: Following Her Footsteps Toward God* (Brewster, MA: Paraclete Press, 2007). Based on the Gospel stories of Mary, Ford Grabowsky offers devotions arranged in a two week cycle for readers to meditate on the life and journey of Mary.

Bibliography

Albrecht, Barbara. "Is There an Objective Type 'Woman'?" Trans. Maria Shrady. In *The Church and Women: A Compendium*, ed. Helmut Moll, 35–49. San Francisco: Ignatius, 1988.

Aldredge-Clanton, Jann. *In Search of the Christ-Sophia: An Inclusive Christology for Liberating Christians*. Mystic, CT: Twenty-Third Publications, 1995.

Allen, John L., Jr. *Cardinal Ratzinger: The Vatican's Enforcer of the Faith*. New York: Continuum, 2002.

Andrews, Edgar H. *Who Made God*. Darlington, England: EP Press, 2009.

Arnold, Fritz. *Like Mary: Towards Christian Maturity in the Twenty-First Century*. Trans. Denis Green. Dublin: Columba Press, 2001.

Ashton, John. *Why Were the Gospels Written? Theology Today* Series, no. 15. Dublin: Mercier Press, 1973.

Augustine. *Confessions*. Trans. R. S. Pine-Coffin. London: Penguin Classics, 1961.

Beattie, Tina. *Eve's Pilgrimage: A Woman's Quest for the City of God*. London: Burns & Oates, 2002.

———. *God's Mother, Eve's Advocate: A Marian Narrative of Women's Salvation*. London: Continuum, 2002.

Beilby, James K., and Paul R. Eddy. "The Quest for the Historical Jesus: An Introduction." In *The Historical Jesus Five Views*, ed. James K. Beilby and Paul R. Eddy, 9–54. London: SPCK, 2010.

Beilby, James K., and Paul R. Eddy ed. *The Historical Jesus Five View*. London: SPCK, 2010.

Benedict XVI (Pope). *Caritas in Veritate*. Dublin: Veritas, 2009. http://w2.vatican.va/content/benedict-xvi/en/encyclicals/documents/hf_ben-xvi_enc_20090629_caritas-in-veritate.html.

———. *Christ and His Church*. London: Catholic Truth Society, 2007.

———. *Church Fathers: From Clement of Rome to Augustine*. Trans. *L'Osservatore Roman*. San Francisco: Ignatius, 2008.

———. *Deus Caritas Est*. Dublin: Veritas, 2006. http://w2.vatican.va/content/benedict-xvi/en/encyclicals/documents/hf_ben-xvi_enc_20051225_deus-caritas-est.html.

———. "Faith, Reason and the University: Memories and Reflections." Speech, Regensburg University, September 12, 2006. http://www.vatican.va/holy_father/benedict_xvi/speeches/2006/september/documents/hf_ben-xvi_spe_20060912_university-regensburg_en.html.

———. *Light of the World: The Pope, the Church, and the Signs of the Times: A Conversation with Peter Seewald*. Trans. Michael J. Miller and Adrian J. Walker. London: Catholic Truth Society, 2010.

———. "Meeting with the representatives of the British Society, including the diplomatic corps, politicians, academies and business leaders Westminster Hall." City of Westminster, September 17, 2010. http://www.vatican.va/holy_father/benedict_xvi/speeches/2010/september/documents/hf_ben-xvi_spe_20100917_societa-civile_en.html.

———. *Saint Paul*. Trans. *L'Osservatore Roman*. San Francisco: Ignatius, 2009.

_____. *Spe Salvi.* Dublin: Veritas, 2008. http://w2.vatican.va/content/benedict-xvi/en/encyclicals/documents/hf_ben-xvi_enc_20071130_spe-salvi.html.

Bergant, Dianne. *Introduction to the Bible.* Collegeville Bible Commentary. Collegeville, MN: Liturgical, 1985.

Bernard of Clairvaux. *Homilies in Praise of the Blessed Virgin Mary.* Trans. Marie-Bernard Said, O.S.B. Introduction by Chrysogonus Waddell. Kalamazoo, MI: Cistercian Publications, 1993.

Borresen, Kari E., ed. *The Image of God: Gender Models in Judaeo-Christian Tradition.* Minneapolis: Fortress Press, 1995.

_____. "God's Image, Man's Image? Patristic Interpretation of Gen 1:27 and 1 Cor 11:7." In *The Image of God: Gender Models in Judaeo-Christian Tradition*, ed. Kari E. Borresen, 146–65. Minneapolis: Fortress Press, 1995.

Boss, Sarah Jane. *Mary.* New Century Theology. London: Continuum, 2003.

_____. *Mary: The Complete Resource.* London: Continuum, 2007.

Bouyer, Louis. *Women and the Church.* Trans. Marilyn Teichert. San Francisco: Ignatius, 1979.

Brown, Raymond E. *The Virginal Conception and Bodily Resurrection of Jesus.* New York: Paulist, 1973.

_____, Karl P. Donfried, Joseph A. Fitzmyer, and John Reumann, eds. *Mary in the New Testament.* London: Geoffrey Chapman, 1978.

Burggraf, Jutta. "The Mother of the Church and the Women in the Church: A Correction of Feminist Theology Gone Astray." Trans. Maria Shrady. In *The Church and Women: A Compendium*, ed. Helmut Moll, 237–58. San Francisco: Ignatius, 1988.

_____. "Woman's Dignity and Function in the Church and Society." Trans. Lothar Krauth. In *The Church and Women: A Compendium*, ed. Helmut Moll, 103–114. San Francisco: Ignatius, 1988.

Carr, Edward H., *What Is History?* London: Penguin, 1987.

Catechism of the Catholic Church. Dublin: Veritas, 1994.

Chadwick, Henry. *Augustine: A Very Short Introduction.* Oxford: Oxford University Press, 2001 (1986).

———. *The Early Church.* London: Penguin, 1993.

Christ, Carol P., and Judith Plaskow, eds. *Womanspirit Rising: A Feminist Reader in Religion.* San Francisco: Harper & Row, 1979.

Clifford, Anne M. "Creation." In *Systematic Theology: Roman Catholic Perspectives*, ed. Francis Schüssler Fiorenza and John P. Galvin, 1:195–248. Minneapolis: Fortress Press, 1991.

Collins, Gregory. *Meeting Christ in His Mysteries: A Benedictine Vision of the Spiritual Life.* Dublin: Columba Press, 2010.

Collins, John J. *Isaiah.* Collegeville Bible Commentary. Collegeville, MN: Liturgical, 1986.

Congar, Yves. *Tradition and Traditions.* Trans. Michael Naseby and Thomas Rainborough. London: Burns & Oates, 1966.

Congregation for the Doctrine of the Faith. "Letter to the Bishops of the Catholic Church On the Collaboration between Men and Women in the Church and the World. 2004. http://www.vatican.va/roman_curia/congregations/cfaith/documents/rc_con_cfaith_doc_20040731_collaboration_en.html.

Copleston, Fredrick. *A History of Philosophy.* Vol. 1: Greece and Rome From the Pre-Socratics to Plotinus. New York: Image Book, 1993.

———. *A History of Philosophy.* Vol. 2: *Augustine to Scotus.* Mahwah, NJ: Paulist, 1950.

Corkery, James. *Joseph Ratzinger's Theological Ideas: Wise Cautions and Legitimate Hopes.* Dublin: Dominican Press, 2009.

Courtney Murray, John, S.J. "Foreword." In Cyril Vollert, SJ, *A Theology of Mary*, 9–11. New York: Herder & Herder, 1965.

Daly, Mary. *Beyond God the Father: Toward a Theology of Women's Liberation.* London: Women's Press, 1986.

Deen, Edith. *All of the Women of the Bible.* New York: Harper & Row, 1955.

De Lubac, Henri. *The Motherhood of the Church*. Trans. Sergia Englund. San Francisco: Ignatius, 1982 (1973).

_____. *The Eternal Feminine*. Trans. René Hague. London: Collins, 1971.

Dogmatic Constitution of the Church. *Lumen Gentium*. November 21, 1964. In *Vatican Council II: The Basic Sixteen Documents: Constitutions, Decrees, Declarations*, ed. Austin Flannery, 1–95. Dublin: Dominican Publications, 1996.

Dogmatic Constitution on Divine Revelation. *Dei Verbum*. November 18, 1965. In *Vatican Council II: The Basic Sixteen Documents: Constitutions, Decrees, Declarations*, ed. Austin Flannery, 97–115. Dublin: Dominican Publications, 1996.

Downey, Michael. *Altogether Gift: A Trinitarian Spirituality*. Dublin: Dominican Publications, 2000.

Dulles, Avery. "Faith and Revelation." In *Systematic Theology: Roman Catholic Perspectives*, ed. Francis Schüssler Fiorenza and John P. Galvin, 1:89–128. Minneapolis: Fortress Press, 1991.

Dunn, James D. G. "Remembering Jesus How the Quest of the Historical Jesus Lost its Way." In *The Historical Jesus: Five Views*, ed. James K. Beilby and Paul R. Eddy, 199–225. London: SPCK, 2010.

Editorial (N.A.). *Vatican II Begins: Fifty Years After. Concilium* (2012/13).

Ehrensperger, Kathy. "Current Trends in Historical Jesus Research." In Leslie Badham, with Paul Badham, *Verdict on Jesus: A New Statement of Evidence*, 5th ed., 239–58. London: SPCK, 2010.

Fergusson, David. "Theology Today–Currents and Directions." *The Expository Times* 123, no. 3 (2011): 105–112.

Flanagan, Donal. *The Theology of Mary*. Cork: Mercier Press, 1976.

_____. "Scheeben and The Basic Principle of Mariology". Irish Theology Quarterly, October 1958 25: 367-381.

Flannery, Austin, ed. *Vatican Council II: The Basic Sixteen Documents: Constitutions, Decrees, Declarations*. Dublin: Dominican Publications, 1996.

Ford Grabowsky, Mary. *The Way of Mary: Following Her Footsteps Toward God* Massachusetts: Paraclete Press, 2007.

Fuchs, Gerhard. "Pope Benedict XVI: 'We Have a Positive Idea to Offer.'" DW-World.com August 13, 2006. http://www.dw-world.de/dw/article/0,,2129951,00.html

Francis (Pope). *Lumen Fidei*. 2013. http://www.vatican.va/holy_father/francesco/encyclicals/documents/papa-francesco_20130629_enciclica-lumen-fidei_en.html.

Fraser, Giles. "The Saturday interview: Justin Welby, Bishop of Durham." *The Guardian.* July 21, 2012. http://www.guardian.co.uk/world/2012/jul/21/bishop-durham-justin-welby-interview.

Fromm, Erich. *To Have or To Be?* London: Abacus, 1979.

Furlong, Monica, ed. *Feminine in the Church*. London: SPCK, 1984.

Galot, Jean. *Full of Grace*. Westminster: Newman Press, 1965.

Galvin, John P. "Jesus Christ." In *Systematic Theology: Roman Catholic Perspectives*, ed. Francis Schüssler Fiorenza and John P. Galvin, 1:249–324. Minneapolis: Fortress Press, 1991.

Gambero, Luigi, S.M. *Mary and the Fathers of the Church: The Blessed Virgin Mary in Patristic Thought*. Trans. Thomas Buffer. San Francisco: Ignatius, 2005.

———. *Mary in the Middle Ages: The Blessed Virgin Mary in the Thought of Medieval Latin Theologians*. Trans. Thomas Buffer. San Francisco: Ignatius, 2005.

Gadzieba, Anthony J. "From the Editor", *Horizon* Volume 40, No. 1 (June 2013)

Graef, Hilda. *Mary: A History of Doctrine and Devotion*. Notre Dame, IN: Ave Maria, 2009.

Hazelton, Lesley. *Mary: A Flesh-and-Blood Biography of the Virgin Mary*. New York: Bloomsbury, 2004.

Hill, Charles E. *Who Chose the Gospels?* Oxford: Oxford University Press, 2010.

Husserl, Edmund. "The Crisis of the Sciences as Expression of the Radical Life-Crisis of European Humanity." Part 1 of *The Crisis of the European Sciences and Transcendental Phenomenology*, trans. David Carr, 3–18. Evanston, IL: Northwestern University Press, 1970.

Hurtado, Larry W. *How on Earth Did Jesus Become a God? Historical Questions about Earliest Devotion to Jesus.* Michigan: Eerdmans, 2005.

Johnson, Elizabeth A. *She Who Is: The Mystery of God in Feminist Theological Discourse.* New York: Crossroad, 1992.

Johnson, Luke Timothy. *The Real Jesus: The Misguided Quest for the Historical Jesus and the Truth of the Traditional Gospels.* New York: HarperOne, 1997.

"Joint Declaration on the Doctrine of Justification by the Lutheran World Federation and the Catholic Church." 1999. http://www.vatican.va/roman_curia/pontifical_councils/chrstuni/documents/rc_pc_chrstuni_doc_31101999_cath-luth-joint-declaration_en.html.

Jung, Carl G. *Aspects of the Feminine.* Trans. R. F. C. Hull. London: Routledge, 1982.

———. *The Archetypes and the Collective Conscious.* 2d ed. Trans R. F. C. Hull. London: Routledge, 2008.

Kant, Immanuel. *An Answer to the Question: 'What is Enlightenment?'* Trans. H. B. Nisbet. London: Penguin, 2009.

Kasper, Walter. *Jesus the Christ.* Trans. V. Green. London: Burns & Oates, 1976.

———. "The Position of Woman as a Problem of Theological Anthropology." Trans. John Saward. In *The Church and Women: A Compendium*, ed. Helmut Moll, 51–64. San Francisco: Ignatius, 1988.

Kelly, J. N. D. *Early Christian Doctrines.* 5th ed. London: A&C Black, 1977.

Kenny, Anthony. *What Is Faith?* Oxford: Oxford University Press, 1992.

Kraemer, Ross S., and Mary Rose D'Angelo, eds. *Women and Christian Origins*. Oxford: Oxford University Press, 1999.

Küng, Hans. *Disputed Truth: Memoirs II*. Trans. John Bowden. London: Continuum, 2008.

———. *Women in Christianity*. Trans. John Bowden. London: Continuum, 2001.

LaCugna, Catherine Mowry. *God for Us: The Trinity and Christian Life*. San Francisco: HarperCollins, 1991.

Lamberigts, Mathijs. "Augustine's Thought on Body and Flesh in Context." In proceedings of the European Society for Catholic Theology's Congress, "Exploring the Boundaries of Bodiliness: Theological and Interdisciplinary Approaches to the Human Condition," Vienna (August 25–29, 2011), 100–110. Vienna: European Society for Catholic Theology, 2011.

Lampe, Geoffrey W. H. "The Reasonableness of Typology." In *Essays on Typology*, ed. Geoffrey W. H. Lampe and K. J. Woollcombe, Studies in Biblical Theology 22, 9–38. London: SCM Press, 1957.

Lehmann, Karl. "The Place of Women as a Problem in Theological Anthropology." Trans. Robert E. Wood. In *The Church and Women: A Compendium*, ed. Helmut Moll, 11–33. San Francisco: Ignatius, 1988.

Lepori, Mauro Giuseppe. "The Individual and Community." Trans. Carol Dvorak. *Cistercian Studies Quarterly* 48, no. 3 (2013): 369–79.

Lombardi, Federico. "The Pope Does Not Reform or Change the Church's Teaching." Trans. Joseph G. Trabbic. http://www.zenit.org/article-31024?l=english.

Lossky, Vladimir. "The Theological Notion of the Human Person." In *In the Image and Likeness of God*. Crestwood, NY: St. Vladimir's Seminary Press, 1974.

Loubser, J. A. (Bobby). "Invoking the Ancestors: Socio-Rhetorical Aspects of the Genealogies in the Gospels of Matthew and Luke." Lecture delivered at the International Meeting of the Society of Biblical Literature, Cambridge (UK), 2003.

Lyons, Enda. *Jesus: Self-Portrait by God*. Dublin: Columba Press, 1994.

MacCulloch, Diarmaid. *A History of Christianity*. London: Penguin, 2010.

Malone, Mary T. *Women and Christianity*. Vol. 1: *The First Thousand Years*. Dublin: Columba Press, 2000.

———. *Women and Christianity*. Vol. 2: *The Medieval Period 1000 to 1500*. Dublin: Columba Press, 2001.

———. *Women and Christianity*. Vol. 3: *From the Reformation to the Twenty-First Century*. Dublin: Columba Press, 2003.

Marmion, Declan, and Rik van Nieuwenhove. *An Introduction to the Trinity*. Cambridge: Cambridge University Press, 2011.

McGuire, Anne. "Women, Gender, and Gnosis in Gnostic Texts and Traditions." In *Women and Christian Origins*, ed. Ross S. Kraemer and Mary Rose D'Angelo, 259–99. Oxford: Oxford University Press, 1999.

McKenna, Mary Frances. "Benedict XVI: A Europe of Faith and Reason." *The Irish Catholic*. September 18, 2008. http://www.irishcatholic.ie/site/content/benedict-xvia-europe-faith-and-reason-mary-frances-mckenna.

———. "The Church in Dialogue with New Scientific Atheism." *The Way* 53, no. 1 (January 2014): 7–22.

———. "Current Problems with the Use of History in Modern Theology and Biblical Interpretation". Unpublished.

———. "A Critique of the Theological Direction the Congregation for the Doctrine of the Faith's Letter on Collaboration between Men and Women, 2004, Provides to Christian Anthropology." Emerging Scholars Conference, European Society for Catholic Theology, Brixen, South Tyrol, August 28, 2013.

———. "The Incalculability of Freedom: A Consideration of Horkheimer and Adorno's critique of Enlightenment in relation to Ratzinger's Notion of Freedom as the Fundamental Structure of the World", 3rd Ratzinger

Symposium, "Christianity, Modernity, and Freedom", Maynooth, 20th of June 2015.

———. "Moral Values and Social Consensus in Democratic Secular Society: Challenges and Responsibilities." *The Heythrop Journal* 56 no. 4 (July 2015): 663–76.

———. "New Directions in Mariology within Fundamental Theology. Mary, Mother of God, Theotokos, Type of the Church, Illuminator of the Fullness of Christian Faith and Theology" *Theology* (March 2016): 119 (2).

———. "Renewing Intellectual Discourse by Means of a New Philosophy of Knowledge for Non-Natural Sciences" *Religion & Education* (Volume 42, Issue 1, 2015), 2-16).

———. "The Role of the Judeo-Christian Tradition in the Development and Continuing Evolution of the Western Synthesis." *Telos* 168 (Fall 2014), 132-144.

McKenna, Megan. *Leave Her Alone.* Maryknoll, NY: Orbis, 2000.

McLoughlin, William, and Jill Pinnock, eds. *Mary for Earth and Heaven: Essays on Mary and Ecumenism.* Herefordshire, UK: Gracewing, 2007.

———. *Mary for Time and Eternity: Essays on Mary and Ecumenism.* Herefordshire, UK: Gracewing, 2007.

Meier, John P. *A Marginal Jew: Rethinking the Historical Jesus.* Vol. 1: *The Roots of the Problem and the Person.* New York: Doubleday, 1991.

Merton, Thomas. *The Last of the Fathers.* London: Catholic Book Club, 1954.

Meyer, Carol. *Discovering Eve.* Oxford: Oxford University Press, 1991.

Meyer, Marvin, with Esther A. de Boer. *The Gospels of Mary: The Secret Traditions of Mary Magdalene, the Companion of Jesus.* New York: HarperCollins, 2006.

Mickens, J. "Pope Tells Theologians to Focus on Truth of Faith." *The Tablet*, December 13, 2008, 31.

Moll, Helmut. "Feminist Theology—A Challenge." Trans. Sigris Nowicki. In *The Church and Women: A Compendium*, ed. Helmut Moll, 259–73. San Francisco: Ignatius, 1988.

———, ed. *The Church and Women: A Compendium*. San Francisco: Ignatius, 1988.

Moynihan, Robert. "Is the Time Ripe for a Fifth Marian Dogma?" March 1, 2010. http://www.zenit.org/article-28508?l=english.

Newman, John Henry. *Certain Difficulties Felt by Anglicans in Catholic Teaching Considered*. London: Longman Green, 1896.

Nichols, Aidan, O.P. *The Thought of Benedict XVI: An Introduction to the Theology of Joseph Ratzinger*. 2d ed. London: Burns & Oates, 2005.

O'Malley, John W. "*Ressourcement* and Reform at Vatican II." In *Vatican II Begins: Fifty Years After. Concilium* (2012/13).

O'Meara, Thomas. *Mary in Protestant and Catholic Theology*. New York: Sheed & Ward, 1966.

Pelikan, Jaroslav. "General Introduction." In *Twentieth Century Theology in the Making*. Vol. 1: *Themes in Biblical Theology*, ed. Jaroslav Pelikan, trans. William Collins, 13–30. London: Collins, 1969.

———. *Mary through the Centuries: Her Place in the History of Culture*. New Haven: Yale University Press, 1996.

Paul VI (Pope). *Marialis Cultus*. February 2, 1974. http://www.vatican.va/holy_father/paul_vi/apost_exhortations/documents/hf_p-vi_exh_19740202_marialis-cultus_en.html.

Popper, Karl. *Conjecture and Refutations*. London: Routledge, 2002.

Radice, Betty, ed. *Early Christian Writings: The Apostolic Fathers*. Trans. Maxwell Staniforth and Andrew Louth. London: Penguin, 1987.

Rahner, Hugo, S.J. *Our Lady and the Church*. Trans. Sebastian Bullough, O.P. Bethesda, MD: Zaccheus Press, 2004.

Rahner, Karl. *Mary, Mother of the Lord*. Trans. W. J. O'Hara. Edinburgh & London: Nelson, 1963.

———. *Theological Investigations.* Vol. 1: *God, Christ, Mary and Grace.* Trans. Cornelius Ernst. London: Darton, Longman & Todd, 1961 (1954).

———. *The Trinity.* Trans. Joseph Donceel. New York: Crossroad, 1997 (1967).

Ranke-Heinemann, Uta. *Eunuchs for the Kingdom of Heaven.* Trans. Peter Heinegg. London: Penguin, 1990.

Ratzinger, Joseph. *Behold the Pierced One.* Trans. Graham Harrison. San Francisco: Ignatius, 1986.

———. "Biblical Interpretation in Crisis: On the Question of the Foundations and Approaches of Exegesis Today." Lecture at St. Peter's Church, New York. January 27, 1988. http://www.catholicculture.org/culture/library/view.cfm?recnum=5989.

———. *The Blessing of Christmas.* Trans. Brian McNeil. San Francisco: Ignatius, 2007.

———. *Called to Communion: Understanding the Church Today.* Trans. Adrian Walker. San Francisco: Ignatius, 1996.

———. *Christianity and the Crisis of Cultures.* Trans. Brian McNeil. San Francisco: Ignatius, 2006.

———. *Church, Ecumenism, and Politics: New Endeavors in Ecclesiology.* Trans. Michael J. Miller, et al. San Francisco: Ignatius, 2008.

———. "Das Problem der Mariologie." *Theologische Revue* 2, no. 61 (1965): 74–82.

———. *Daughter Zion: Meditations on the Church's Marian Belief.* Trans. John M. McDermott, S.J. San Francisco: Ignatius, 1983.

———. "Dogmatic Constitution on Divine Revelation." In *Commentaries on the Documents of Vatican II*, vol. 3, Herbert Vorgrimler, gen. ed., 155–98. London: Burns & Oates, 1969.

———. *Eschatology: Death and Eternal Life.* 2d ed. Trans. Michael Waldstein and Aidan Nichols. Washington, DC: Catholic University of America Press, 1988.

———. *God and the World: Believing and Living in Our Time: A Conversation with Peter Seewald*. Trans. Henry Taylor. San Francisco: Ignatius, 2000.

———. *God Is Near Us: The Eucharist, the Heart of Life*. Trans. Henry Taylor. San Francisco: Ignatius, 2003.

———. *The God of Jesus Christ: Meditations on the Triune God*. Trans. Brian McNeil. San Francisco: Ignatius, 2008.

———. *Gospel, Catechesis, Catechism: Sidelights of the* Catechism of the Catholic Church. San Francisco: Ignatius, 1997.

———. *Images of Hope: Meditations on Major Feasts*. Trans. John Rock and Graham Harrison. San Francisco: Ignatius, 2006.

———. *'In the Beginning . . .': A Catholic Understanding of Creation and the Fall*. Trans. Boniface Ramsey. Grand Rapids: Eerdmans, 1995.

———. *Introduction to Christianity*. 2d ed. Trans. J. R. Foster. San Francisco: Ignatius, 2003.

———. *Jesus of Nazareth*. Trans. Adrian J. Walker. London: Bloomsbury, 2007.

———. *Jesus of Nazareth: Holy Week: From the Entrance into Jerusalem to the Resurrection*. Trans. Vatican Secretariat of State. San Francisco: Ignatius, 2011.

———. *Jesus of Nazareth: The Infancy Narratives*. Trans. Philip J. Whitmore. New York: Image, 2012.

———. *Journey towards Easter: Retreat Given in the Vatican in the Presence of Pope John Paul II*. Trans. Mary Groves. New York: Crossroad, 1987. (Reprint edition, 2006, subtitled *Spiritual Reflections for the Lenten Season*, under the name Pope Benedict XVI.)

———. "Man between Reproduction and Procreation." Trans. Thomas A. Caldwell, S.J. *Communio* 16, no. 2 (1989): 197–211.

———. *Many Religions—One Covenant: Israel, the Church, and the World*. Trans. Graham Harrison. San Francisco: Ignatius, 1999.

_____. "Maria Heimsuchung. Eine Homilie." *Bibel und Leben* 3 (1962): 138–40.

_____. *The Meaning of Christian Brotherhood*. Trans. W. A. Glen-Doepel. 2d ed. San Francisco: Ignatius, 1993.

_____. *Milestones: Memoir 1927–1977*. Trans. Erasmo Leiva-Merikakis. San Francisco: Ignatius, 1988.

_____. *The Nature and Mission of Theology: Essays to Orient Theology in Today's Debate*. Trans. Adrian Walker. San Francisco: Ignatius, 1995.

_____. *A New Song for the Lord: Faith in Christ and Liturgy Today*. Trans. Martha M. Matesich. New York: Crossroad, 1996.

_____. "On the Position of Mariology and Marian Spirituality within the Totality of Faith and Theology." Trans. Graham Harrison. In *The Church and Women: A Compendium*, ed. Helmut Moll, 67–79. San Francisco: Ignatius, 1988.

_____. *On the Way to Jesus Christ*. Trans. Michael J. Miller. San Francisco: Ignatius, 1987.

_____. *Principles of Catholic Theology: Building Stones for a Fundamental Theology*. Trans. Sister Mary Frances McCarthy, S.N.D. San Francisco: Ignatius, 1987.

_____. "Retrieving the Tradition concerning the Notion of Person in Theology." Trans. Michael Waldstein. *Communio* 17, no. 3 (1990): 439–54.

_____. *Salt of the Earth: The Church at the End of the Millennium: A Conversation with Peter Seewald*. Trans. Adrian Walker. San Francisco: Ignatius, 1997.

_____. "Sign of Cana." *Communio* 33, no. 4 (2006): 682–86.

_____. "The Sign of the Woman." Introduction to John Paul II, *Mary: God's Yes to Man: John Paul's Encyclical* Redemptoris Mater. Trans. Lothar Krauth. San Francisco: Ignatius, 1988.

———. *The Spirit of the Liturgy.* Trans. John Saward. San Francisco: Ignatius, 2000.

———. *Theological Highlights of Vatican II.* Trans. Gerard C. Thormann. New York: Paulist, 1966.

———. "Thoughts on the Place of Marian Doctrine and Piety in Faith and Theology as a Whole." Trans. Adrian Walker, *Communio* 30, no. 1 (2003): 147–60.

———. "Truth and Freedom." Trans. Adrian Walker. *Communio* 23, no. 1 (1996): 16–35.

———. *Truth and Tolerance: Christian Belief and World Religions.* Trans. Henry Taylor. San Francisco: Ignatius, 2004.

———. *A Turning Point for Europe? The Church in the Modern World—Assessment and Forecast.* Trans. Brian McNeil. San Francisco: Ignatius, 1994.

———. *Values in a Time of Upheaval.* Trans. Brian McNeil. New York: Crossroad/San Francisco: Ignatius, 2006.

———. *What It Means to Be a Christian.* Trans. Henry Taylor. San Francisco: Ignatius, 2006.

———. *Without Roots: The West, Relativism, Christianity, Islam.* Trans. Michael F. Moore. New York: Basic, 2006.

———. *The Yes of Jesus Christ: Spiritual Exercises in Faith, Hope, and Love.* Trans. Robert Nowell. New York: Crossroad, 1991.

———. "'You are full of grace': Elements of Biblical Devotion to Mary.'" Trans. Josephine Koeppel, *Communio* 16, no. 1 (1989): 54–68.

———, and Hans Urs von Balthasar. *Mary: The Church at the Source.* Trans. Adrian J. Walker. San Francisco: Ignatius, 2005.

———, and Jürgen Habermas. *The Dialectics of Secularization.* Trans. Brian McNeil. San Francisco: Ignatius, 2006.

———, with Vittorio Messori. *The Ratzinger Report.* Trans. Salvator Attanasio and Graham Harrison. San Francisco: Ignatius, 1985.

Rausch, Thomas P. *Pope Benedict XVI: An Introduction to His Theological Vision.* New York: Paulist, 2009.

Rowland, Tracey. *Ratzinger's Faith: The Theology of Pope Benedict XVI.* Oxford, Oxford University Press, 2008.

Rubin, Miri. *Mother of God: A History of the Virgin Mary.* London: Penguin, 2010.

Ruono, Anthony. *The Greatest Marian Titles: Their History, Meaning, and Usage.* New York: St Paul's, 2008.

Schelkle, Karl Hermann. *An Introduction to the New Testament.* Trans. Gregor Kirstein. Cork: Mercier Press, 1969.

Schneider, Sandra M. *Beyond Patching: Faith and Feminism in the Catholic Church.* Rev. ed. Mahwah, NJ: Paulist, 1991.

_____. *With Oil in Their Lamps: Faith, Feminism, and the Future.* Mahwah, NJ: Paulist, 2002.

_____. *Women and the Word: The Gender of God in the New Testament and the Spirituality of Women.* Mahwah, NJ: Paulist, 1986.

Schüssler Fiorenza, Elizabeth. *But She Said: Feminist Practices of Biblical Interpretation.* Boston: Beacon, 1992.

_____. *In Memory of Her: A Feminist Theological Reconstruction of Christian Origins.* New York: Crossroad, 1989.

Schüssler Fiorenza, Francis. "Marriage." In *Systematic Theology: Roman Catholic Perspectives*, ed. Francis Schüssler Fiorenza and John P. Galvin, 2:305–346. Minneapolis: Fortress Press, 1991.

_____, and John P. Galvin, eds. *Systematic Theology: Roman Catholic Perspectives.* 2 vols. Minneapolis: Fortress Press, 1991.

Semmelroth, Otto. *Mary: Archetype of the Church.* Trans. Maria von Eroes and John Devlin. Dublin: Gill & McMillan, 1964.

Sheldrake, Rupert. *The Science Delusion: Freeing the Spirit of Inquiry.* London: Coronet, 2012.

Smit, Peter-Ben. "Something about Mary? Remarks about the Five Women in the Matthean Genealogy." *New Testament Studies* 56 (2010): 191–207.

Soskice, Janet M. *The Kindness of God*. Oxford: Oxford University Press, 2007.

Stacpoole, Alberic, ed. *Mary's Place in Christian Dialogue*. New York: Morehouse-Barlow, 1982.

Storr, Anthony, ed. *The Essential Jung*. London: Fontana Press, 1998.

Suarez, Federico. *Our Lady the Virgin*. New York: Specter, 2003.

Suelzer, Alexa, and John S. Kselman. "Modern Old Testament Criticism." In *The New Jerome Biblical Commentary*, student edition, ed. Raymond E. Brown, Joseph A. Fitzmyer, Roland E. Murphy, 1113–29. London: Geoffrey Chapman, 1989.

Tate, W. Randolph. *Biblical Interpretation: An Integrated Approach*. 3d ed. Peabody, MA: Hendrickson, 2008.

Taylor, A. J. P. *Bismarck: The Man and the Statesman*. London: Penguin, 1955.

Thurian, Max. *Mary, Mother of the Lord, Figure of the Church*. Trans. Neville B. Cryer. London: Faith Press, 1963.

Trible, Phyllis. "Eve and Adam: Genesis 2-3 Reread." In *Womanspirit Rising: A Feminist Reader in Religion*, ed. Carol P. Christ and Judith Plaskow, 74–81. San Francisco: Harper & Row, 1979.

Twomey, D. Vincent. *Pope Benedict XVI: The Conscience of Our Age*. San Francisco: Ignatius, 2007.

Viviano, Pauline A. *Genesis*. Collegeville Bible Commentary. Collegeville, MN: Liturgical, 1985.

Von Balthasar, Hans urs. *A Theology of History*. London: Sheed & Ward, 1965.

———. *The Glory of the Lord: A Theological Aesthetics*. Vol. 1: *Seeing the Form*. Trans. Erasmo Leiva-Merikikis. Edinburgh: T&T Clark, 1982.

———. "How Weighty is the Argument from 'Uninterrupted Tradition' to Justify the Male Priesthood." Trans. Lothar Krauth. In *The Church* and Women: A Compendium, ed. Helmut Moll, 153–60. San Francisco: Ignatius, 1988.

———. *The Theology of Karl Barth: Explorations and Interpretations.* San Francisco: Ignatius, 1992 (1976).

Vollert, Cyril. *A Theology of Mary.* New York: Herder & Herder, 1965.

Wansbrough, Henry. The Story of the Bible; How it Came to Us. London: Darton Longman and Todd, 2006.

Williams, Rowan. "The Person and the Individual." Theos, London, annual lecture. October 1, 2012. http://www.theosthinktank.co.uk/comment/2012/10/09/theos-lecture-transcript.

———. "Holiness and the Sovereignty of Grace: Mary's Discipleship." Lecture at the Ecumenical Society of the Blessed Virgin Mary Congress, Magdalene College, Cambridge. September 23, 2014.

Woollcombe, K. J. "The Biblical Origins and Patristic Development of Typology." In *Essays on Typology*, ed. Geoffrey W. H. Lampe and K. J. Woollcombe, Studies in Biblical Theology 22, 39-75. London: SCM Press, 1957.

Yoder Neufeld, Thomas R. *Recovering Jesus: The Witness of the New Testament.* Grand Rapids: Brazos, 2007.

Index of Names and Subjects

Abel (biblical figure), 222
Abraham (biblical figure), 45–46, 149, 154
Adam (biblical figure): creation of Eve and, 140–41; Fall and, 204; hierarchical gender relations and, 139; as human being, 136–40; Jesus Christ as second Adam, 1, 12–13, 19, 23, 67, 106, 137–38, 173–74, 203, 211; line from, 104–5; original sin, 143–44, 173–74, 204; origin of, 162n70; as representative figure, 138
Adam, Karl, 122
`adam, meaning of, 3, 139, 140n11, 222
AIDS, 95
Albrecht, Barbara, 179
Alcuin, 196n86
Aldama, José Antonio de, 31

Allen, John, 77, 96
Altogether Gift (Downey), 205
Ambrose, 182, 194
Anamnesis, 81. See also conscience, nature of
`anawin, 146
Annunciation: incarnation, link to, 223–24; in Mariology, 101; redemption and, 198–99
Anthropology and Christology, 14, 21–24, 211–12
Appolinarius of Laodicea, 17
Arianism, 92, 125–26
Aristotle, 53
Ark of the Covenant, 216
Arnold, Fritz, 197
Ashton, John, 128
Assumption of Mary, 35, 38, 182, 194–99
Athanasius, 138

245

Augustine: Christology, 12–14; on faith, 71n155, 92; Mariology, 181–82; on person, 20, 24

Babylon, 151
Balthasar, Hans Urs von, 7; on development of dogma, 56; on faith, 45, 48–50; on feminine, 174–77; on human father of Jesus, 190–91n68; on Mary, 156, 174–75; on person, 15, 174; on reality of faith, 56; theology of history, 68–70
Baptism, 140, 185–86, 190n66, 194n76
BarAbbas, 117
Bar Kokhba, 117
Barth, Karl, 91
Bathsheba (biblical figure), 147–48
Beattie, Tina, 179
Beilby, James K., 119
Bergraff, Jutta, 179
Bernard of Clairvaux, 169–72
Bibel und Leben (journal), 101
Biblical interpretation: faith in, 119–30, 218; of female line in Bible, 112–13; as multidimensional, 129–30; principles of, 113–17; trust in sources, 121

Biblical interpretation, principles of, 113–17
"Biblical Interpretation in Crisis" (Ratzinger), 128–29
Bingermer, Maria Clara, 73
Birth control, 94–95
Bismarck, Otto von, 97
Boethius, 21
Bonaventure, 65
Book of Laws, 220
Bouyer, Louis, 109, 176
Brown, Raymond, 148, 186–87, 188, 190n66

Cain (biblical figure), 221–22
Canonization, 113, 114, 120
Cappadocians, 53
Catholic Mariology. *See* Mariology
Celestine V, 7
Chalcedon, 126, 127
Christianity: authentic, 30–39, 86–90; historical nature of, 51–52, 53n103, 62, 66–71, 118, 153–54; purification of, 118; women in, 108–10; *see also* specific topics
Christology: anthropology and, 14, 21–24, 211–12; epistemology and, 51; historical-critical method and,

117–18; incarnation in, 13–14; Mariology and, 30–31, 34, 141, 164–65, 201, 217; Pauline Augustinian, 12–14; person/human being and, 16, 19, 21

Church: abstraction of, 36; as body of Christ, 60; faith as foundation, 56; as feminine, 36, 174–75; innovation within tradition, 90–97; Mary as type, 34, 36–39, 100–101, 166–76, 188–89; memory, guarding, 79; motherhood of, 35–36; as parallel to Mary, 35; state duality, 83–85; tradition through, 56–66, 71–77

Church Fathers, 52, 140n11, 167

Clement, 150

Collins, Gregory, 131

Communio (journal), 7, 73, 158

Church, 110, 140–41; faith in, 132–33, 216; of humanity, 144, 189, 204, 207; inclusive, 156n60; personal, 138n8; person/individualism in, 26–30; relationality in, 132–33; survival and, 151n46; trinitarian, 212–13; women in, 215, 221

Concilium, 73

Congar, Yves, 44, 45, 53, 60–66, 68, 71n155

Congregation for the Doctrine of Faith, 5, 6, 7, 13, 80, 94

Conscience, nature of, 79–82

Corkery, James, 74–75

Council of Chalcedon, 181

Council of Ephesus, 33–34, 180–81

Council of Nicea, 125n51

Council of the Three Hypostases, 18

Council of Toledo, 158

Covenant, theology of, 152–54

Crucifixion and salvation, 66–67

Cyril of Alexandria, 138

Daly, Mary, 179, 197

Daughter of Zion, 39, 103, 172–74, 191–92, 203, 216–17

Daughter Zion (Ratzinger), 103–4, 152, 154–55, 163–64, 179–80, 187, 189–91

David (biblical figure), 148, 149

Deborah (biblical figure), 149–50

Dei Verbum, 59, 61, 88, 91, 101, 106–7, 113

De Lubac, Henri, 7, 35–36, 38, 156n60, 175, 176–77

Dialog, use of term, 202

Dissent in theology, 77–90

Docetism, 92
Downey, Michael, 205, 209
Dwelling of God, 39

Early Christian Doctrines (Kelly), 181–82
Eddy, Paul R., 119
Enlightenment, 53n103, 81, 124, 130, 133
Ephrem, 167–68
Epistle to the Ephesians (Peter), 185–86
Eschatology (Ratzinger), 7, 40, 92–93, 96, 123
Essence: of Christianity, 52, 116; vs. existence, 15, 21; God as, 18n22; of humanity, 5, 162n72, 212
Esther (biblical figure), 149–50
Eternal Feminine, The (Teillard de Chardin), 175
Eucharist, 140, 153
Eve (biblical figure), 155, 182; as ambiguity of life, 195; childbirth pain, 221–22; creation of, 139–40, 221; eating forbidden fruit, 203–4; Fall, reading of, 142–45, 194n76; female line from, 1, 99, 103, 104, 106–7, 225; interpretations of, 140–42; original sin, 143–44
"Eve and Adam" (Trible), 139
Exegesis: in Church tradition, 219n2; Gnostic, 109–10; medieval, 114n32; modern, 118–19, 123; patriarchal, 138–39, 142–43n22, 218; prosopographic, 19; scriptural, 19, 102; traditional, 138, 149–50; typological, 114–15, 138, 146–47, 194
`ezer, use of term, 142

Faith: Augustine on, 92; Balthasar on, 45, 48–50, 56; in biblical interpretation, 112, 119–30, 218; in community, 216; in history, 130–34; illumination of knowledge and, 48–49; of Israel, 47; Judeo-Christian notion, 49; matriarchs and, 145–46; Old Testament, 199; in perfect love, 47; as philosophy, 52; protection of, 84; Ratzinger on, 43–56, 112, 222; reality of, 56; reason and, 48, 49, 50–55, 53n103, 165; relationality and, 132–33; sacraments and, 43–44; self-

INDEX OF NAMES AND SUBJECTS

revelation and, 30, 44–45, 117; truth and, 40, 48, 50–51
Fall, story of, 142–45, 194n76, 204, 208
Female line in Bible: biblical interpretation approach, 112–13; influences and context, 105–12; introduction of concept, 1–2, 99–105; Mary as link, 103–4, 210–11; in New Testament, 163–213; in Old Testament, 135–62; person and, 224–25; Ratzinger's themes on, 135–36; salvation and, 2, 105–6, 157, 179, 205–6, 215–16; in Thurian framework, 39; Wisdom literature and, 156–57n60; *see also* Eve (biblical figure); Mary (biblical figure)
Feminine: Balthasar on, 69–70, 174, 176–77; Church as, 36, 174–76; femininity, 4–5, 69–70, 177; God's traits, 160–61; in salvation, 1–2, 105–6, 157, 176n34, 205–6
Feminist theology, 100, 111, 156–57n60, 158, 179, 218
Fertility cults, 109
First Epistle to the Corinthians (Clement), 150

Francis (pope), 45
Freedom: divine being and, 84; incalculability of, 54–55; Jesus Christ and, 67–68; limits and humanness, 162n72; revelation and, 23–24; in truth, 207; Western notion, 82
Frings, Josef, 7, 72
Fromm, Erich, 8
Fundamentals of Catechetics (Halbfas), 77

Gabriel (archangel), 172
Galvin, John, 126–27
Gamaliel (rabbi), 87
Gira, Dennis, 73
Glory of the Lord, The (Balthasar), 48–49
Gnilka, Joachim, 187
Gnosticism, 109–11, 186–87
God: as person, 19–21; relationality of, 3, 14–16, 26; Tri-Unity and, 17, 20, 202–4; Word of God, 47, 65, 116–17, 184–85, 202–3; *see also* Self-revelation of God; Trinity
God For Us (LaCugna), 125
Godzieba, Anthony J., 55
Gospel of Philip, 185
Gospel of the Egyptians, 110
Gospel of Thomas, 110

Gospels of Mary (Meyer/de Boer), 111

Grace; faith and, 133, 136; genealogy of, 147, 149; of God, 150–51, 179, 186, 194; of Holy Spirit, 28; individuality and, 18, 25; in Mary, 37, 100, 102, 168, 172, 191–98, 200; matriarchs and, 145–46; of mission, 69; theology of, 184

Greek philosophy, 51, 53n103, 62, 153–54

Guardian, The (newspaper), 76

Guardini, Romano, 122

Hagar (biblical figure), 145
Halbfas, Hubertus, 77
Hannah (biblical figure), 103, 145–46
Hazelton, Lesley, 179
Hilary, 182
Hippolytus, 167
Historical Jesus, The (Beilby/Eddy), 119
Hitler, Adolf, 6
Hodegetria, 210
Holofernes (biblical figure), 150
Holy Spirit: activity of, 58–59, 64, 66, 119–20; Church in remembrance, 56; faith and, 45; immaculate conception and, 185, 202, 204, 210–11; tradition and, 65–66; in Trinity, 14, 19, 23, 28, 29, 89, 162, 168, 198–99, 210, 217, 224

Homoousios, 31, 124, 125n51, 159

Huldah (biblical figure), 220

Humanae Vitae (Paul VI), 94

Hypostasis, 16, 18–19, 20, 26, 31, 127, 156n60

Ignatius, 185–86

Immaculate conception, 146, 182, 186–88, 191–94, 198

Incarnation: annunciation, link to, 223–24; belief in, 12–14, 117; as concrete unity of life, 183n47; divinity and, 17, 181, 202; faith and, 216; in Mariology, 35, 42, 103, 163, 170, 179; Mary as person and, 198, 199; redemption and, 198–99; salvation and, 66–67, 103, 157; as theological/historical, 30, 66–67, 70; in trinitarian theology, 205, 209, 211–12, 217

Individualism: in community, 28–29; person, 26–30

Infancy narratives, 87, 165, 184–85

Infancy Narratives (Ratzinger), 87, 187
Innovation within tradition, 90–97, 171, 215–25
Introduction to Christianity (Ratzinger), 35, 92–93, 103, 190
Irenaeus, 167
Isaac (biblical figure), 145
`*ishshah*/`*ish,* use of terms, 141–42
Israel: communion with God, 208; as Daughter Zion, 152, 172, 174, 216; embodiment of, 103, 150, 155; exile to Babylon, 151; faith of, 47; genealogy of, 146–49; God's covenant with, 14, 136, 152–54, 189; God's indwelling in, 199, 221; infancy narratives of, 184–85; link to Christianity, 165, 168; Mary and, 165, 168, 173, 188–89; patriarchy and, 144; relationship with God, 142, 152–54, 212; women of, 103, 215

Jeremiah (biblical figure), 183
Jerome, 182
Jesus Christ: Christ-Sophia image, 159n60; communion through prayer, 13, 59–60; faith in, 84, 112, 121; freedom and, 67–68; fully open, 140n14; historical, 118–19, 122–25; *homoousios,* 31, 124, 125n51, 159; human/divine nature of, 17, 24, 112–13, 126–27; human father of, 190–91; incarnation, 12–13; Matthew's genealogy of, 146–49, 184n51; as person, 199–201; salvation through, 12–13; as second Adam, 1, 12–13, 19, 23, 67, 106, 137–38, 173–74, 203, 211; as Son of God, 12, 17, 217; in theology of history, 68–70; tradition and, 59–60, 64, 85, 88, 108; truth of, 121; typological interpretations of, 114; *see also* Christology
Jesus of Nazareth (Ratzinger), 8, 118, 158
John (apostle), 167
John Paul II (pope), 7, 95, 104, 207
John the Baptist, 183
John XXIII (pope), 31–32, 102
"Joint Declaration on the Doctrine of Justification by the Lutheran World Federation and the Catholic Church," 75–76, 92
Jonah (biblical figure), 114

Joseph Ratzinger's Theological Ideas (Corkery), 74
Judah (biblical figure), 147, 148
Judith (biblical figure), 149–50
"Justification and Liberty," 76

Kant, Immanuel, 79n173, 123
Kasper, Walter, 178
Kelly, J. N. D., 181–82
Küng, Hans, 108, 110, 159–60, 164, 180–81, 193–94, 197

LaCugna, Catherine Mowry, 125, 130, 205
Lampe, G. W. H., 115
Langemeyer, Bernhard, 192–93
Laurentin, René, 31, 39, 173
Leah (biblical figure), 145, 147
Lehmann, Karl, 178
Leo XIII (pope), 76
Lepori, Mauro Giuseppe, 28–29
"Letter to the Bishops of the Catholic Church on the Collaboration between Men and Women in the Church and the World," 2–4, 177–78
Light of the World (Ratzinger), 94
Like Mary (Arnold), 197
Liturgy: faith and, 47, 83, 131; feasts, 223–24; Marian devotion and, 155, 164, 196; Ratzinger on, 74, 155; Wisdom and, 155, 156n60
Lombardi, Federico, 94–95
Lossky, Vladimir: on person, 15–19, 20, 21, 24–26, 29, 88; on relationality, 15, 26, 28–29; on Trinity, 20
Loubser, J. A., 148
Love: faith and, 47; freedom and, 55; reason and, 54
Lumen Fidei, (Francis/Benedict XVI) 45–46, 48–50, 101, 130–31, 133
Lumen Gentium (Paul VI), 14, 32–33, 36, 101, 166–67
Lutheran Church, 92
Lutheran World Federation, 75, 92

Magnificat, 146
Man, use of term, 8–9
Many Religions—One Covenant (Ratzinger), 153
Marcion, 120
"Maria Heimsuchung. Eine Homilie" (Ratzinger), 101
Marialis Cultus (Paul VI), 163–64
Marian dogmas, 35, 165, 169, 172, 173, 175, 179–83, 196–98
Mariology: assumption in, 38; Augustinian, 181–82; from

below, 193–94; of Bernard, 169–72; Christology and, 30–31, 34, 141, 164–65, 201, 217; Church-centered, 33–39, 100–101, 166–76, 188–89; in ecclesiology, 33, 169, 172; faith interconnectedness and, 189; goddess tradition and, 180–81; John XXIII on, 31–32; pre-Vatican II, 30–31; problematic aspect, 178–79; role in Trinity, 38, 162, 205–6, 209–10, 217; trinitarian framework, 38; unresolved issues in, 2–3; Vatican II debates, 32–34; Wisdom literature and, 155–57, 159–60; *see also* specific topics

Marmion, Declan, 206–7

Marriage covenant, 152–54

Mary (biblical figure): as Ark of the Covenant, 216; assumption, 35, 38, 182, 194–99; in authentic Christianity, 30–39; as Church type, 34, 36–39, 100–101, 166–76, 188–89, 199; as daughter of Zion, 172–74, 191–92, 203, 216–17; dialogue with Triune God, 202–4; faith of, 149, 199; grace in, 37, 100, 102, 168, 172, 191–98, 200; historical, 122, 197–98; as *Hodegetria,* 210; as human, 31, 33, 34, 198; immaculate conception, 182, 191–94, 198; Israel and, 165, 168, 173–74, 189; as person, 199–201, 210–11; piety of, 31–32, 164; as special to women, 178–79; as Theotokos, 33–34, 168, 179, 180–81, 197–98, 199, 201, 206, 210, 217; veneration of, 101; virginity and maternity, 31–32, 87, 182, 183–94, 202; Yes of, 192, 204, 224–25; *see also* Female line in Bible

Mary, Mother of the Lord (K. Rahner), 36–37, 38, 205

Mary, Mother of the Lord, Figure of the Church (Thurian), 38–39

Matriarch narratives, 145–46

Matthew, Gospel of, genealogy in, 146–49, 184n51

Maximus the Confessor, 15

McKenna, Megan, 151n46

Meeting Christ in His Mysteries (Collins), 131

Merton, Thomas, 170, 193

Miraculous births, 145–46. *See also* Immaculate conception

Moses (biblical figure), 14, 47, 106, 154, 167, 219–21
Mother, use of term, 209–10, 217–18
Motherhood of the Church, The (de Lubac), 35–36, 38
Murray, John Courtney, 131
"Mystical Body of Christ" (Pius XII), 197

Nazianzus, Gregory, 204
Nestorius/Nestorianism, 17, 92
Newman, John Henry, 61, 81
New Testament: depiction of Jesus, 159; development of, 60, 120, 155; Gentile women in Matthew, 146–49; interpretation of, 114–15, 137; Marian dogmas, 165, 179, 182–83; philosophical methodology and, 52; salvation history in, 204; Wisdom literature, 155–57; *see also* Female line in Bible; Scripture
Nicaea, 125–26
Nicene Fathers, 159
Nichols, Aidan, 96
Nieuwenhove, Rik van, 206–7
Nowell, Irene, 146

Old Testament: canonization and, 120; covenant in, 152–54; female judges in, 149–51; God's self-revelation, 14; idolatry in, 109; interpretation of, 114–15, 137, 152, 157–58; matriarch narratives, 145–46; Wisdom literature and, 155–57; womb imagery, 157–62; *see also* Female line in Bible; Scripture
O'Malley, John W., 74–75
One humanity (concept), 138, 141
"On the Position of Mariology and Marian Spirituality within the Totality of Faith and Theology," 164
Ordo hypostaticus, 31
Original sin, 58, 143–44, 174, 191–93, 204
Our Lady, cult of, 171–72
Our Lady of the Church (H. Rahner), 34, 156, 166, 181–82
Ousia, 16, 20, 26

Passion, 224
Pastoral of the German Bishops, 164
Patriarchy, 142–43n22, 219–21
Paul (apostle), 114; Christology, 12–14; interpretation of letters,

128; on salvation, 13, 49; on second Adam, 12, 67, 138, 211; on transformation, 44–45; typology, use of, 114, 137–38; on voice of God, 81–82; on wisdom, 130; Paul VI (pope), 2, 33, 163–64. *See also* specific works
Pelagianism, 92
Penina (biblical figure), 145
Person: Balthasar on, 15, 174; Christ as, 199–201; as communion with Triune God, 202–4; in community, 29; complementary presentations of, 24–26; divine vs. human, 17, 18, 22; vs. essence, 21; female line and, 224–25; freedom and, 23; individualism and, 26–30; Lossky on, 15–19, 16–19, 20, 21, 24–26, 29, 88; Mary as, 199–201, 210–11; prosopographic exegesis, 19; Rahner, Karl on, 17–18; Ratzinger on, 15–16, 19–26, 210; relationality and, 15, 20, 25–26, 28–29; transition to human being, 15–16, 19, 21; two-nature, 21
Peter (apostle), 114, 185–86
Pilate, 117

Pius IX (pope), 193–94
Pius XII (pope), 102, 197
Plato, 53, 71n155
Polycarp, 167
Post-Chalcedonian theology, 15
Prayer, 13, 59–60, 69, 159, 193n74, 202
Principles of Fundamental Theology (Ratzinger), 191
"Problem der Mariologie, Das" (Ratzinger), 31, 102
Prosopon, use of term, 19–20
Protestantism, 38, 42, 62, 109–10n21, 115

Rachel (biblical figure), 147
Rahab (biblical figure), 147–48
Rahamin, use of term, 158, 175. *See also* womb imagery
Rahner, Hugo: on immaculate conception, 194n76; on Marian dogma, 196–97; on Mary and Church, 34, 36, 39, 166–73, 181–82, 193–94
Rahner, Karl: on human/divine person, 17–18; on Mary and Church, 36–39, 168n15; on Trinity, 205–6
Rationality, 51–52, 53n103, 62, *see also* Reason
Ratzinger, George, 6

Ratzinger, Joseph: background, 5–9, 72; life work, 90–91; resignation from papacy, 86; *see also* specific topics; specific works

Ratzinger Report, The (Ratzinger/Messori), 30–31

Rausch, Thomas P., 71n155

Reason: faith and, 48, 49, 50–55, 53n103, 165; tradition and, 58–59; *see also* Rationality

"Reasonableness of Typology, The" (Lampe), 115

Rebecca (biblical figure), 147

Redemption: annunciation and, 198–99; incarnation and, 198–99; *Redemptoris Mater* (John Paul II), 104

Reflection, 51–52, 53n103, 62–63, 83, 95, 105, 131, 206, 208

Relationality: faith and, 132–33; of God, 3, 14–16, 26; Lossky on, 15; person and, 15, 20, 25–26, 28–29; pure, 20–21; Ratzinger on, 20–24, 28–29; of Trinity, 14–16, 204–5, 207, 223

Rerum Novarum (Leo XIII), 76

Resurrection: belief in, 77, 127; as divine intervention, 186; in Mariology, 38; salvation and, 66–68; as theological/historical, 77, 194–95; Revelation. *See* Self-revelation of God

Richard St. Victor, 21

Ruth (biblical figure), 147–48

Salvation: female role in, 1–2, 105–6, 157, 176n34, 179, 188, 205–6, 215–16, 222–23; incarnation and, 66–68, 103, 157; male/female lines and, 157, 218; Pauline, 13, 49; Ratzinger on, 67–68, 105–6; through Jesus Christ, 12–13, 222–23

Samson (biblical figure), 145–46

Sarah (biblical figure), 103, 145–48

Scatena, Silvia, 73

Schelkle, Karl H., 120

Scholasticism, 21, 96

Schüssler Fiorenza, Francis, 95

Second Epistle of Peter, 128

Self-revelation of God, 14–16, 20, 53n103, 64, 113–14, 133–34; Christianity as, 168; faith and, 44–45, 48, 117; incarnation and, 30; love/thought and, 54; meaning of person and, 26; reason and, 48, 54; textual origins of, 129; tradition and, 86, 89; Trinity as, 208, 217; womb imagery and, 158

INDEX OF NAMES AND SUBJECTS

Sermon on the Mount, 60
"Sign of the Woman, The" (Ratzinger), 104–5, 113
Smit, Peter-Ben, 148
Sobrino, Jon, 73
Solomon (biblical figure), 114, 147
Solus Christus movement, 42, 109–10, 111
Sophia. *See* Wisdom *(Sophia)*
Soteriology, 13, 138. *See also* Salvation
"Summorum Pontificum" on liturgy, 74
Sympathia, 119. *See also* Faith

Tamar (biblical figure), 147–48
Teillard de Chardin, Pierre, 175
Ten Commandments, 60, 64
Teresa of Avila, 213
Tertullian, 20, 24, 52–53
Theological Investigations (K. Rahner), 37, 38
Theology of Ratzinger, 11–12; as Christian, 92–93; Christology, 12–13; of history, 68–70; as innovation, 91–97; interpretation of Scripture, 128; key aspects of, 51; Mariology in, 165–79; role of dissent in, 77–90; *see also* specific topics; specific works

Theotokos, Mother of God, 33–34, 168, 179, 180–81, 197–98, 199, 201, 206, 210, 217
Thomas Aquinas, 129
Thurian, Max, 38–39
To Have or To Be? (Fromm), 8
Totalitarianism, 82–83
Tradition: apostolic, 63–64, 115–16; authentic, 61–62, 63, 86; Congar on, 60–66; ecclesiastical, 63–64; Holy Spirit and, 64–65; innovation within, 90–97, 171, 215–25; Jesus and, 59–60; misunderstanding of, 33–34; Ratzinger on, 39–42, 56–66, 71–77; reason and, 58–59; role of dissent in, 77–90; Scripture and, 63, 65–66; on self-revelation of God, 86, 89; through Church, 56–66; truth and, 39–42; Vatican II on, 71–77
Tradition and Traditions (Congar), 53, 61, 63
Transfiguration, 190n66
Trible, Phyllis, 139–44
Trinity: alienation from God and, 208; communion with, 28, 206; existence and, 21; Mary's

257

role in, 38, 162, 204–13, 217; relationality of, 14–16, 204–5, 207, 223; as self-revelation, 208, 217; *see also* Holy Spirit

Truth: authority/subjectivity and, 81; Balthasar on, 49–50; faith and, 40–41, 49–50; freedom in, 207; rationality and, 51–52; Ratzinger on, 49–52; tradition and, 39–42

Twomey, Vincent, 79–80

Typology, 114–15, 137

Vashti (biblical figure), 220

Vatican II, 6; on church tradition, 71–77; as continuity, 75–76; discontinuity of, 73–75, 76; Mariology debates, 32–34; Ratzinger contributions/ commentaries, 7, 31, 42, 96, 101–3; *see also Dei Verbum; Lumen Gentium*

Virginal conception. *See* immaculate conception

Vollert, Cyril, 168

Welby, Justin, 76

Williams, Rowan, 26–29, 88, 198

Wisdom *(Sophia),* 154–57

Wisdom texts, 156–57

Womb imagery, 157–62, 175

Women and the Church (Bouyer), 176

Women in Christianity (Küng), 108

Yahwist creation account, 142

"'You are full of grace'" (Ratzinger), 200

Zeno of Verona, 182

Zur Theologie de Ehe (Ratzinger), 95

Index of Scripture References

1–3 John......90
1 Samuel 1-3......145
2 Chronicles 3:14–33......220n2
2 Corinthians 11:2......181n44
2 Kings 22:3–23:3......220n2
2 Timothy 4:2-5......92
3 John......40

Acts......90
Acts 5:38-39......87
Acts 7......115n34
Acts 9:2......73
Acts 19:23......73

Deuteronomy 33:13......167

Ephesians 2:6......195
Ephesians v 31-2......69
Esther......149–150, 151n46
Esther 1:9-22...... 220
Esther 1:16-21...... 220
Ezekiel 16......153–54

Galatians 2:20......44, 217
Galatians 3:27......196n86
Genesis......18, 136–7, 139, 143–44, 145, 178, 183, 208, 216
Genesis iii 15...69
Genesis 2......139
Genesis 2:4b–23......140n11
Genesis 2–3......143n22
Genesis 3:2–6......204
Genesis 3:16......221n3
Genesis 4:1......222
Genesis 12:2......106
Genesis 13:15......106
Genesis 13:16......46
Genesis 15:5......46
Genesis 18......145
Genesis 22:17......46

Hebrews......90, 114
Hebrews 10:5-7......211
Hebrews 1:1-2......106–7

Isaiah 7:14......185
Isaiah 49:15......158
Isaiah 62:5......39
Isaiah 62:11-12......39
Isaiah 66:13......158

Jeremiah 31:3-6......39
Job 10:8–10......162n70
Joel 2:21......172
John......20, 165, 184, 202, 210
John 1:1......137
John 1:3......106, 137
John 2:19......114
John 3......137
John 3:14......114
John 5:19......20
John 10:30......20
John 12:32......211n108
John 15:5......20
John 17:11......20–21
Judges 13:2ff......145–46

Lamentations 4:21......172
Luke......161n68, 165, 184, 187, 195
Luke 1:28......172
Luke 1:35-36......217
Luke 1:48......195
Luke 13:34......161

Malachi 4:2......196n86

Mark 2:19f......153
Matthew......146–49, 184, 187
Matthew 1:22......185
Matthew 12:24......114
Matthew 12:39......114
Matthew 23:37......161

Numbers......219
Numbers 27:7-9......220; as revelation, 115–16

Philippians 2:5-11......209
Proverbs......156n60
Psalms 40:5-8......211
Psalms 119:73......162n70
Psalms 139:13, 15......162n70
Revelation 12......221–22
Revelation 12:14......17, 196
Romans 1:19-20......106
Romans 2:1-16......82
Romans 2:6-7......106
Romans 5......137; as text of Bible, 113–14
Ruth......147–48

Song of Songs......152–54

Timothy 4:2-5......92; tradition and, 63, 65–66

Wisdom literature......159–60

INDEX OF SCRIPTURE REFERENCES

Zechariah 9:9......172

Zephaniah 3:14......172

CPSIA information can be obtained at www.ICGtesting.com
Printed in the USA
LVOW06s0837110815

449577LV00003B/4/P

9 781451 487992